THE PARLIAMENT OF MAN

RANDOM HOUSE

NEW YORK

THE PARLIAMENT OF MAN

*The Past, Present, and Future
of the United Nations*

PAUL KENNEDY

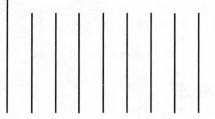

Copyright © 2006 by Paul Kennedy

Published in the United States by Random House,
an imprint of The Random House Publishing Group,
a division of Random House, Inc., New York.

RANDOM HOUSE and colophon are
registered trademarks of Random House, Inc.

LIBRARY OF CONGRESS CATALOGING-IN-PUBLICATION DATA

Kennedy, Paul M.
The parliament of man: the past, present,
and future of the United Nations / Paul Kennedy.
p. cm.
Includes index.
ISBN 0-375-50165-7
1. United Nations—History. 2. International relations. I. Title.

JZ4984.5.K46 2006
341.23—dc22 2005044785

Printed in the United States of America on acid-free paper

www.atrandom.com

1 2 3 4 5 6 7 8 9

FIRST EDITION

Book design by Dana Leigh Blanchette

To the new members of my lovely extended family,
Cynthia, Sophia, Catherine, and Olivia

and

To the constant friends of my life,
Jim, John and Cinnamon, and Matthew Kennedy

For I dipt into the future, far as human eye could see,
Saw the Vision of the world, and all the wonders that would be;

Saw the heavens fill with commerce, argosies of magic sails,
Pilots of the purple twilight, dropping down with costly bales;

Heard the heavens fill with shouting, and there rain'd a ghastly dew
From the nations' airy navies grappling in the central blue;

Far along the world-wide whisper of the south-wind rushing warm,
With the standards of the peoples plunging thro' the thunder-storm;

Till the war-drum throbb'd no longer, and the battle-flags were furl'd
In the Parliament of man, the Federation of the world.

There the common sense of most shall hold a fretful realm in awe,
And the kindly earth shall slumber, lapt in universal law.

—ALFRED, LORD TENNYSON,
  "Locksley Hall" (1837)

A Note on the Title

In 1837, the young, promising English poet Alfred Tennyson wrote a lengthy, rambling work called "Locksley Hall" (named after a run-down mansion in Staffordshire), in which he ruminated about the future of the world. It is a curious, moving work, full of inventions, lurid language, and juvenile optimism. It foresees the coming of airpower and the bombing of cities ("there rain'd a ghastly dew") but also forecasts that the nations of the world, realizing they could destroy one another, might mutually agree to form a political federation, the Parliament of man.

Tennyson's vision influenced many people in the English-speaking world, especially those who urged the end of mass warfare and the creation of international organizations to resolve disputes peacefully. A century or so later, one of Tennyson's fans was a junior senator from Missouri named Harry Truman, who had recently been elected vice president of the United States. On April 12, 1945, he became the most powerful man in the world following the death of Franklin Roosevelt. On his shoulders was laid the responsibility for much of the postwar order. Those were, fortunately, very broad shoulders.

"Locksley Hall" had a profound effect upon Truman, and for years he kept a clipping of the lines used as this book's epigraph. When puzzled senators and staffers asked Truman about his commitment to international organization, at the 1945 San Francisco conference and later, he was happy to reach into his wallet and read that passage from "Locksley Hall." Most times, his listeners got the point. Mankind was going to destroy itself unless it invented some form of international organization to avoid conflict and advance the common humanity. The ghost of Tennyson, but also that of Harry Truman, runs through the present work.

Preface

In the course of the twentieth century, there occurred a development unique in the story of humankind. States, which had defined themselves from Thucydides to Bismarck by their claims to sovereign independence, gradually came together to create international organizations to promote peace, curb aggression, regulate diplomatic affairs, devise an international code of law, encourage social development, and foster prosperity. The emergence of this network of forms of global governance was not straightforward. It involved many setbacks and aroused much resistance from those who felt their power and privileges threatened by such a trend. For every voice favoring global cooperation there was another, warning against the erosion of national sovereignty. The debate is just as heated today as it was generations ago. Nevertheless, were a diplomat or editor of the year 1900 to be transported to our present world, he or she would be astonished at the role that international bodies play on behalf of global society.

The best-known and most ambitious of these bodies is the United Nations organization. Established in 1945 by the victor states of the Second World War, it inherited many of the features of that earlier experiment in global cooperation, the League of Nations. Yet it also represented a great increase in the League's functions and powers, whether in the realms of conflict resolution, human rights, or economic affairs. To be sure, this increase was conditional and constrained, for the United Nations could never escape the central paradox of all international bodies. The paradox is this: Since the world organization was created by its member states, which acted like shareholders in a corporation, it can function effectively only when it receives the support of national governments, especially those of the larger powers. Nations can ignore the world body, as did the USSR in 1950 and the United States in 2003 (and many a "rogue state" in recent years), but that usually comes at a price. Conversely, the organization cannot pursue proposed actions if a Great Power—that is, one of the five countries possessing the veto—is opposed. This tension between sovereignty and internationalism is inherent, persistent, and unavoidable. Unless the reader understands that this tension was built into the system from the beginning, it is impossible to follow the United Nations' story over the six decades since 1945.

This study traces the evolution of the United Nations during that length of time, assesses what it has done well and where it has failed, and considers its prospects in the years to come. It rests upon the reasonable assumption that whether we approve of the organization's past record or not, the changes taking place in world society will make us turn to it again and again. If international bodies did not at present exist, we would be compelled to create them, though probably in a somewhat different fashion from what exists. But they are there, and we often need them. It therefore follows that an understanding of how and why the world organization was established, what it can and cannot do, and what potential exists to enhance its usefulness should be the common property of every educated man and woman.

It is hard to describe the purpose and form of this book in a single sentence. It might be described as an "intellectual history" of the United Nations, but it is not quite that because it ventures into many other genres of history and politics and is just as interested in policy outcomes as in the ideas that caused them. It is a study of changing visions of international structures and how they were used to achieve common human purposes in fields where individual nations could not satisfactorily act alone. It is less concerned with formal UN institutions and proceedings per se and much more with the way in which the organization worked, how it was altered to carry out a new activity, and, especially, why that new activity came to be seen as a further, proper role for the world body. It is a study of evolution, metamorphosis, and experiment, of failure and success. It is, most certainly, not a handbook to the "alphabet soup" of the acronymic UN offices or a bureaucratic history of how this hydra-headed organism grew over time. In sum, the subject matter is too complex and entangled to allow for easy categorization. Let us just say that it is a story of human beings groping toward a common end, a future of mutual dignity, prosperity, and tolerance through shared control of international instruments. It is also a tale of multiple setbacks and disappointments.

This book's structure is reasonably clear. Following this Preface, Part One tells a tale of the first, tentative steps that humankind—really, their governments—took toward international accords, codes of ideas, and cooperative behavior. It notes those intellectuals and public officials who urged the case for greater global cooperation and even the idea of global governance. If the latter seemed wildly improbable in times of large-scale fighting, conquests, and arms races, the idea itself began to develop a momentum by the middle of the nineteenth century and surfaced again when the rivalries among the Great Powers culminated in the catastrophic bloodshed and waste of the First World War.

In consequence, the first half of Chapter One tells the story of the creation, evolution, and slow collapse of the League of Nations, that significant but flawed institution that preceded the United Nations and from whose fate the founding fathers of the latter body drew many important conclusions. This offers a lead-in to the greater part of the same chapter, which looks at the work of policy makers and their advisers in 1941–45 in fashioning improved international structures to serve the global community, as well as serving their own best interests. Since it was in this furnace that the key parts of our contemporary United Nations organization were forged, it is important to get into the minds of the UN's artificers and understand why they shaped the various parts of the world body (for instance, the Security Council) the way they did. Without a knowledge of the intentions and arguments of the UN's founders, most of the rest of this work will be unintelligible.

Part Two of this book constitutes its core and thus claims most of the text. Here are six loosely linked chapters that examine the chief aspects of the world organization's missions and how well or poorly each purpose has been fulfilled in the decades between 1945 and our present times. The logic for arranging the central part of the book into parallel, thematic chapters is simple. A chronological account from 1945 to 2005 would be too dense and tedious, a sort of narrative that within each chapter hopped from security and peacekeeping matters to human rights issues or environmental accords, making it difficult for the reader to follow how things were evolving overall. The second reason for the thematic approach is that it reflects the different ways in which governments and peoples regard the United Nations itself. Anyone who has watched the UN on the ground in, say, Africa or looked at the agenda of items and reports placed before the General Assembly will be forced to the conclusion that, even if the world body is constitutionally one large organism, there are in practice many UNs. To some observers, it is best known as the UN of peacekeeping and Security Council resolutions; to others, it is the UN of economic development; to others, it is the UN of advancing civil rights worldwide; and to others, it is the body chiefly responsible for rebuilding the social fabric of broken-down societies, protecting the environment, and encouraging cultural understanding among peoples. Like the blind men feeling the various parts of an elephant, different groups in today's world see the UN in different ways—just as they did in 1945.

Thus, the first of these parallel chapters (Chapter Two) tells the story of the Security Council, what it did in its early years, how it responded to changes over time—and how puzzling it remains. The next chapter (Three) devotes itself to "peacekeeping and warmaking," matters that are intimately linked to the Security Council but which, concerning what happened in the field, require study on their own. The important and ever growing agendas of global economic relations, especially in the field of "North-South" development, are handled in the following chapter (Chapter Four), which itself is closely linked to the next field of study, an analysis in Chapter Five of the UN's efforts in pushing for social and environmental progress. The story of the evolution of international human rights is one deserving its own telling and receives it in Chapter Six. The final strand of these parallel attempts to fulfill the aims of the UN Charter deals with the vaguer yet still important matter of representativeness within the present world body, as well as the role of those players outside the member states in forging a global discourse; Chapter Seven also considers the various notions of how to establish higher forms of global governance. Ultimately, all these stories and actions have to be brought together in order to establish a holistic understanding of the world organization; but that aim is best achieved by looking at the strands separately before weaving them together.

Part Three of this book is an attempt to fuse those strands in the form of an extended essay about the United Nations today and, especially, tomorrow.[1] There is a change in tone here, since Chapter Eight seeks more to persuade than to describe. Its purpose is to point to the future. It assumes that since this is the only world organization that we possess, we need to make it work in the best way possible, in order to help humankind navigate our present turbulent century.

In sum, I believe that the canny junior senator from Missouri was right. Like it or not, humankind requires something out there that is more than egoistical nation-states. Today and into the future we will need a United Nations organization, duly modified from the world of 1945 but still recognizable to its founding fathers and still dedicated to their lofty purposes. The question is, can we do it, practically? Can we modify our fears and egoisms to the common good and our own long-term advantage? Much of the history of the twenty-first century may depend on our collective response to that challenge.

Contents

PART 1

The Origins

CHAPTER 1

The Troubled Advance to a New World Order, 1815–1945

The idea of a universal association of humankind goes back hundreds if not thousands of years. Some works claim that ancient Chinese philosophers or Greek sages were arguing even then for the establishment of a world order. Others suggest that Catholic theologians in the Middle Ages proposed some form of universal governance, no doubt Christian in construction but reaching out to all peoples. All sorts of institutional and scholarly names are tossed out here: the federation of Greek city-states, the Stoics, various disciples of Confucius, Dante, William Penn, the Abbé de St.-Pierre with his "Project to Render Peace Perpetual in Europe" (1713), the American founding fathers in their pursuit of a "more perfect union," and then, perhaps especially, the Prussian philosopher Immanuel Kant's *Perpetual Peace* of 1795. The list is long; later, even Lenin wrote in favor of "the United States of Europe," while H. G. Wells and Arnold Toynbee pleaded for a new international system of affairs.[1]

It comes as no surprise that most of these texts were composed near the end of, or shortly after, a great and bloody war. They were efforts to find a way out of the international anarchy, to escape the repeated struggles between cities, monarchies, and states, and to establish long-lasting peace. All of them sought to constrain selfish, sovereign power, usually by some form of league of nations that would take action against a country that broke the existing order. The mechanisms were therefore reactive, assuming humankind's propensity to conflict but trusting that such dangerous drives could be headed off.

They were devices to chain national egoism; as St.-Pierre argued, all members must be placed in a "mutual state of dependence." From this negative intent there would flow positive benefits: global harmony, rising prosperity, the pursuit of the arts, and so on.

To say that this was idealist would be a gross understatement. We might note that Kant's great treatise was composed just a few years before Napoleon began his rampage across Europe, leaving damaged and raped communities everywhere. Nonetheless, these early writings contained ideas that would not go away. They were ideas, moreover, that formed a central part of the intellectual architecture of the Enlightenment, the rise of the free trade movement, and the advance of Western liberalism. There was, to be sure, no real move toward a universal monarchy in the early nineteenth century, nor toward any parliament of man. Indeed, the only international structure at that time was the rather informal Concert of Europe, run by the five Great Powers, which was usually conservative in hue. However, since each of those powers was reluctant to risk another expensive and potentially destabilizing war, a general peace obtained.[2]

Despite that conservatism, there also existed an urge toward the more liberal conduct of affairs, especially in Western Europe and the United States. Advocates of perpetual peace may not have had their hopes fulfilled (there were many smaller wars outside of Europe in the decades following 1815, and revolutionary movements within the Continent were usually crushed), but reformers applauded the news of the increasing legislation against slavery and the slave trade, the emancipation of Catholics in Britain and of Jews in France and the Habsburg Empire, and the reduction or elimination of protectionist tariffs such as the Corn Laws—not because any single change was of itself transforming, but because collectively they comprised movement in the direction of greater peace, tolerance, and interdependence. Tennyson, in the flush of composing "Locksley Hall," was not alone in his optimism about humankind's capacity for progress. He was preceded, joined, and followed by some of the greatest names in the Western liberal tradition—Smith, Ricardo, Bentham, Comte, and Mill—as well as by his great contemporary and former classmate, the later prime minister William Gladstone, who with like-minded politicians sought to turn these notions into practice.

In such progressive yet pragmatic fashion, the nineteenth century thus witnessed a series of measures, both legal and commercial, that, it was hoped, would move the world away from international anarchy. The coming of free trade to Britain, later championed across Europe by its ardent disciple Richard Cobden, was hailed not just as an act of economic liberalization, but as a bonding together of peoples, their mutual dependency preventing future war. The creation of the International Committee of the Red Cross (1864) was recognition of the need to treat prisoners of war fairly and a signal advance in "the laws of war"; it was, arguably, the first treaty-bound international organization. By century's end, the two Hague peace conferences (1899 and 1907) would codify the treatment of civilians and neutrals in wartime and provide a mechanism for the peaceful settlement of disputes.[3] Meanwhile, the technical innovations that fascinated Tennyson and his fellow Victorians continued apace. The laying of the first submarine cable between Britain and the United States was hailed by both governments as a bond of harmony; the Universal Postal Union provided a similar bond; and the free flow of capital across the globe was praised as if it were the lubricant to ease the world's troubles and bring prosperity to all. In John Maynard Keynes's gorgeous description, a gentleman before 1914 "could secure forthwith, if he wished it, cheap and comfortable means of transit to any country without passport or other formality, could dispatch his servant to the neighboring office of a bank for such supply of the precious metals as might seem convenient, and could then proceed abroad to foreign quarters, without knowledge of their religion, language, or customs, bearing coined wealth upon his person, and would consider himself much aggrieved and much surprised at the least interference. But, most important of all, he regarded this state of affairs as normal, certain, and permanent, except in the direction of further improvement."[4]

Yet, as the great economist would readily have conceded, there were other, more daunting elements within the international system.

The first was that it remained in essence a European-centered pentarchy, right up until the 1890s; and when Japan and the United States joined the club at the end of the nineteenth century, it simply shifted a little to become a septarchy. The Great Powers still did bilateral or multilateral deals. The Treaty of Portsmouth (1905), for example, whereby Teddy Roosevelt brokered an end to the Russo-Japanese War, seemed more an affirmation of the old order than a harbinger of any new way of dealing with such matters, despite the award to him, as a result, of the Nobel Peace Prize. Second, advancing cosmopolitan tendencies did not stop the larger nations from their most massive bout of colonization, in Africa, the Middle East, Southeast Asia, and the Pacific; 1870–1914 was the age when the "North" really did take over the "South." International civil society was thus confined to the Western nations, the British dominions, Japan, and the independent states of Latin America; it would remain so until the late 1940s. Subjugated to imperial rule, other peoples remained excluded.

Nor did growing international integration prevent the biggest armaments buildup in history up to that time. The Prussian army's decisive defeats of the Habsburg Empire in 1866 and of France in 1870 spurred an anxious reform of all armies, both qualitatively and quantitatively—conscription of millions of men in peacetime became the norm, except within the Anglo-American nations. Defense spending soared to dizzying heights. Following Otto von Bismarck's initial and secret contract with Vienna in 1879, the Great Powers began to assemble into combinations, each of which was pledged to war if an ally was threatened. In parallel with the military buildups, there was the proliferation of naval "races"—the Royal Navy against the French and Russian navies, the rise of the American and Japanese fleets, the Anglo-German antagonism across the North Sea. Truly, the era from 1871 to 1914 was a bizarre and puzzling one, with great and increasing evidence of international integration existing side by side with ethnic-nationalist passions, warmongering, and social Darwinist notions about the primacy of struggle. In many regards it is not unlike today's world, where theories about the rise of new Asian superpowers and growing awareness of the possibility of a terrorist cataclysm jostle with evidence of the ever greater globalization and interdependence of all peoples.

This contest between "merchants and warriors" was won by the latter, decisively, in August 1914.⁵ Sparked by an assassination and a long-standing conflict in the Balkans, which then escalated through the alliance system across most of Europe, the Great Powers marched to war, as traditionally they had done, in defense of perceived national interests. Bankers like the Rothschilds were dismayed beyond measure; generals everywhere were confirmed in their beliefs. There was no parliament of man, only the god of Mars.

But this war was different from that of 1870 or even the hegemonic struggle of 1793–1815. World War I fatefully combined international anarchy on the one hand and modern mass industrialized warfare on the other. The losses of human life, along the western front, the Isonzo, and the eastern front, in the Balkans, the Atlantic, and Mesopotamia, were beyond all measure and comprehension. When, for example, the British army retired, bloodied and hurt, at the end of the *first day* of the Battle of the Somme in July 1916, it had taken nearly sixty thousand casualties, around twenty thousand fatal. (To give some perspective, U.S. forces' losses in more than twenty-five years' fighting in Vietnam were around fifty-eight thousand.) This mutual leaching of the strength and manhood of all the combatant nations had immense consequences, unintended by the decision makers of 1914 who had disregarded the warnings of prewar liberals that modern industrial conflict would shake the pillars of Western life and society. The war shifted the balance of economic power across the Atlantic and undermined Europe's hegemony. It led to the collapse of the Hohenzollern, Romanov, and Habsburg empires and to the creation of myriad successor states. It transformed the Middle East. It advanced Japan's claims in the Pacific and Far East. It allowed the Bolshevik Revolution and boosted the tendencies toward Fascism elsewhere in Europe.

The war also led, in almost equal measure, to unexpected and radical domestic consequences. It furthered the cause of labor, since modern warfare could not function without the recruitment of the masses. It advanced the liberation of women, at least in the West,

since they, too, could not be recruited without trade-offs. It encouraged the growth of the welfare state, since politicians on all sides
promised their warring proletariats "a home fit for heroes." It increased the Exchequer's penetration into the economy, since this total
war called for vastly increased expenditures, and vastly increased
taxes, upon virtually everything that moved or stayed still. The First
World War, in a nutshell, created the modern age.[6]

This catastrophe stimulated, as a reaction, the revival of the
Tennysonian idea that humankind simply had to bring their nations
together before they destroyed the world. Within a year or so of
the first battles, individuals in various countries—Lord Robert Cecil
in Britain, Léon Bourgeois in France, the South African general Jan
Smuts, President Woodrow Wilson, and his adviser Colonel Edward
House—drafted schemes for a postwar organization of states that
would prevent any future conflagration, through structures of consultation and arbitration. The victory of the Allied Powers in November 1918 allowed those ideas to become the matter for serious
political negotiations at the Paris Peace Conference (it is doubtful if
the victory of Wilhelmine Germany would have led to talks leading
to world organization). The result was the Covenant of the League
of Nations, a treaty whose clauses laid out a set of rules and procedures that League members pledged to observe in the pacific settlement of all future disputes. Every sovereign nation, large or small
(except for a while the defeated Central Powers), could register for
membership and participate in the deliberations and decisions of this
new body.

While contemporaries marveled at the revolutionary and unprecedented nature of the League, with Wilson in particular praising the
arrrival of a new international setup, it is important to notice the extent to which the Covenant built upon the nineteenth-century Concert system rather than replacing it. The committee that drafted the
Covenant consisted of representatives of the five victor powers (the
British Empire, France, the United States, Italy, and Japan), joined by
some smaller states. Essentially, though, this critical document was
the work of Wilson and House on the one hand and Cecil and Smuts
on the other. All were for a more open and inclusive international

order, but none intended to rock the boat. Inis Claude, the great historian of the United Nations, puts it beautifully and wryly:

> [The founders of the League] accepted the independent sovereign state as a basic entity, the great powers as the predominant participants, and Europe as the central core of the world political system. They felt no sense of failure or inadequacy when they created a League which did not represent a fundamental alteration of the old system, since they regarded that system as basically sound and workable. World War I was to them not an indication that war is the typical and necessary result of the existence of sovereign states, but a warning that accidents can happen. The task to which they set themselves was that of creating safety devices to obviate the repetition of such an unfortunate breakdown as had occurred in 1914.[7]

Thus, there would be an Assembly of all the (noncolonized) nations of the globe, but its meetings in neutral Geneva would be occasional, and real weight would lie with the Council of the League of Nations, whose nine members automatically included the five victor powers, the other four seats being for rotating members, usually elected on a regional basis. The world system had indeed advanced from the mere pentarchy of states that ran the show after 1814; yet the League's arrangements, like those that emerged from the San Francisco conference in 1945, were a compromise between the more egalitarian instincts of the smaller and medium-size nations and the claims to privilege of the powerful few—with the latter having the upper hand.

Nevertheless, this was the closest the world community had come to creating a parliament of man, and its proceedings generated much excitement and hope throughout the 1920s and into the 1930s. It was only later that the view developed that the League experiment had been worthless. In its early stages, though, the optimism seemed justified. Here, for the first time in the history of humankind, there existed an international organization, with headquarters in a settled neutral state, which was committed to ways of solving problems through peaceful means and thus avoiding the recourse to war. Much of the world was to be fascinated at the regular and extraordinary meetings in Geneva, and many rejoiced at the promise it offered. Small states especially—such as Belgium, Czechoslovakia, Finland, and Colombia—felt that at last they had some place at high table.

Progress toward international cooperation advanced on four parallel fronts during the 1920s. The first was at what might be described as the merely technical level—except that much of their work was not "merely" at all. The International Labour Organization (ILO) had commenced its important reviews of labor standards. There was an Opium Commission and an older committee to prevent what was called "white slave traffic" (international forced prostitution). There were agreements on civil aviation, which was swiftly exploding in the 1920s. International postal and telegraph unions flourished, as did maritime arrangements. Most of these were intergovernmental organizations and thus not directly under the League's control. Still, they were a part of the evolving international architecture and were increasingly associated with the League. Even the Americans and Soviets, usually suspicious of entanglements abroad, began to appreciate that international structures were not always a bad thing. It is interesting to note that it was these technical bodies that were to enjoy the greatest respect and that most of them would be absorbed into the larger United Nations family by the late 1940s.

It was obvious to all why air traffic control, or opium control, was uncontentious. They simply were needed for civilized life to go on. By contrast, it was at the political level, and especially the territorial level, that serious quarrels occurred. Even here, the League had successes. It brokered a Finnish-Swedish dispute over the Aaland Islands as early as 1920. It supervised, through a high commissioner, the Free City of Danzig. It carried out a plebiscite in the disputed districts of Eupen and Malmédy, awarding both to Belgium. It had a far harder task to achieve settlements of the Polish-Lithuanian disputes over Vilna and Memel and even more over the Council's 1922 boundary award on the impossible German-Polish disputes over the future of Upper Silesia, where the two populations lived cheek by jowl. Rejecting British and Turkish arguments, it decided in 1924 that the former

Ottoman province of Mosul should go to Iraq—and Britain accepted. Although there was much grumbling (and, in the case of the division of Upper Silesia, nationalist fury in Germany), Zara Steiner is surely correct in remarking that the League's participation in these tricky disputes "made it easier for the loser to accept unwelcome judgements."[8]

Other positive aspects of the League's political endeavors are worth noting. The first was the insistence (chiefly by the Anglo-Americans at Versailles) upon the recognition and protection of ethnic rights. This was first pushed upon the new Polish regime in 1919 (including the recognition of Jewish rights), then extended to a slew of other new states in Central and Southeastern Europe. There were complaints against this double standard of requiring only new states to be fair in their treatment of minorities, although it was also true that pogroms and other injustices were most likely to occur in recently established and precarious nations such as Albania, Latvia, Poland, and Yugoslavia. There was no need to require, say, Norway to preserve the rights of ethnic minorities. Not all, or many, of the thirteen states that had recognized minorities as "collective entities" carried out their League pledges. But at least they knew they were under some sort of international scrutiny.

In an ironic way, so, too, were the imperial Great Powers themselves subject to scrutiny, since in the Versailles arrangements they had agreed to inspect—or at least to report on—their "mandated" territories, those lands seized from the German and Turkish empires during the First World War. The British complied best, though coolly. The French hated any oversight of what they were doing in Syria and Lebanon. And the Japanese simply refused all requests to report on how they were administering the central Pacific islands they had seized from Germany in 1914. Still, however unevenly the mandate reports turned out to be in practice, precedents were being set regarding accountability to some higher body than the nation-state.

The third area in which advances occurred in the international system lay *outside* the League itself, in a set of Great Power treaties, very much in Bismarckian style. Yet they were significant nonetheless. In 1921–22, the United States, the British Empire, Japan, France, and Italy signed a series of accords in Washington, D.C. These were very detailed agreements upon comparative naval strengths, fortified bases, and respect for China's independence, along with solemn pledges for perpetual peace in the Far East. The real point to note is that, while producing the first ever treaty to limit naval strength (not only in overall numbers of various classes of warship, but in their displacement and the size of their guns) and being thus in its way a remarkable breakthrough in arms negotiations, it was still an "old boy" deal, as among the five largest naval powers.

The same might be said about the famous 1925 Treaties of Locarno. This was the contract that was widely supposed at the time to have "buried" the First World War. Germany, France, and Belgium agreed to recognize their 1919 boundaries in Europe and not transgress them—a critical French anxiety. Britain and Italy declared they would take up arms against any or each of the three prime signatories that violated the deal. Locarno was, alas, full of inconsistencies, but it didn't seem to matter.[9] There was general rejoicing at this act of reconciliation. In the giddy age of the mid-1920s, all was well in the world.

This frivolity was driven by a fourth factor, the remarkable (and yet fragile) economic recovery of the era. Europe had of course been badly hurt by the First World War, and the years immediately following were grim. But the economic stabilization projects regarding war debts and reparations (the Dawes Plan of 1924 and the Young Committee of 1929), plus the flow of short-term American investments into Europe during the 1920s, created a minor miracle. Industries such as automobiles, aircraft, and chemicals boomed. Housing starts were up, and the middle classes began touring abroad again. The new system of peace seemed to be working.

Yet for all the hopes placed in the League, and the various advances made in the growth of international civic society after 1919, the system failed within less than two decades of its founding. Perhaps no global machinery for keeping the peace could have survived the lingering ideological hatreds, economic dislocations, and primal passions that coexisted with the Locarno optimism. But the League was in any case cruelly flawed from its inception, and as the 1920s moved into the 1930s, its weaknesses became more and more evident.

To begin with, it was never a real world organization, only a partial one. About half of the globe was still in a condition of colonial dependency, lacking representation (and at least two advanced nations, Japan and Italy, were out to increase their imperial holdings). The vast Russian lands, torn by civil war and then transformed into the mysterious, isolated Soviet Union, had no place in the system— indeed, although Moscow joined certain technical agencies, it regarded the League itself as a form of capitalist conspiracy that had to be opposed (until, that is, the mid-1930s, when the USSR deftly joined the organization following Germany's departure). Japan paid mere lip service to the League. The defeated Germany was not allowed membership until 1926; Hitler marched it out in 1933. That was a seven-year stint, beaten only in its brevity by that of the Soviet Union, which was expelled in early 1940 after its invasion of Finland—the one country to be voted out of membership of the League. Wilson had argued years earlier that only nations committed to democracy should be members of the League; he would have been sorely disappointed at the list of those within the club by the mid-1930s.

Most important, the Geneva-based body lacked American participation as a result of Wilson's angry confrontation with, and defeat by, the U.S. Senate. Thus, the country that had pushed hardest for the creation of an international security system—and by that time was the most powerful nation on the planet—was absent from the world stage. Not only was it absent; its actions, and more often its inaction, operated as a drag upon efforts at international cooperation. Its angry demands for the repayment of Allied war debts soured transatlantic relations throughout the 1920s and complicated negotiations over German reparations. Its wariness during the 1931–34 Manchurian crisis prevented any possible coordinated action by the West that might have made Japan act more cautiously. Its continued trading with Italy (especially in oil supplies) during the Abyssinian crisis of 1935–36 caused a worried British government to drop the idea of a total commercial blockade of Mussolini's Fascist regime. And Roosevelt's habit in the late 1930s of encouraging Britain and France to be stalwart against Hitler's aggressions while at the same time publicly insisting upon American neutrality drove Neville Chamberlain crazy.[10] This was not helpful at all.

With so many of the major players not in the League, it fell upon Britain and France to occupy the center of the stage, attended by those minor actors mentioned earlier—the smaller European powers, the dominions, the nations of Latin America. This itself, although only a "rump" parliament of man, might have worked reasonably well had it not been for the fact that London and Paris possessed such fundamental differences about what the League was to do.[11]

France, traumatized by two massive, punishing German invasions within the preceding half-century, was insistent upon creating "a League with teeth"—that is, a body that would act collectively and physically to prevent any territorial revisionism. Germany simply had to be pinned down, like Gulliver in Lilliput. In this aim, France was joined by newly created Central and Eastern European nations such as Poland, Czechoslovakia, and Yugoslavia, all worried about large ethnic minorities that might agitate for border revisions of the 1919–23 deals, all clearly fearful of Germany and desirous of a system that punished aggression. Britain, by contrast, saw the League as a pacifier, an emollient, not as a stern international policeman. Successive governments in London felt that they had too much on their plate already without becoming embroiled in Continental Europe's myriad problems. Britain's electorate had recoiled, massively, against any idea of a Continental commitment to France and pushed for social and economic improvements at home rather than strong armed forces. The dominions were straining for greater independence. India, Egypt, and much of the Middle East were full of unrest. The British economy was dislocated, a nineteenth-century creation in a twentieth-century world. The country's navy, army, and air force were reduced and stunted, yet required to police one-quarter of the globe. This was not a time for generosity toward an agitated France or toward far-off countries of which Britain (to paraphrase Chamberlain after his return from Munich in 1938) knew nothing.

There was, of course, a larger structural problem concerning the maintenance of security, arising from the unbalanced nature of the League's membership. It was all very well that a member of the Assembly such as Finland or Chile or that most consistent antiappeaser, New Zealand, should call for economic sanctions or a naval blockade against an aggressor during some crisis in the 1930s, but who actually was to provide the warships and the men? With Japan in smoldering resentment and the United States in high-minded isolation, the burden fell upon the Royal Navy, with the possible help (though probably only against Germany) of the French. This obligation was strongly resisted by the Admiralty, not without due cause. The fact that the League's Covenant did not compel member states to take economic or military actions against an aggressor, but required them only to consider a collective response—which any single member could object to—indeed made the organization toothless except in those cases where the interests of the Great Powers were not involved and they could compel a smaller state to cease a rogue action.

In sum, the classical balance of power was fatefully upset and dismantled. Over the preceding four centuries, as the great German historian Ludwig Dehio reminds us, the European-centered states system had enjoyed "a precarious balance."[12] Every so often, a European aspirant—Philip II of Spain, Louis XIV, Napoleon—had attempted to upset that balance to gain mastery; but those ambitions were contested by other nations (Austria, Sweden, the Netherlands) and ultimately destroyed by the interventions of the two "flank" powers, Britain and Russia. The 1814–15 settlements made that system clearer than ever, guaranteeing a century of Great Power peace. However, the architecture of international affairs that followed the First World War was totally different. The "flank" powers, now the United States and the USSR, seemed to have pulled out of the system, and Japan, another outlier nation, was distracting rather than supporting.

The order of states was thus fundamentally unstable. Two of the seven nations, Britain and France, though often in severe disagreement, played the lead roles at Geneva. Three dissatisfied powers, Germany, Japan, and Italy, nursed revisionist aims and waited on their chances to achieve them, adding further to the confusion of the status quo countries—just who was the greatest danger to the peace by 1935, Germany in Central Europe, Italy in the Mediterranean, or Japan in the Far East? And if you stood forthright against one, surely you had to appease the other two, or at least look away from their transgressions? Finally, there were the two giant continentwide powers, the United States and the USSR, both contemptuous of the old order, not willing to help, and waiting in the wings. Seen from this structural perspective, the League of Nations had no chance of fulfilling Wilson's dreams; perhaps one should salute it for doing what little it did. The peacemakers felt they had done the best they could; but the small child weeping behind the marble pillars at Versailles (see opposite page) had a better instinct about the future than Woodrow Wilson, Georges Clemenceau, or David Lloyd George.

The power imbalances were fateful enough, but the miserable financial and commercial circumstances in Europe after 1919 were even more out of joint—perhaps more than the world had been at any time since the Black Death. The colonies had been drained for their material and military resources. The defeated powers had been devastated by the war—in Russia, where civil war had followed, manufacturing and production in 1920 was only 13 percent of what it had been in 1913. That great conquering nation Britain did not recover its 1913 levels until 1929, when it tumbled into the Great Depression. A few outsider nations—Japan, the United States, Argentina, dominions such as Australia—benefited economically from the war. But the center of the global economy—Europe itself—was dreadfully hurt. This was a massive depressant upon international trade and a great curb upon capital flows. Europe's economic health had seemed to recover by the mid-1920s owing to the inflow of American funds, but when the Wall Street Crash occurred, many of those investments were recalled. And the League of Nations, though not much involved in monetary affairs, took a body blow because its major players were so at odds with one another.

The fact was that the post-1919 Wilsonian system did not provide

The Tiger: "Curious! I seem to hear a child weeping!"

This remarkable *Daily Herald* cartoon of 1919 shows a child under the heading "1940 Class"—that is, recruited to the French army in 1940. Clemenceau is saying to Wilson and Lloyd George: "Curious! I seem to hear a child weeping." Surely the most prophetic cartoon of the twentieth century.

strong international machinery to soften, or contain, blows to the turbulent currency and stock markets. Before 1914, the exchange system ran on its own, based upon the gold standard and upon the Bank of England's role as the lender of last resort that would always repay. By 1919, and given the cost of the war, Britain was an international debtor, no longer a lender. The weight of financial power had moved from Lombard Street to Wall Street. Therein lay the problem. The British strove mightily after 1920 to recover their prewar eminence in global economic matters but never had the resources to do so. The Americans had resources enough but not the will to take the lead. The result produced yet another structural flaw that could be cured only by unusual—indeed, unnatural—American broadness of spirit. This would come in the 1940s. In the 1920s, in the age of isolationists like Senator William Borah, this was not going to happen.

The financial and commercial implosion had its political and social consequences, of course. As economic activity spiraled downward after 1929, the damage intensified; fiscal collapse hit many countries, brutally; budgetary worries led to decreased spending; decreased spending hurt orders, and sales, and stores; this led to manufacturers and retailers dismissing many of their employees; they, in turn, could not purchase goods, which led to further decreases in economic activity. And what was happening, disastrously, at the national level was even more rampant on the stage of international finance and commerce. With millions of their workers thrown out of jobs, every nation retreated into its hole and abandoned the Cobdenite dream. Those mid-Victorian forecasts of free trade, liberal internationalism, and goodwill among nations collapsed in a world of anger and suspicion. The center, as Yeats noted, could not hold. Desperate citizens across Europe and Japan marched into the camp of the extreme Left, assured that they would soon achieve a brave new egalitarian order, or into the camp of the extreme Right, assured in turn that they would witness defeat of the un-Christian, radical, and unhealthy elements of society.

It was in these troubled times that several of the Great Powers, driven by their own internal throbbings and dissatisfied with the

1919–22 border settlements, took advantage of the League's weakness and kicked down the flimsy artifice of international order. The first to move was Japan, badly affected by the global commercial crisis, stung by the sense that it was regarded (by the Washington treaties) as a second-class nation, hard-pressed by a militant nationalism that threatened and even murdered liberal political figures, and irritated beyond measure by Chinese irregular attacks upon its holdings (chiefly railways) on the continent. The Japanese invasion and conquest of Manchuria of 1931–33 was the first big challenge of the post-1919 system. And the system failed. The British government was paralyzed by its financial crisis, the collapse of the Labour administration, and domestic unrest—which included the first mutiny in the Royal Navy since 1797. This was not a time to be bold-faced in the Far East, especially when London was renegotiating relations with the dominions that would give them the right to separate foreign policies, including the right to neutrality. France was obsessed by the power rising again across the Rhine and horrified that Britain might be drawn into an Oriental conflict. The United States preached but did nothing. Germany and Italy watched with interest as Japan shattered the League's principles and then, after the unfavorable Lytton Report of 1933, walked out of the organization. The USSR, scared about Japan's intentions, and with Stalin just about to instigate large-scale internal repressions, kept very quiet. What use, then, was there for the Chilean and New Zealand navies? What could they do? Nothing.

It has often been said that had the Western powers, particularly Britain, France, and the United States, stood firmly against Japan's invasion of Manchuria, the Second World War would have been averted. As the argument goes, this was the first domino, and if it had been held upright, the others would not have tumbled. It may be possible that Benito Mussolini, with his weaker resources, would have been deterred by the example of firm action against territorial revisionism; one doubts if Adolf Hitler would have been persuaded out of his manic plans to undo Versailles. In any case, the damage was done, and Japan was not to be deterred. A large nation had blatantly ignored the governing principles of 1919, and the other large nations had done little, apart from making plain their divisions and incapacities. And the League's real weaknesses were clearly exposed.

There was more to come. In 1932–34, the German-French-British negotiations over land and aerial disarmament fully collapsed. Germany (even Weimar Germany) demanded the right to rebuild its armed forces, thus casting off the Versailles restrictions upon its possession of an air force, armored units, and a larger navy. But France would agree only if Great Britain would give ironclad military guarantees in the event of German aggression, something that London had been dodging since 1919 and was even less inclined to offer a decade later, given the turmoils caused by its economic weaknesses, its running financial rows with America, Japan's moves in the Far East, and the acute reluctance of the dominions (other than New Zealand) to commit to anything. As the disarmament talks foundered, the Nazi Party assumed power in Germany and Hitler instigated a program of massive rearmament. France, not helped by repeated changes of government and a worsening economy, began to lose its nerve. Its caution was mirrored by that of the British cabinet, although the latter reluctantly agreed that it was time to augment its run-down armed forces, albeit slowly at first. The ghosts of the First World War were gathering again, and the stormclouds of another great conflict were gathering.

With Hitler, too, joining the Japanese by walking out of the League in 1933, the world organization took another hit. A decade later, Viscount Cecil gallantly described the world body as "a great experiment," but it was an experiment that was failing, like a balloon rapidly losing air. Seeing this, Mussolini, long dissatisfied with the status quo and increasingly envious of Hitler's successes, decided to make his move. Italy had already practiced its aggressiveness by genocidal bombings and other atrocities in Libya. Now it attacked Ethiopia, which ironically was one of the few independent states in Africa and a member of the League of Nations. The case here was even more blatant than that of Manchuria, where Japan had acted against a devolved province of the Chinese Empire in which it itself had considerable extraterritorial rights. Italy's invasion of 1934–35 was a plain act of aggression by one League member against another.[13]

The response by the League to this invasion of Ethiopia was pathetic. It was also a striking confirmation of the argument, which realists love and consensualists hate, that international organizations work effectively only when the Great Powers, motivated by their own interests, are agreed to take action. It is now clear from the archival record that Italy's economy was so precarious, and its armed forces so overstretched and dubious, that firm action by the French and British navies would have settled the issue very quickly—and, in turn, given a great boost to the League. But for the reasons noted earlier, this did not happen. Britain was far too distracted by other items, domestic and imperial. France was paralyzed by a rising Germany and the fear of driving Italy into Hitler's camp (which, sadly, was soon to happen). America did nothing except to insist on its trading rights, the USSR again stayed on the sidelines, and Japan was gearing up for an invasion of China proper. A clumsy attempt by the British and French foreign ministers—the Hoare-Laval Pact of 1935—to let Mussolini have the lion's share of Ethiopia but to offer fringe territories from Somaliland as compensation to the much reduced Abyssinian state produced enormous criticism in Britain, where public opinion was simultaneously pacifist *and* in favor of strong League action (provided no fighting was called for). The whole thing was a mess. In the meantime—March 1936—Hitler's divisions reoccupied the Rhineland, and territorial revisionism had now moved to Europe.

The story from then on, at least from the perspective of the League, was downhill all the way. Reacting with much irritation to the Ethiopian debacle, the new British prime minister, Neville Chamberlain, described the League's efforts, and failure, as "midsummer madness." It would be far better, he was convinced, to talk with Hitler and Mussolini directly. Meetings in Geneva no longer made sense. In light of what we now know about the ambitions of the Fascist dictators, that was surely an accurate conclusion. But it dealt a deathblow to the League. If its major player, the British Empire, no longer believed in it, the United States, Germany, Japan, and Italy were not members, and the USSR was busy with its own internal purges, the League was essentially reduced to France and its increasingly despairing Eastern European allies, some of which were edging toward Berlin. The first attempt at a parliament of man, the rickety 1919 version, had fallen to the ground.

Moreover, as the British antiappeasement politician Duff Cooper remarked (when he resigned from the cabinet after the Munich accords of 1938), negotiating with Hitler and Mussolini made sense only if you put the Royal Navy to sea, patrolling offshore as the diplomats came to agreement. A few *Queen Elizabeth*–class battleships, their fifteen-inch guns bristling off Wilhelmshaven or Genoa, would have been a remarkable reminder. If the Fascist states acted aggressively, their economies would be ground to dust by maritime blockade. But with the French economy in free fall by the mid- to late 1930s, the French army petrified by the prospect of a joint war against Germany and Italy, the British air chiefs giving terrifying warnings about the Luftwaffe's massive superiority, the Royal Navy obsessed by dangers in the Far East, the army reduced to pitiful levels, the dominions threatening to stay neutral, India in revolt, and the USSR and United States sitting on their hands, Cooper's belligerent arguments—and those of his fellow antiappeaser Churchill—seemed risky and ridiculous to their contemporaries. So they were, by normal reasonings. But they were right in the long run.

The result was that dismal catalog of attacks upon the international order that finally led to the Second World War. In the summer of 1937, Japan invaded China itself, with terrifying brutality (the "rape of Nanking," among others) and deliberate attacks upon Western warships (the bombing of the USS *Panay*) to drive them out of the Yangtze and treaty ports by the end of the year. Diplomatic protests really did nothing; the conquest proceeded. A few months after those bombings, in March 1938, Hitler ordered his troops into Austria, where the population received him (a fellow Austrian) with delirious joy—all except the Jews, the Socialists, the trade unionists, and the more thoughtful, liberal Catholics. It was a typical Sunday morning coup d'état, the French being frozen in political crisis and most members of the British cabinet enjoying an early spring weekend on their country estates. The League did nothing. How could it when their largest powers were somnambulant and with so much public opinion believing that, since the Austrians spoke German and had petitioned to join Germany in 1919 (but been refused), this was not an improper act?

Then came the greatest crisis of all to the international rule of law. Hitler's move in the summer/autumn of 1938 and then again in the spring of 1939 against the sovereign state of Czechoslovakia—a pure creation of the Versailles order—constituted the largest assault upon the system, partly because of its drama, chiefly because of its gravity. Even those who were not appeasers might agree that the recovery of the German-speaking Saarland and the Rhineland to the Reich, and the Anschluss with Austria, conformed to Wilsonian rules of national self-determination. It was harder to justify the forcible splitting up of Czechoslovakia, even if there were many German speakers (though never, historically, part of Germany) in Bohemia. And it was impossible to justify Hitler's march into Prague and takeover of the Czech rump state, possessing few if any German speakers at all. But the main point, for our purposes, is that these critical issues of war and peace were settled without the League playing any role at all. This is why the Munich conference of early October 1938 forms so large a part in the story of the failure of those earlier dreams. Four Great Powers—since Japan and the United States kept their distance, and the USSR was excluded, at Hitler's insistence—met together in traditional form in a European city (one thinks of the congresses of Berlin, Paris, Vienna) to settle a territorial dispute and to tell a smaller nation to accept the loss of its western lands. So the Czechs surrendered Bohemia. Six months later, Hitler reneged on his promises, humiliated Britain and France, and conquered the rest of Czechoslovakia. This was the rule of brute force.

The German invasion of Poland in September 1939 simply completed the tale of a low, dishonest decade. The hopes, the visions, of Wilson, Cecil, Smuts, and their millions of equivalents, collapsed into rubble. Hitler began to crush his eastern neighbor, starting with the bombing of Warsaw. Chamberlain's government, forced by a now outraged British public and a reawakened Parliament, went to war. The empire, apart from Eire, followed suit. France, reluctantly, had to come in. Stalin soon took his share of the spoils in eastern Poland and the Baltic states. Everyone else stood on the sidelines, except for the clumsy Mussolini, who waited until the fall of France in 1940 before joining what he believed would be the victorious side. Poland first, then Denmark, Norway, Belgium, the Netherlands, France, Romania, Bulgaria, Yugoslavia, and Greece fell under the Axis yoke. The settlements of 1919–23 were destroyed. The cartoon about the weeping child had been uncannily right.

The League had failed, completely. There had been late-in-the-day efforts to rethink it, including the Bruce Report of August (!) 1939, whose main suggestion was for the creation of a Central Committee for Economic and Social Questions, separate from the League's political functions—as if tacitly recognizing that territorial issues could not be supervised by the present rump Assembly, whereas the technical agencies might continue with their work. With Hitler's panzer divisions revving their engines on the Polish border, no one cared much for the Geneva organization; all eyes were focused elsewhere. The world seemed no different from the way it had been in 1914, or even 1648. The nations of Europe now marched, sailed, and flew to the war, as they had done so often in the past. The League's final gasp of breath, to expel the Soviet Union for its attack upon Finland that winter, seems more symbolic of its pathos than of its powers. The show was over, and the curtains had closed.

The League was put into a sort of "receivership" after mid-1940, its appeasement-prone secretary-general, Joseph Avenol, being succeeded by Sean Lester, who administered a skeleton organization in Geneva throughout the war, indeed until April 18, 1946, when it was formally wound up.[14]

As the League's main chambers thus gathered dust, the dramas of World War II overwhelmed everything around them. The German conquests of Poland and much of Western Europe, the fall of France and the Battle of Britain, the entry of Italy into the war and the struggle's extension into the Mediterranean, Balkans, and Middle East, the Nazi attack upon the USSR, and the Japanese onslaughts in the Far East grabbed all the popular attention between 1939 and 1942.

These were not circumstances in which leaders as hard-pressed as Churchill and Stalin had time to reflect upon improved world structures.

Yet some early thinking occurred at less august levels. American internationalists, long frustrated by their country's inertia during the 1930s, formed the Commission to Study the Organization of Peace and as early as 1940 had produced a report on the need to move from a league of nations to a world federation (thus making the case several years before the publication of Wendell Willkie's astonishingly popular book, *One World*).[15] Roosevelt himself was encouraging the State Department to thoughts about the postwar order, even before the United States was in the war. The British Foreign Office, which possessed a department for international organizations and treaties, was also developing some early thoughts, albeit with Churchill's tart proviso that this was only for those who had time on their hands! And when the prime minister and president met in August 1941 to proclaim the Atlantic Charter, they agreed on the "establishment of a wider and permanent system of general security." It is worth observing that Roosevelt's public emphasis in these years upon the "Four Freedoms" speech (freedom of speech and expression; freedom of religion; freedom from want; and freedom from fear) anticipates the lofty language of the Preamble to the UN Charter itself. But this was all very vague, deliberately so.

Obviously, substantial thought and planning could get under way only from 1943 onward, as the tides of war changed in favor of the Grand Alliance and the various players were compelled to consider what sort of world they wanted after the fighting was over. Before assessing the decisions taken that were to lead to the future international order, however, we should examine the ideas and anxieties that influenced Allied policy makers, especially since some of those concerns have faded into the mists of time.[16]

In the security field, there were at least three reasons why the Great Powers behaved as they did. The first was simply their natural egoism. Powerful animals see no reason to be circumscribed by lesser, weaker ones. The second was the result of the powers' interpretations of recent history. The third concerned their worries for the immediate

future. These last two reasons have almost been forgotten and have
scarcely been mentioned in the recent debates on changing the Security Council's membership. However, all three motives contributed to
the care and thought with which those governments crafted the critical chapters of the UN Charter that dealt with security issues.

The egoism and wariness of the discussions of 1944–45 were exhibited above all by the two emerging superpowers, the USSR and the
United States. This is understandable enough. France was being re-
suscitated into Great Power status at Churchill's urgings, but how
could Paris affect the deliberations at Dumbarton Oaks, Yalta, and
San Francisco? China was embroiled in civil war and regarded with
bemusement and without credibility by Moscow and London. One
might have thought the waning British Empire might have been the
state most wary of restrictions upon its sovereignty, and it certainly
wanted to ward off interference in the internal affairs of its colonies;
but by 1945, its policy makers were even more concerned about the
need to enmesh the somewhat wayward Americans and Russians into
a web of international obligations.

Thus it was that the two real Great Powers of the time, whose
growing bipolar influence had been predicted more than one hundred
years earlier by Alexis de Tocqueville, exhibited most suspicions about
restraining their future actions through international charter. Neither
country had fond memories of the League of Nations. America, as we
have seen, had abandoned it even before signing. The USSR had not
been permitted membership in 1919, was belatedly brought in during
the mid-1930s, and was then expelled after the invasion of Finland.
Each also believed that it would gain victory chiefly through the
power of its own resources and will. So why be hamstrung now?
More specifically, Stalin, whose bursts of paranoia at this time were
breaking new bounds, feared entrapment by the capitalist architects
of the new world order. A triumvirate or, if necessary, a five-state
cabal of world powers, warily circling but respecting one another's
stated interests, was just acceptable. But he would never allow voting
in the new forum to lead to common actions against Soviet interests.
A veto was, therefore, essential. Ironically, the same position was held
by many in Washington—for example, by Senator Arthur Vanden-

berg, that profoundly anti-Communist American who is reported to have told a protesting Mexican delegate at San Francisco that he could either have a United Nations with a Permanent Five veto—or no UN at all.[17]

The second reason was this: The American, British, and Soviet policy makers who were intent upon fashioning the world order in 1945 had all come through the harrowing experience of systemic international collapse during the preceding fifteen or twenty years. One suspects that by 1939 they had already drawn grim conclusions about what worked and what didn't in the pursuit of peace, or at least in the avoidance of catastrophe. The cathartic events of the Second World War can only have burnished and intensified those judgments. By the time policy papers and draft charters had to be submitted about their next attempt at deterring war, they were in little mood for any of the flaccid well-meaning declarations that, they suspected, had given the League of Nations such weak legs. The new security system had to have teeth.

Their charges against the former League system, some stated openly, some held privately, were many, various, and withering. It had been simply too democratic and too liberal. As we have seen earlier, this meant that small, earnest states such as Finland and New Zealand could make proposals and object to necessary deals, with results that worked like casting sand into the wheels of old-diplomacy negotiations. It was one thing for international law to recognize that all states are sovereign, Denmark as much as the USSR, Costa Rica as much as the United States; but that democratic tendency had not worked to deter the aggressors of the 1930s. On the contrary, the evidence was that it had encouraged the dictators, who observed the League's paralysis, to be bolder and bolder. This was not to happen again.

Therefore, the potentially isolationist Great Powers, the United States and USSR, had to be kept inside the camp and not allowed to bolt into distant mistrust and obstructionism. On this point, the British government was most clear. It had no intention of being put in the same position it had occupied after 1919, with all the other players having left the stage except itself and a weakened (and, on this

second occasion, seriously weakened) France. If the "Big Two" had
to be enticed to remain on board, whether it be through guarantees to
the U.S. Senate about sovereignty or special voting privileges to the
Great Powers, then so be it. If they could be "embedded" by postwar
military coordinations or some negative control over how things
might go, that was also worth the price. It might weaken certain uni-
versalistic principles and compromise the effective response to possible transgressions of international law where a large nation was
involved, but that was a lot better than no security system at all. This
could be worked out, if everyone was reasonable.

But perhaps the most important motive in the planners' minds was
their assessments of the different capacities—different qualities—of
large versus small states. The belief was simply this: What the 1930s
taught them was that militarily weak countries like Czechoslovakia,
Belgium, Ethiopia, and Manchuria were inherent "consumers" of security. They could not provide for themselves, not because of some
lapse of national character, but because they lacked the demographic,
territorial, and economic resources to resist the aggressions of larger
neighbors. By contrast, the big powers were, or had been forced to
become, the "providers" of international security—again, not because of any special virtues of character, but because only they had
the capacity to withstand and then defeat Germany, Italy, and Japan.
The basic distinction between countries requiring outside help to preserve their security and countries that committed themselves to provide it had to be made clear this time. If it was fudged, the world's
democracies might once again be thrown into confusion should a future Manchurian crisis or Austrian Anschluss occur.

This, then, leads to the third reason, which is that the wartime
planners felt an acute need to anticipate the possibility of renewed aggressions by Berlin and Tokyo or, perhaps, some other ambitious
state in the mid-1950s or thereafter. If this seems an astonishingly bad
piece of forecasting from today's perspective, given the deep cultural
revulsion in postwar Germany and Japan at being drawn into any
foreign entanglements, it made sense at the time. The British and, to
a lesser extent, the French certainly had this on their minds. It is
worth recalling that when these Allied plans for the postwar order

were being drafted, both Axis powers were still in possession of vast swaths of captured territory and still fighting hard. An eventual victory for the Grand Alliance seemed increasingly likely, but German and Japanese resolve was impressive, and who knew what dreadful secret weapons the Germans (especially) might be developing from their massive technological resources? These were not folks to be taken lightly. Only fifteen years after Germany's epic defeat in the last war, it had been ready to challenge the prevailing system again. Most people in the West and USSR were convinced that their foes possessed a "natural," inexorable tendency toward aggression and atrocity.[18]

True, the Allies had extensive plans for the democratization of Germany and Japan, but after the crushing of those rosy Wilsonian hopes for lasting peace only two decades earlier, the victor powers knew they had to be more careful this time and stiffen the security provisions of the Charter. Small nations ought therefore to cease carping about the unfairness of the veto and be grateful that the Great Powers were now going to take their international responsibilities seriously. Finally, and despite the rising suspicions between East and West as the 1939–45 conflict came to a close, there was still hope that the wartime alliance might be maintained in some transformed way to achieve a new era of peace. Historians are perhaps a little too fast to fasten upon those 1945 discussions at Yalta and Potsdam, where the "Big Three" were in disagreement, and often pay less attention to the sessions during which the military staffs reported on their respective operations and plans. Keeping up this cooperation, albeit at a much lower level and slower pace, was not out of the question.

Ultimately, two things were clear. First, unlike in 1919, in 1945 every one of the Great Powers was willing to help construct and then enter into a new international security system. Second—although this awkward fact was never spelled out openly—despite all the language of the UN Charter requiring compliance with Security Council resolutions, if a powerful state should decide to defy the world body and go it alone, there was little that could be done to prevent that happening, unless, of course, the other powerful states were willing to move to military enforcement and thus run the strong risk of starting World

War III. If lesser states broke the rules, they might well get spanked. In this regard, at least, little had changed—Great Powers would do what Great Powers choose to do. The planners were well aware of that reality but crossed fingers that the harmonious and mutually beneficial workings of a new international structure, plus improved measures for cooperation, reinforced by the memories of two bloody world conflicts, would be sufficient to keep all countries from crossing that dread boundary between peace and war. For institutional and also moral reasons, governments would feel the global pressure to settle disputes without recourse to the sword, or the bomb.

The other great lesson that Western planners and politicians drew from the interwar years related to the economic and social collapse of the open market system, a disaster that they believed was the root cause of the political unrest and extremism that led to the wars: Desperate men do desperate things. American and British working parties (obviously the Soviets had no interest here) therefore spent much time exploring ideas for improved financial, banking, and commercial architecture that would, positively, advance international prosperity and interdependence and, negatively, head off any dire threats to instability in currency and stock markets. The exploration of these economic schemes ran parallel to the negotiations to construct a postwar security order, and the idea of grand socioeconomic reconstruction was wildly popular in the Western liberal press. Yet, unsurprisingly, the plans for that new international financial system (as detailed further in Chapter Four) that were hammered out at the famous Bretton Woods conference in the summer of 1944 ended up by placing much more emphasis upon fiscal responsibility than upon any global mission to improve humanity regardless of cost. The need for stability—a stability controlled by the larger powers—always took priority, even when employing the rhetoric of advancing universal human goods. It was no coincidence that voting rights on the future International Monetary Fund (IMF) and World Bank (first known as the International Bank for Reconstruction and Development, IBRD) were "weighted" to reflect the greater resources of the rich capitalist nations, above all the United States.

These, then, were the broad assumptions about the provision of future military and economic security that motivated the Big Three powers and shaped their plans for the new world organization, when they met, variously, in Moscow, Bretton Woods, Dumbarton Oaks, Yalta, and San Francisco (by which time China and France were also playing a role). Given their special place in the security scheme, the Great Powers were willing to see the establishment of more democratic decision making and parliamentary structures in other parts of the United Nations. It was all right, for example, to have some additional nonpermanent members on the Security Council, since none of them would possess the veto. And a deliberative body such as a General Assembly representing the governments of all UN member states, and with various committees and agencies whose membership rotated and could be regionally representative, was to be welcome—always provided they respected the special powers of the Security Council.

Not much attention was given at the top to matters of culture and ideology or to the important issue of human rights. Those all came in a rush, in 1945, as the negotiators strove to put a loftier context to the more prosaic language regarding the UN's security apparatus, its quasi-parliamentary constitution in the Assembly, and the hard-nosed arrangements for economic cooperation. Even before the acceptance at San Francisco of the high-minded language of the Charter, and later of the Universal Declaration of Human Rights, officials inside and writers on the outside were describing the new world organization as a sort of three-legged stool:

Leg one involved measures to obtain international security and therefore stressed cooperative diplomacy and arbitration to settle disputes, backed up by shared military force to deter aggression or, if that failed, to defeat the aggressors.

Leg two rested upon the belief that military security without economic improvement was short-term and futile. Instruments, whether within the UN family or "in relationship" to the world body (such as the Bretton Woods institutions), therefore had to be devised to rebuild the world economy.

Leg three was arguably the most interesting of all and clearly picked up the idealist legacies of Kant, Wilson, and others. It argued that however strongly the first two legs were constructed, the system would fold—would collapse—if it did not produce ways of improving political and cultural understandings among peoples. Since war begins in the minds of men, it was (and is) in that realm that important advances were required.

Physically, a three-legged stool is a very strong structure; all three poles tilt inward, reinforcing the others. It is hard to damage it or pull it apart. Nonetheless, it is a human creation and therefore dependent upon the great craftsmen who forged it. If the carpenters gave more strength to one of the legs, leaving the others weaker, the stool would soon be tilting. In fact, thanks to a number of compromises (and some very clever drafting), the document that emerged from the San Francisco conference—the UN Charter—was remarkably balanced. What seems clear from the historical record is that it was the Americans who most touted the idea of cultural and ideological community, the Soviets who stressed the need for security above all else (what need had Stalin for the World Bank?), and the British who were most anxious for a deal that offered both military and economic stability for the postwar order, giving the new international bodies more power than the League ever possessed, but without intrusion into domestic or colonial affairs. This seemed a fair arrangement, assuming (a large assumption) that the Big Three continued to respect the compromises hammered out among themselves between 1943 and 1945.

All this helps to explain the particular form of the Charter's text (which, for convenience, is reproduced in the Appendix). After the lofty Preamble, which "hereby establish[es] an international organization to be known as the United Nations," Chapter I reminds members of the purposes and principles to which they had pledged themselves by signing the Charter. They were extensive and commanding obligations: All members "shall fulfill in good faith," "shall settle their international disputes by peaceful means," and "shall give the United Nations every assistance in any action it takes." As if to compensate for the boldness of these pledges, the chapter ends with the famous declaration (Article 2, Part 7), "Nothing contained in the present Charter shall authorize the United Nations to intervene in matters which are essentially within the domestic jurisdiction of any state."[19]

The second chapter is a brief one, simply defining membership of the UN as being open to all peace-loving states and outlining the processes for admission—and expulsion. It reads rather like the statutes for membership in a London or New York gentlemen's club. The third chapter is even briefer, identifying six "principal organs" of the world body—the General Assembly, the Security Council, the Economic and Social Council, the Trusteeship Council, the International Court of Justice, and the Secretariat. These six were not equal in real weight, as we shall see; but they were now established in international law. The Charter also declared that "such subsidiary organs as may be found necessary may [also] be established." The founding fathers were giving themselves a lot of leeway.

The really critical sections come in the center of the Charter: Chapter IV on the General Assembly, Chapter V on the composition, powers, and procedures of the Security Council, Chapter VI on the pacific settlement of disputes; and the explosive Chapter VII, "Action with Respect to Threats to the Peace, Breaches of the Peace, and Acts of Aggression." Both at the time of drafting and in subsequent decades, all governments and their diplomats viewed these four chapters as the key elements in a new international order. How could they not, composing the text in the midst of the most destructive war in history and determined to produce something better than the League of Nations had offered?

The articles relating to the functions, powers, and procedures of the General Assembly are most artful in nature. At first sight, it looks as if Tennyson's Parliament of man—at least in the form of a parliament of governments—is to be realized, and so in a sense it was. All nation-states could apply for membership, and voting was by majority rule, with decisions on "important questions" needing a two-thirds majority.[20] The Assembly was charged to consider and approve the UN's annual budget, to approve trusteeship arrangements, and to supervise international cooperation "in the economic, social, cultural, educational, and health fields." It was to assist "in the realization of human rights and fundamental freedoms for all." This was a heady list. Here, surely, was the political center of gravity for the international order in the decades to come.

But closer inspection of the Charter's delicate language suggests that the Assembly did not have the innate powers possessed by, say, the British House of Commons. The careful reader will note the frequent use of the conditional word *may* (as opposed to *shall*) at many points. Thus, while the General Assembly "may call the attention of the Security Council to situations" that threatened the peace, it was also made plain in Article 12, Part 1, that it should not make any recommendations at a time when the Security Council was wrestling with a particular dispute. Perhaps the greatest measure of the power "gap" between the two organs was that Assembly resolutions, while always carrying an important symbolic weight, were not binding; Security Council resolutions were binding upon all members—indeed, a condition for permitting them to sign the Charter. One wishes that all governments remember that fact.

There were two further distinctions between the General Assembly and the Security Council, again of much weight. The first was that the Assembly would normally meet in "regular annual sessions," which in practice reduced its capacities and flexibility; it tended to make such sessions honorific and ideological.* The Security Council, by contrast, could meet at very short notice, even at night or over a weekend, in emergency session, which once more suggested that it was a sort of executive branch of the world organization. The second was that, whereas the Security Council was supreme in the realm of security (save where a Great Power could not be stopped from going its own way), the General Assembly did not enjoy equivalent authority and monopoly in the areas of economic and social matters. As previously noted, the new and powerful machinery for international financial cooperation that emerged from the Bretton Woods conference was never within the domain of the Assembly and soon distanced itself further. From its very birth, then, the parliament of governments was restricted in its financial powers.

The Charter's language about the Security Council (Chapters V–VII, plus, in a way, VIII upon regional arrangements) is even more

---

*The custom was gradually established that the annual sessions would commence each September in New York, with the world's leaders flying in to make speeches on behalf of their current political hobbyhorse.

artful. Most commentators rush in to examine the sections upon the peaceful/diplomatic settlement of disputes (Chapter VI) and then upon the economic and military measures to do the same (Chapter VII). But it is wise to spend some time on Chapter V, which deals with the composition, functions and powers, and voting and procedures of the Security Council, for this was where the negotiators of 1943–45 devoted their largest energies. They established that the Council would consist of the five great victor powers, all with permanent seats (the P5), plus six rotating two-year members, a number not increased for another two decades (to ten nonpermanent members). It is worth noting that the Charter insists that the most important criterion for nonpermanent membership would be a country's contribution "to the maintenance of international peace and security and to the other purposes of the Organization" (Article 23, Part 1). Equitable geographic distribution was only the second criterion. It seems fair to observe that this priority has suffered badly during the past six decades of regional horse trading and "it's my turn now" deals. It may be worth resuscitating the principle that if you can't carry the load, don't even try to join the club.

All members were to agree to confer primary responsibility for international peace and security upon the Security Council, which was charged to act on their behalf; and they had to "accept and agree to carry out" each of its decisions. The Council, as previously noted, was to be organized to be able to function continuously, day or night. It could hold its meetings away from its normal seat, establish subsidiary organs, plan a system of arms control, adopt its own rules of procedure, and bring in for discussion non–Security Council members when it saw fit. The chief object was to get things done.

The most contentious part of this section concerned the P5's right of veto, although it is coded in such nifty language (see Article 27) that one is obliged to read the text several times. Essentially, it says that Security Council decisions on procedural matters may be made by an affirmative vote of roughly 60 percent of its members (that is, seven out of eleven in the early decades, nine out of fifteen later). That sounds reasonable enough, but the same article also adds that "decisions on all other matters shall be made by an affirmative vote of seven [later nine] members, including the concurring votes of the permanent members." Here, in opaque form, lies the veto. Even if only one of the P5 is against a resolution, declaring it to be more than a procedural issue, it fails. When a bewildered non-P5 ambassador once asked the Soviet representative how one could tell the difference between a procedural matter and a substantive matter, he was informed dryly, "We shall tell you." And so it remains today.

With this proviso in place—recall that its intent was to stop the United States and USSR from bolting the tent—the articles in Chapter VI, "Pacific Settlement of Disputes," make a lot of sense. The section begins by declaring that the parties to any dispute (always assumed to be nation-states) shall seek for solution "by negotiation, enquiry, mediation, conciliation, arbitration, judicial settlement, resort to regional agencies or arrangements, or other peaceful means of their own choice" (Article 33). It reads as if it were co-drafted by a psychiatrist and a labor relations lawyer and clearly is meant to express that hopeful Wilsonian notion that reasonable men should always be able to arrive at a peaceful solution by themselves or with some outside help.

The Charter also insists that the Security Council is entitled to investigate any dispute that threatens the common peace and that any member state can bring a cause to the Council (also, interestingly, to the General Assembly, which can offer its view, but not more than that, to the Council). The Security Council is fully empowered to recommend appropriate procedures or methods of adjustment, though it is noted that legal disputes should normally be taken by the disputing parties to the International Court of Justice at The Hague. If the contenders fail to agree, the Council can make its own recommendations in order to achieve "a pacific settlement of the dispute."

This is precisely where Chapter VI ends. The reader, plus all those governments that sign the Charter and pledge to fulfill its terms, are being walked up the garden path. It is all very logical. It is based upon the supposition that "the parties in dispute" can settle things through various means. If they can't, then the Security Council will play a helpful role, offering recommendations to get things resolved. One party might feel that it has received a worse deal than the other at a

Council decision, but all nations would agree that the pacific settlement of disputes process to which they are contractually agreed is an impartial one. It is so reasonable that this entire chapter takes a mere six articles, namely, numbers 33–38.[21]

But then comes Chapter VII concerning the enforcement of the peace, should an aggressor or threatening state refuse the route of pacific settlement. Here the Security Council was given complete authority to determine the crisis situation, recommend provisional measures to solve it, "duly take note of failure to comply" (Article 40), and then decide what instruments to employ in enforcing its own decisions. Taken literally, the text is breathtakingly bold and was meant to be. Little wonder that the Charter's authors needed a full thirteen articles to elaborate on how this new security system would work. After six years of total war, placing much faith in the pacific resolution of disputes among nations seemed unwise, and downright foolish, despite what was said in Chapter VI.

The Security Council was given the power to decide upon nonmilitary measures against an offending nation, most notably economic sanctions and the severance of air, rail, sea, and telegraphic communications. Here it was not unlike the League of Nations, although some of the planners must surely have remembered the failure of economic sanctions in the past, such as those applied against Italy after its attack upon Abyssinia. If, therefore, the Council determined that nonmilitary measures were inadequate, it was empowered by the Charter to undertake peacekeeping operations and, if necessary, was also authorized to pursue all possible actions by air, sea, or land against an aggressor state. To achieve this goal, it required all members—thus, not just those on the Security Council—to make available armed forces, assistance, and facilities, including rights of passage, when asked to do so. Such contributions would be negotiated by "special agreement" (Article 43), and no one expected that small states could offer much, except perhaps vital rights of passage. But the message was plain: Any nation that signed the UN Charter had to pull its weight. In fact, Article 45 was bold enough to declare that in order for a Security Council operation to take place fast, "Members shall hold immediately available national air-force contingents for combined international action." (There is much stress upon the value of airpower and forward air bases in the planning documents, and it emerges also in the Charter.)

Clearly, all this would require serious military preparation and planning, and thus the Charter went so far as to establish a Military Staff Committee to advise and assist the Security Council on all questions relating to military requirements, the command of forces in the field, and even "possible disarmament." This was a hugely ambitious idea, and had it been pursued, it would have transformed the nature of international politics.[22]

To the American and British officials who drafted this section, the wartime experience was obvious: Since victory in the present campaigning was impossible without carefully coordinated Allied staff planning, it followed that a lasting peace would also be impossible without such expert military support for the Security Council. Yet here again, the hierarchical nature of the system was clear. The membership of the Military Staff Committee was restricted to "the Chiefs of Staff of the permanent members of the Security Council or their representatives." Any other UN member would be invited to be associated only "when the efficient discharge of the Committee's responsibilities requires the participation of that Member in its work." And the Great Powers alone had the right to decide what constituted the necessary level of efficiency to merit such a special invitation to help them.

This seriousness about military capacity and efficiency also explains the very detailed plans that were made to establish an array of UN army bases, airfields, and naval harbors in different parts of the world, from Wilhelmshaven and Naples to the Far East. The best planners on earth were of little use if there were not also powerful, multinational forces stationed in forward positions, to deter aggression in the first place but also to be deployed at the Security Council's will in any future crisis. As to other members, they also were called upon to make available to the Security Council such military resources as they had; at the very least, they could offer base facilities to the larger peace enforcement operations. If every signatory to the

Charter was committed to these responsibilities, any future version of, say, the 1935 Abyssinian crisis ought to be quickly quashed.[23]

This chapter runs on to reassert (Article 49) that all members shall afford assistance to ensure the Security Council's resolutions are carried out, then reassures dubious governments that if UN enforcement measures create "special economic problems" (Article 50)—one imagines because of blockade or disruption of communications—they have the right of swift consultation with the Security Council. Both are clear messages that collective security should indeed be exactly that. This is really strong stuff. Those Victorian realists Henry Palmerston and Otto von Bismarck, even perhaps the archliberal William Gladstone, would have been astonished.

The final article in this assertive Chapter VII then takes an abrupt turn, and since it has proved for sixty years exceedingly difficult to parse, I am including its full text below, so that readers may judge what to make of the remarkable Article 51:

> Nothing in the present Charter shall impair the inherent right of individual or collective self-defence if an armed attack occurs against a Member of the United Nations, until the Security Council has taken measures necessary to maintain international peace and security. Measures taken by Members in the exercise of this right of self-defence shall be immediately reported to the Security Council and not in any way affect the authority and responsibility of the Security Council under the present Charter to take at any time such action as it deems necessary in order to maintain or restore international peace and security.

The first part is easy to understand. Nations that had witnessed a series of Fascist surprise attacks across Europe, the unprovoked Operation Barbarossa, and the sneak assault upon Pearl Harbor were not going to wait for Security Council approval before reaching for their weapons if they were the subject of aggression. But what exactly do the qualifying clauses in the second sentence about maintaining the authority and responsibility of the Security Council mean in practice? And how elastic is the term *self-defence*? To man your guns as the Luftwaffe flies overhead is one thing, but can you act preemptively if your intelligence tells you that those bombers are still on the ground a thousand miles away and that a state of open war does not yet exist? Can you act even before then, by a preventive strike against a growing and perceived threat—and does not that make you the aggressor? It is an issue that has dogged UN debate on "security" from the beginning, and perhaps never more bitterly than in the run-up to the second Iraq war.

Ultimately, the Great Powers themselves would decide, according to their perceptions of their national interests. Clearly, Article 51 is placed in the center of the Charter to assuage the suspicions both of American senators and of Joseph Stalin that this new organization would weaken their right to fend for themselves. Both were determined that nobody was going to take that right away, and surely Winston Churchill and Charles de Gaulle were, too; yet at the same time there also existed a desperate yearning to escape the international anarchy of the past and establish an effective rule of law that would head off disastrous conflicts in the future. In various ways, this article captures the ambivalence: "Yes, I will surrender certain powers to the international organization, but I insist on retaining my freedom of action in cases I judge to be important." The UN optimists hoped that, were Chapters VI and VII shown to work successfully, this mistrust would fade. The realists kept their powder dry.

So much for the core chapters dealing with the General Assembly and the Security Council. It would be wrong to dismiss the other sections of the Charter—on regional arrangements (VIII), the Economic and Social Council (IX–X), trusteeship (XI–XIII), the International Court of Justice (XIV), and the Secretariat (XV)—as being ephemeral. On the contrary, the fact that the text of these chapters consumes almost twice the length as those on the General Assembly and the Security Council suggests that the creators of the Charter attached much significance to the additional organs. If they have faded in prominence over the intervening decades, they were regarded as important in 1944–45 and may still be of use today.

Take, for example, the brief Chapter VIII, "Regional Arrangements," which allows for the making or existence of regional pacts for the maintenance of international peace, provided their activities are consistent with the purposes of the UN itself. Indeed, it seems to encourage regional groups to seek to resolve local disputes and states that the Security Council may use such instruments as a sort of buttress to the global security architecture. The language used here sought to satisfy two needs. The first was Churchill's strong feeling that security in the future would best be assured through regional groups led by one of the Great Powers, simply because the countries involved would have the most immediate reason to deter or halt aggression in their neighborhood. Still warm in the prime minister's memory was the undeniable fact that most members of the League had found it difficult to think of committing resources to stop a *distant* violation of the peace. Even certain Americans like Cordell Hull, who worried that this option might lead to Great Power "spheres of influence" policies, could see the merits of at least recognizing that regional arrangements (under Security Council purview) might be helpful.

The second reason (expressed in Articles 53 and 54) was the Soviet, British, and French desire to be able to act collectively and swiftly "against renewal of aggressive policy" on the part of "enemy states"—never mentioned by name but clearly intended to mean Germany and Japan. This seems very anachronistic six decades later, and the wording ought to be amended in any general revision of the Charter. Still, in today's troubled world, the existence of an authorization to recruit regional security groups may have increasing utility, as an overstretched UN looks to subcontract the handling of a crisis, or war, to the members of that region—always, of course, conditional upon respect for the Charter's principles.

Truly anachronistic seems the remarkably lengthy section (Articles 73–91 of Chapters XI–XIII) on the issue of non-self-governing territories and the formation of a Trusteeship Council as one of the principal organs of the world body. Since the UN was going to inherit supervision of those lands in Africa, the Middle East, and the Pacific that had been League of Nations "mandate" territories in 1919, something had to be said here, and in fact these chapters contain much high-minded and generous language about advancing the inhabitants of those territories to all their rights. Almost fully concealed from the layman's eye, however, lurked the secular concerns of the Great Powers.

The USSR had little concern here, just as long as others recognized the special controls in areas it was acquiring for strategic purposes. And China in 1944–45 played hardly a role. But the other three had strong interests in mind. Britain and France were the two overseas colonial powers par excellence. To them, a too intrusive supervision of the mandated League territories and swift advance to independence might, even in small dependencies, have reverberations upon their far larger and richer colonial estates. In this area, the United States again exhibited ambivalence. Publicly, its position against colonialism had been trumpeted, it had put much pressure upon Churchill about India and Africa, and it was keen to attract the non-Communist world into the Western, free market camp. Moreover, the granting of basic constitutional rights to all peoples was a passion of that remarkable African American Ralph Bunche, already a rising star in the State Department.[24] But the U.S. military was also determined to retain control of the Japanese-mandated islands it was seizing in the Pacific, in order to possess additional strategic bases.

All this explains the strained language of the Charter, describing how future trusteeship arrangements were to work: Dependent peoples were to be advanced toward statehood, but not yet. Bunche himself, as the first director of the UN Secretariat's Trusteeship Division, led a staff determined to advance this cause despite the old colonial powers and more conservative Americans. As it happened, most of this effort turned out to be overtaken by history. Within a period far shorter than the policy makers (even the most progressive) could have imagined, the age of decolonization began; and the Trusteeship Council looked increasingly like some ancient, rusting battleship, its engines removed, its crew long departed.

There are some nowadays who would say that the Economic and Social Council (ECOSOC) has come perilously close to a similar end. This is not true, but it will be better to analyze its history in the pages that follow. Yet no one who reads the pertinent sections of the UN Charter—Chapter IX ("International Economic and Social Co-operation") and Chapter X ("The Economic and Social Council")—can come away without being impressed (and amazed) at the boldness of this part of the UN's architecture. Read literally, it is to replicate the Security Council in most other spheres. What that powerful body was to do in the realms of international peace and security, the ECOSOC would provide in regard to economic, social, health, environmental, human rights, and cultural advancement.

In retrospect, and as we shall discuss further in Chapters Four and Five, it is clear that this was an overambitious remit. It is also noticeable that the Great Powers do not insist on a special place here. Having achieved their privileged positions on the Security Council and the Bretton Woods institutions, they were content to see an ECOSOC of eighteen rotating members, reporting to the General Assembly and taking instruction from it, drafting its own rules, creating its own commissions, initiating studies and calling conferences, going "into relationship" with the specialized agencies, consulting with nongovernmental organizations (NGOs), and anything else it chose to do. To an enthusiast of international social and economic cooperation, this must have looked wonderful. A realist, by contrast, would have noted that "consulting with NGOs" appears nowhere in the description of the Security Council's powers and functions.

The chapters on the International Court of Justice (XIV) and the United Nations Secretariat (XV) have much less guile to them. They are plain and factual and necessary inheritances from the earlier international system. The segment on the Court is exceedingly brief, in part because the "Statute of the International Court of Justice" was to be attached to the Charter and regarded as an integral part of it. The statute itself was chiefly given over to definitions of membership, election, competence, and procedures. In many regards, it was the successor to the Permanent Court of Arbitration established by the 1907 Hague Convention—that is, it offered a judicial structure only for states that agreed to take their rival claims to arbitration. No other entities could initiate the process, and the governments concerned had voluntarily to submit to the judicial outcome. Should one of the parties not agree to the Court's decision, the latter could refer the case to the Security Council, in essence to the Great Powers. The International Court of Justice was thus another "firewall" to slow down any need by the Security Council to undertake Chapter VII actions against a member state. Still, should a nation be in blatant defiance of the Court's carefully rendered opinion, the Security Council reserved the right to intervene. On issues of power, all roads led back to it.

The Secretariat was also an echo of how the League of Nations had functioned. It was a principal organ of the United Nations, but a servant to all. Its job, under the secretary-general, was to make the many facets of the organization work on a daily basis. Three items in the text of Chapter XV stand out. The secretary-general was to be appointed by the General Assembly "upon the recommendation of the Security Council," so once again the P5 had a controlling interest. Second, and more encouraging, the personnel of the Secretariat (who would staff the General Assembly, the Security Council, the ECOSOC, the Trusteeship Council, and all other principal and subsidiary organs) would be international civil servants, who would not take instruction from the governments of their land of birth and had to meet "the highest standards of efficiency, competence, and integrity" (Article 101). This important demand was then followed by a pious hope for recruiting staff "on as wide a geographical basis as possible." No method was suggested for how one reconciled sheer competence with geographic entitlement, a problem that haunts the UN to this day.

Third, the secretary-general was to bring to the Security Council's attention any matter that might threaten the maintenance of international peace and security. This was a critical point (Article 99), since it created an office separate from both the Security Council and the General Assembly that could initiate at least examination, if not action, in regard to threats to, or breaches of, the peace. It therefore gave the Secretary-General's Office some claim to independent intelligence and assessment, even if it remained the servant to many masters. It also represented an organ to which member states, or the General Assembly itself, could turn for information, provision of reports, and budgetary data. Since one of its tasks—perhaps its chief task—was to be the general staff to the Security Council, it was also obliged to think hard and deeply about post–World War II peace-keeping and enforcement and responses to any manner of crises. These were heavy loads for a fledgling bureaucracy.

The final articles of the Charter are typical "tidy up" and miscellaneous measures relating to transitional arrangements, international immunity for UN personnel, ratifications procedures, and signature. Only two are worth mention: the article (103) asserting that the obligations of members to the UN prevail over all and any of their other international obligations; and the important statement (Article 109, Part 2) that any amendment to the Charter required the vote (ratified by home parliaments) of two-thirds of the Assembly's members, "including all of the permanent members of the Security Council." All was fastened nicely in place.

The Charter thus consists of many parts, and as the parallel stories of the fate of those parts are unfolded in the chapters ahead, we will gain a sense of its meaning and effect, of what worked well and what didn't, of what could be adjusted to meet changing circumstances and what was frozen in stone. The Charter itself was a curious combination of inflexibility on the one hand (the repeated insistence of the special rights of the P5) and the utmost flexibility on the other (in regard, for example, to the variety of possible responses to a threat to the peace). This was surely no coincidence. The men who had labored long and hard to compose the Charter were well aware that they had to give the world organization a strong inner core—the Security Council—but also use language that was adaptable enough to allow application under unforeseen circumstances in years to come.[25] In addition, the Charter had to incorporate the broad yearnings for more than military security alone and give structure and process to them.

What is incontestable is that the UN's founders had, in some way, created a new world order. The structure of international politics after 1945 was different from that after 1648 and 1815; different even from that after 1919, because it now brought all of the Great Powers into the tent (even the difficult United States) and had given the new international entity a broader remit to address the economic, social, and cultural reasons that it believed drove people toward conflict. There were, of course, many challenges that the drafters of the Charter did not foresee, perhaps especially a future world in which threats to the peace would often be due less to external acts of aggression than to internal disintegration and civil wars. But should we really expect such foresight from a generation of overworked politicians, diplomats, legal experts, and military advisers who were required to think about the future of the world when enormous battles were raging across Europe and the Pacific? I do not think so.

There is one further conundrum here, not yet mentioned. The United Nations "system" had come into being, and altered the political landscape, to the great applause of World Federalists and other internationalist bodies. But in 1945, another massive transformation was taking place: The multipolar, chiefly Eurocentric order of states was swiftly giving way to a bipolar world, and one that would be nuclear at that.[26] Thus, the international system was changing, both in regard to the entry of new global organizations and in the eternal story of the rise and fall of the Great Powers. How these two, totally different, new "orders" would relate to each other was a massive puzzle. For large nations are rarely good members of an international club designed to restrain the exercise of national power.

The politicians' speeches about the creation of the United Nations, whether at San Francisco itself or when the first sessions of the General Assembly and Security Council opened in London in January 1946, were emotional, triumphant, and optimistic about the future of humankind. Truman himself, in a brilliant address to the final plenary session on the UN conference that was meeting some two months after San Francisco to sign the Charter and record membership, concluded with: "This new structure of peace is rising upon strong foundations. Let us not fail to grasp the supreme chance to establish a world-wide rule of reason—to create an enduring peace under the guidance of God." The diplomats who had toiled day and night in the Dumbarton Oaks, Yalta, and San Francisco vineyards were altogether more secular and apprehensive. In the State Department, George Kennan was already venting his view that the Charter promised too much and its wording was too ambiguous and that this would lead to future quarrels with the suspicious and untrustworthy

USSR. And Gladwyn Jebb, the British diplomat who had worked so hard on so many of the drafts, came away from the whole experience fearing that the negotiators had aimed too high for "this wicked world."[27]

This, of course, was and is the UN's permanent dilemma. Since its beginning, the organization's high ambitions have contrasted sharply with the constant jostling of peoples and governments and with the assertive claims of sovereign states. It was, perhaps, President Dwight Eisenhower who offered the best justification for the world body when he said: "With all the defects, with all the failures that we can check up against it, the U.N. still represents man's best-organized hope to substitute the conference table for the battlefield."[28] This is, many voices will claim, no less true today. But that justification remains, for all the reasons to be discussed in the pages that follow, a long way away from the early vision of a federation of the world, lapt in universal law.

PART 2

*The Evolution of the Many UNs
Since 1945*

CHAPTER 2

The Conundrum of the Security Council

There have always been Great Powers. The Roman Empire had much more power and exercised many more privileges than the Gauls, the ancient Britons, and the tribes of Spain, and the Ch'in dynasty had no comparable rivals in Asia. After 1500, the major European powers were always seen as being in a different league from the midsize states and lesser kingdoms around them. In 1814–15, a pentarchy of Austria, Britain, France, Prussia, and Russia created—and then ran—the peace system that followed the great wars of the long eighteenth century. And when that Concert of Europe finally collapsed in 1914, the hideous conflict that followed prompted a new constellation of large victor powers to recast the system to their own liking in 1919, often against the howls and protests of smaller actors. As the Second World War was drawing to its close, another select group of Great Powers came together to hammer out the new world order of 1945—so why should we be at all surprised that they arrogated particular privileges to themselves? Contemporaries would have been staggered had they not done so.

However, to any reasonable person nowadays, it is outrageous that a mere 5 of the 191 sovereign states that make up the United Nations have special powers and privileges. Five countries—Great Britain, France, the People's Republic of China, Russia, and the United States—are permanently sited at the core of the UN Security Council, which, as described in the preceding chapter, itself is the heart of our global security system. Upon what they do, or decide not to do, and upon what they agree to, or veto, lies the fate of efforts to achieve peace through international covenants. Even more amazing and disturbing is that any single one of the Permanent Five, were its national government determined upon it, can paralyze Security Council action; moreover, it would be fully within its charter rights to do so. Some states *are* more equal than others.

The power calculations, historical judgments, and fears for the future from which the Security Council was forged were explained in the previous chapter. As we saw, the Great Powers took upon themselves the greatest responsibility, that of deciding war and peace. The challenge, as the Security Council entered the postwar world, was to turn the carefully chosen words of the Charter into practice. It was then that the realities of the nascent Cold War intruded, showing up first in an early use of the veto by the USSR, on a matter that could not in any sense be interpreted as one in which Soviet interests were directly threatened. In February 1946, Soviet commissar Andrei Vishinsky cast a "nyet" vote in a dispute over the withdrawal of French forces from Lebanon and Syria, because the USSR regarded the successor regimes there as being Western imperialist lackeys. The most interesting aspect of this incident, now largely forgotten, was the reaction of Senator Vandenberg. As he reported to his colleagues in the U.S. Senate, the Soviet action should be seen by the West not as a smack in the face, but rather as a confirmation that "the system worked." Here was one of the permanent members exercising its veto right against something with which it disagreed, and the United States should be the last to complain. Indeed, what Vishinsky had done was to prove the correctness of Vandenberg's impassioned argument to wavering senators the previous year that the UN Charter would never threaten their own claims to sovereignty. To the smaller states, this incident simply confirmed their earlier apprehensions that the playing field was tilted against them.[1]

To the early internationalists, it was not unreasonable to claim that the veto power ought to be deployed for war-and-peace matters, not lesser issues. Indeed, the Charter states that a permanent member cannot veto if it is a party to a "pacific" dispute, only if it is involved in a (Chapter VII) "threat to the peace" quarrel. But the vagueness of the language, the decisiveness of Vishinsky's move, and American acquiescence meant that an important precedent had already been set in the Security Council's infancy. If a permanent member could negatively control the process of decolonization, what else might it obstruct if it so wished?

The answer seems to be: An awful lot of things. In the beginning, it was USSR vetoes all the way, save for an occasional French veto on a colonial issue. Some Soviet interventions were perhaps understandable, relating to conflicts within and between Greece and its Communist neighbors. But the most frequent use of the veto by Moscow was to block admission to the UN of countries that had previous or current Fascist leanings, were still seen as neocolonial satellites, or were Catholic conservative states. On September 13, 1949, alone, Moscow held up admission to Austria, Ceylon, Finland, Ireland, Italy, Portugal, and Transjordan; in September 1952, it held out against Libya, Japan, Cambodia, Laos, and South Vietnam. Some countries had to keep coming back, only to find the same obstacle. On December 13, 1955, Moscow vetoed all of the above, plus a few more: sixteen in total. Occasionally, there were serious vetoes over security issues, as when the British and French blocked condemnatory resolutions during the 1956 Suez crisis (see page 57). Yet even in the UN's early years, the veto was being applied to matters not involving international conflict, such as the choice of secretary-general. Again, it was Moscow that created the precedent, but once begun, it was established. In the years following, China also would use its veto to block a candidate to the secretary-generalship that Beijing deemed unsuitable, and the United States would later deny renewal to Secretary-General Boutros Boutros-Ghali. France, for its part, threatened to oppose anyone proposed who was not fluent in the French language.[2] Here, if anything, the privilege of the Permanent Five was further underlined. One of them simply had to threaten that the veto might be wielded, and the others were forced to compromise, usually during a confidential chat in one of the private meeting rooms in the UN building itself. That was certainly better than the Great Powers coming to blows, but it definitely froze or slowed down the decision-making process and, most disturbingly, reduced the number of things that the world organization could actually do.

Remarkably, for the first twenty-five years the United States found no cause to use the veto—which, of course, suggests that the UN agendas normally went in America's direction. Its first veto was in March 1970, paralleling a British vote against General Assembly interference in the Southern Rhodesian question. But that now forgotten action by London and Washington was a harbinger of changed times, of the world organization becoming dominated, in the General Assembly, at least, by countries from Africa, Asia, and Latin America, and of the agenda turning to issues like decolonization, North-South relations, and civil wars in Africa. Increasingly, the United States found itself blocking resolutions concerning places where it deemed it had important interests to protect—the Panama Canal, North Korean membership, Angola, Nicaragua. Above all, it found itself drawn into Middle East matters, especially in blocking hostile votes against Israel. Thus, ironically, the Russian and American record on the veto became reversed: For example, between 1985 and 1990 there were no Soviet vetoes but twenty-seven U.S. ones. Yet the fact that Washington and the other four powers could block proposed resolutions and actions provided in its way a pressure valve. Few foreign representatives at the UN would acknowledge it, but it was better that the United States be obstructionist than that it walk out of the organization altogether. What some critics saw as a terrible weakness in the system could be viewed by realists as a redeeming feature, affirming in fact that it was better to have the larger nations inside the UN system rather than on the outside.

If the Cold War led to the veto being applied too often, and over too many matters, it had an even more decisive impact upon the Military Staff Committee: There were simply too many things to quarrel about, given mutual East-West suspicions. And in July 1948, "with a frankness not always characteristic of divided UN committees," to use Professor Nicholas's phrase, the committee reported to the Security Council that the situation was hopeless.[3] Any early planning ground to a halt, the bases idea was abandoned, and this whole part of the Charter was forgotten about. The committee still survives on paper even today, a skeleton in the cupboard, meeting regularly but without agenda. Regrettably, and as we shall see in the next chapter, the fact that it became a casualty of the early Cold War meant that the Security Council and the Secretary-General's Office were ill equipped in all sorts of practical ways when later confronted with crises that demanded peacekeeping and peace enforcement measures.

Within a couple of years of the San Francisco conference, then, the larger ambitions for the Security Council had been dashed. Optimists at the time had claimed that this body would have greater authority than any others in history, but they forgot to remind their readers and listeners that everything depended upon agreement among the veto powers. From time to time, a frustrated General Assembly passed resolutions urging unanimity upon the Big Five; and in late 1947, it set up its own interim committee to be able to respond to sudden international crises if the Security Council was divided. But that committee lacked enforcement power and slowly faded away. In October 1950, under American coaxing and to circumvent Soviet vetoes, the General Assembly passed the famous Uniting for Peace resolution, which authorized itself to meet and discuss possible actions in the event a Security Council action was blocked by a veto but a majority of Council members wanted movement. This was perhaps the boldest attempt ever to shift power between the UN organs and had great appeal—it resurfaced, unsurprisingly, in the General Assembly's resolutions during the 1956 Suez crisis. But it had no constitutional (that is, Charter) power and could not constrain an obdurate permanent veto member, as we shall see.

The record of the Security Council during its first forty years was a fair barometer of Great Power tensions in the second half of the twentieth century: Korea, Suez, Berlin, the Congo, the Arab-Israeli conflicts, Central America, and Africa. All engaged the Security Council, but how they were resolved depended not only on the situation on the ground, but on whether the P5 were in agreement.

The first landmark event was North Korea's invasion of the South in 1950. This was a classic case of international aggression as envisaged in the Charter, yet by that time East-West tensions in the Security Council and the USSR's frequent resort to the veto suggested that there was little chance of a collective UN response. But Moscow's temporary boycott of the Council (in protest at the exclusion of the People's Republic of China in favor of Nationalist China) allowed a U.S.-led move to authorize and then take a "police action" against the aggressor. The war itself was long, tense, and difficult, the greatest of all UN peace enforcement campaigns. Obviously, there was no unanimity among the Permanent Five: The USSR was furious at what was happening, and at its own mistake, and protested vigorously but in vain against the UN's role. It would never again be absent from the Council and showed itself willing to veto more frequently, as a form of payback to the West. And when Communist China eventually replaced the Nationalists as the UN member, it nursed a direct grudge against the United States not just for battlefield losses, but more generally because America represented the hated capitalist system. If anything, and after the death of Stalin, Mao's China was to be an even more revisionist and unpredictable player than the USSR, on the Council itself and within the international system as a whole. Finally, Beijing would resist (and still does today) any action that might suggest a precedent for interference in a member's sovereign domestic affairs. For all these reasons, Permanent Five unanimity, upon which so much rested, became harder and harder to obtain except on matters of small import.

Thus, the Korean War produced a curious mixture of Charter and non-Charter activities. The UN operations clearly fell under Article 42, allowing any form of actions to maintain or restore international peace and security. But neither the full Security Council nor its Military Staff Committee had much of a role. Everyone could see that the operation was in essence an American-led campaign, barely clothed by the necessary UN resolutions—not unlike the First Gulf War (1991) in many respects, save that on the later occasion there was not a furious, obstructive USSR. The U.S. commander in Korea reported to Washington, D.C., not to UN headquarters in New York City, and the armed forces employed in the conflict were, along with the South Korean troops themselves, overwhelmingly American (although many other pro-Western nations participated and fought very well). Since only the fluke absence of the Soviets had allowed the intervention to happen in the first place, the operation gave few lessons or little guidance as to future actions that might be authorized by the Security Council.

The next landmark was the Suez-Hungary double crisis of 1956, which had at least two consequences for the position and practices of the permanent members. To indignant neutrals, the Anglo-French-Israeli military action against Egypt and the Soviet crushing of the Hungarian uprising were in principle basically the same—aggressions by big powers against smaller ones; an angry General Assembly strove to have a say, though not to much effect. Both Britain and France on the one hand and the Soviet Union on the other used vetoes in the Security Council to protect their interests against hostile resolutions. But the real difference was that when a frustrated and angry Eisenhower put pressure (especially financial pressure) on London and Paris to reverse their actions, the two Western European nations were eventually forced to give way—Britain drawing the conclusion that it could not pursue independent policies against American disfavor, and France that it had to make itself less dependent upon the prevailing U.S. hegemony. By contrast, none of the protests against the Soviet Union for its crushing of the Hungarian uprising were effectual; Hungary was within the Soviet sway of influence and could not be rescued from it without a major (possibly nuclear) war. This no one, even the U.S. secretary of state, John Foster Dulles, who had flirted with the idea of the "rollback" of Communism, could risk. Thus, even among the Permanent Five, a military gap had opened between the weaker members and the stronger powers, albeit somewhat disguised by their individual possession of the veto and their permanency on the Council.

The second interesting consequence of the Suez crisis was the peacekeeping operation that was set up in Sinai after the hostilities. Details of this will be covered in the following chapter, but what was pertinent here was the weakening of the connection between the Permanent Five and national military contributions to peacekeeping and enforcement work. The Great Powers agreed, tacitly, to stand aside. Here was another casualty of Cold War tensions and a massive step away from the intentions of the UN's founders. Although it is true that the British and French would participate in some missions in the decades to follow, the two superpowers kept a lower profile, offering logistical support instead. Thus, instead of the Great Powers being the chief "providers" of security, they let those tasks be undertaken by nonpermanent members, especially neutrals like Sweden and India. Given that Moscow and Washington were engaged in a bidding war for the favor of nonaligned states, and that each side in the Cold War suspected the other would take advantage of unfolding events should it have forces in the field, this was the only way to go. But it made nonsense of the principle that countries with the broadest backs should carry the greatest weights in maintaining international security. It also made the privileges of the Permanent Five appear even more anachronistic; they would continue to fix the rules and agree on which proposed operations to approve (or at least not veto). But the blue helmets in the field would not be theirs.

This is why international crises of the 1960s and 1970s like the Congo catastrophe and the recurrent Arab-Israeli wars, although of the greatest importance in the story of the evolution of peacekeeping and peace enforcement, had little effect upon the structures and powers of the Security Council. The Council was, of course, dramatically and repeatedly involved in both regions. Both East and West had client states that they tried to support, positively through diplomatic support and military supplies and negatively by use of the veto to block actions against their satellites. Soviet political assistance to Congolese prime minister Patrice Lumumba during the Katanga secession and consequent civil war was deployed time and again. Moscow also protected Egypt's interests in these years, and by the early 1970s, the United States itself began to use the veto in earnest, chiefly to quash hostile resolutions against Israel. At times it was feared that the Egyptian-Israeli conflict, flaring up in the 1967 and 1973 wars, would drag in both superpowers, with incalculable consequences, and there was much diplomatic brinkmanship to avoid that dire prospect. Consequently, the Security Council met frequently, in tense and often verbally confrontational sessions, a sign that the Cold War now ranged all the way from the Gaza Strip to the Council's meeting chamber in New York City.[4]

But each permanent member recognized that it could not disregard a veto, since that in turn undercut its own privileges. Very often there had to be a sullen agreement to disagree at the political level when one superpower insisted that its vital interests were at stake, leaving the UN Secretariat to delegate, say, the necessary administrative work on the ground—as was carried out, for example, by the Palestine Refugee Agency through the United Nations Relief and Works Agency (UNRWA), whose task was to assist the refugees without getting politically involved. When an issue was less divisive, as in West New Guinea or Cyprus, the Security Council was willing to authorize the Secretary-General's Office to initiate and coordinate a new peacekeeping operation. Cynics could not resist pointing out the paradox: It was far easier to get agreement about *less* momentous regional problems than upon really serious matters (the Korean peninsula, Taiwan, Arab-Israeli tensions) that might lead to a major war and the collapse of the international security system. But that dual standard had been implicit from the beginning.

One promising development emerged from this impasse at the UN's center—namely, the increase in the activities and profile of the secretary-general. Chapter XV of the Charter had made him "the chief administrative Officer" of the world organization, and commentators in recent years have called him the world's number one civil servant. The latter isn't a bad description, since the secretary-general clearly is a "servant," not just of the Security Council, but of many other UN organs, especially the General Assembly. Yet his actual powers had been kept weak, save for his public image and ability to capitalize on it. Still, names like "secretary" and "civil servant" obscure the fact that the position was not merely an administrative one, like that of a recording clerk or a cabinet secretary. While it is clear that the secretary-general's declared function is to service the workings of the world organization, it is also true that the person holding that office had been given political responsibilities by the Charter, especially in working with the Security Council on matters that threaten international peace (Article 99) and in reporting to the General Assembly (Article 98).

The secretary-general, while bound to impartiality and to decline taking orders from any single power, is therefore required to make the UN organization work. In addition, it became a common assumption, at least in Western liberal circles and in developing countries, that he should represent world opinion and speak to world concerns, especially perhaps those affecting weaker members and distressed societies. Even at the best of times those are tough requirements, since they are potentially in conflict. Being a successful executor of the Great Powers' wishes may not be appreciated by the smaller developing countries, and focusing too much on security matters may draw the criticism that the secretary-general is putting social justice concerns on the back burner. Yet to offend one of the Permanent Five is usually fatal. Even the nimble hero of Carlo Goldoni's *The Servant of Two Masters* might slip up here.[5]

During the tensions of the Cold War, the task was truly forbidding. The first secretary-general, Trygve Lie, had an expansive view of his political functions almost from the very beginning of his tenure, but his actions during the Korean crisis—pushing the anti–North Korean resolutions in the Security Council, urging the General Assembly to favor the Uniting for Peace resolution—meant that he had little influence once the enraged Soviets returned to the UN. Ironically, just at the time the USSR was refusing to work with Lie and vetoing his prolongation in office, Joseph McCarthy and his followers were launching an attack upon the world body as being a clandestine center of Communist influence in America. After Lie's reluctant resignation in late 1952, his successor, Dag Hammarskjöld, turned out to be the perfect person for this impossible job—firm, politic, a pragmatic idealist, and an innovator. Even in his first few, relatively quiet years, he developed a special place in discreet, behind-the-scenes diplomacy to solve tricky issues. Where Lie had proclaimed, a little too publicly, the so-called good offices role of the secretary-general, Hammarskjöld simply performed them.

The high point of that performance undoubtedly occurred during the Suez-Hungary double crisis. The story deserves a much fuller telling than is possible here, for Hammarskjöld came close to producing miracles: shuttling among the Permanent Five, three of whom stood accused of violating international law and the Charter itself;

moving from emergency General Assembly sessions to emergency Security Council meetings, then back to the Assembly again; crafting language that would advance the peace process and get the Great Powers off the hook; formulating—in less than forty-eight hours—the plan to insert an international peacekeeping mission (UNEF) to deploy between Egyptian and Israeli troops along the Gaza-Israel border; and mollifying everyone's sensitivities in the most remarkable way. When, a year after the crises, he was reelected unanimously to a second five-year term, he told the General Assembly that while he always preferred to be instructed in his duties, there were times he had to act without guidance "in order to help in filling in any vacuum that may appear in the systems which the Charter and traditional diplomacy provide." This was an acute self-assessment of the office, and no one, not even the Soviets, protested, despite their increasing unhappiness at his roles. Still, as later disagreements revealed, it would have been rash to assume that the UN's sovereign members would automatically accord such discretion to secretaries-general in the future. Both his successors U Thant and Kurt Waldheim had rough encounters with various permanent members, and Boutros Boutros-Ghali, as noted already, was not renewed in office because of American opposition in 1996.

Yet something had been happening that was significantly more than the stringent articles of Chapter XV that spelled out the Secretariat's role. In the Congo crisis of 1960–61, Hammarskjöld and his extraordinary team, including Bunche himself, Andrew Cordier, and Brian Urquhart, were at the heart of the action; it was symbolic that Hammarskjöld died in an airplane while flying from the Congo to Northern Rhodesia precisely in the midst of his "good offices" and "vacuum-filling" mission. By this time, the General Assembly was looking to him to be the world's troubleshooter, and even the Permanent Five had found his office increasingly useful.

The danger of overload, and of backlash by important members if things went wrong, was great. It was one thing, for example, for Secretary-General Kurt Waldheim to fly to Algeria in 1977 and bring back hostages of the Polisario liberation movement. Who could object to that? But the stakes had been much bigger when his predecessor U Thant sought, despite U.S. suspicions, to negotiate an end to the Vietnam conflict; and bigger still earlier, in 1962, when he had taken initiatives to defuse the Cuban missile crisis.[6] In the latter case, it was clear that the ultimate decisions about war and peace were going to be made in Washington and Moscow and that everyone else played a minor or nonexistent role: This was the nature of the bipolar, Cold War world. Crudely put, the UN and the Secretariat would play second fiddle during larger emergencies, while the "Big Two" tacitly agreed to leave the world body to handle decolonization, development, and so on, provided this did not interfere in their security interests. But the very fact that the secretary-general was playing the parts he did confirms that the world had moved on from 1914 or 1870. In many smaller conflicts, his office was often given, or assumed, the lead role. Even during Great Power disagreements, it had, in theory, a place as an impartial agency that was willing to help settle disputes or simply act as confidential messenger.

Slowly, often reluctantly, then, more and more nations came to recognize the importance of having a Secretariat that did not play politics but did play an active role in settling disputes. Professors Franck and Nolte put it nicely:

> [By the mid-1980s] Secretaries-General had felt justified, at times, in acting on their own to safeguard what they perceived to be minimum standards of world order; and they had been completely successful in drawing a line between their role and the role played by the political organs at the behest of member states. . . . The General Assembly could make more noise, and the Security Council could act more decisively, if there ever was unanimity among the Permanent Members. But to the limited extent that the UN was having any salutary effect on the real world outside its own compound, it was primarily because of the functions being performed by the Secretary-General.[7]

The same authors then go on to describe no fewer than seventeen "good offices" actions in the 1980s and early 1990s alone—some authorized by the Security Council, others by the General Assembly, and yet others undertaken at the secretary-general's own initiative. Clearly, the ending of the Cold War helped a great deal, lessening suspicions in both Moscow and Washington against any third parties playing a role in world affairs—indeed, causing them on many occasions to view the secretary-general as a useful instrument to solve tricky problems. Very often it was the secretary-general's handpicked special envoy or special representative who conducted the shuttle diplomacy, either in the region of tension or in some neutral place like Geneva. Certain of the issues were small-scale in nature, such as the Guyana-Venezuela border dispute or New Zealand–French squabbles over French nuclear testing in the Pacific; but others were truly important for the maintenance of international peace and security, like supervising the Cambodian elections and achieving the Central American peace accords. Not all these diplomatic missions were glowing successes—witness the Vance-Owen efforts, in vain, to stop the bloodshed in Bosnia in 1992–93, responsibility for which continues to be disputed to the present day. The blunt fact was that if one or both parties to a conflict preferred fighting to negotiation, or if a Great Power poured cold water on a mission, neutral mediation could not work.

Thus the transformation in the role of the UN Secretariat in international affairs was welcomed in progressive circles everywhere, but the irony was that this expansion of the secretary-general's activities depended solely upon the consent of the superpowers. There really was no change in the underlying power structures. United Nations missions were now more frequent simply because the frosts and snows of the Cold War had begun to melt, from around 1987 onward, gently at first and then with a more regular drip, as the new Soviet leader Mikhail Gorbachev started to push through his liberalization policies and the West cautiously responded. Not the least beneficiaries of this thaw were the United Nations, the Security Council, and the Secretary-General's Office, since Gorbachev frequently asserted that Moscow would now like to work with, and indeed empower, the United Nations as a conciliatory move that would complement his domestic reform agenda.

The results of this Great Power transformation upon the Security

Council were nothing short of revolutionary.[8] The five permanent members worked together on topic after topic in a way they had never done before. They thus recovered their original Charter function but also made many more demands upon the Secretariat and authorized more and more peacekeeping actions. Often, it is true, the Chinese representatives simply abstained on the Security Council, cautioning that they didn't like the new activism since it might set precedents for interference in the internal affairs of member states. But it was a caution, not a veto. (It is worth noting here that over time, the Great Powers had decided among themselves that an abstention would meet Article 27's requirement concerning "the concurring votes of the permanent members.") What was more remarkable was that the USSR not only voted positively, but also was now willing to play a major diplomatic role in helping to settle regional struggles and take the Cold War dimension out of Third World disputes. A Security Council resolution devised by the Permanent Five and negotiated by yet another of the secretary-general's "good offices" missions brought the Iran-Iraq war to an end in 1988. The secretary-general also negotiated a Soviet withdrawal from Afghanistan in the year following, saving Moscow's face in the process. In the same period, Cuba withdrew from Angola, and Namibia achieved independence, in both cases under the keen gaze of the Security Council. It was scarcely surprising that President George Herbert Walker Bush began to talk about a "new world order." So it was, though not, alas, for all that long.

Then came another surprise—the blatant act of Iraqi aggression against Kuwait in August 1990. In retrospect, it is clear that Saddam Hussein made many miscalculations in launching that attack— miscalculations regarding American resolve, U.S. military technology, Arab attitudes, and world opinion. But perhaps one of his greatest mistakes was to fail to realize that he had offered the classic case for the Security Council to authorize military action under Chapter VII of the UN Charter. Here was the perfect example of what the planners of 1944–45 contemplated, even more than the Korean case because it did not involve an absent and angry veto power. None of the Permanent Five had an interest in blocking Security Council action— Gorbachev was bracing himself to transform the USSR and wanted

Western friendship, China could hardly veto on a matter involving clear aggression by one member against another, and Britain and France went along with an aroused United States. Besides, Hussein had many enemies in the region and was a renowned abuser of human rights, and he even looked like a classic villain (not unlike Hitler, with his mustache, decided many Western cartoonists). Here was the new Abyssinian or Rhineland crisis, but without League of Nations ineffectiveness. Even critics who claimed that the U.S. government had specific, selfish motives in taking military action—such as securing oil supplies, inserting itself further into the Middle East, or proving that its vast defense expenditures of the 1980s had been well spent—had to concede that the war against Iraq was perfectly justified in international law.

Yet it was still amazing that the Security Council had condemned the Iraqi invasion by the afternoon of the same day. Over the next few months, it passed another eleven resolutions, which authorized first economic sanctions, then a naval embargo, and finally the use of force. To be sure, the implementation of those resolutions did not fully follow the Charter; with the Military Staff Committee defunct, for example, and Russia and China willing to sanction but not participate, the military campaign against Iraq became a de facto alliance, led and orchestrated by the United States and with American firepower providing the greater part of the coalition forces. Nor did the success of the operation lead to some more permanent security measures, such as governments agreeing to make ready military forces (as under Article 43) for UN purposes in this area. Thus, there was no guarantee that any future crisis regarding Iraq would evoke a response identical to that which occurred in 1990–91.

The same sort of ad hoc treatment of an international crisis had a precedent, incidentally, in the Falkland/Malvinas war of 1982. Neither China nor Russia had any interest in that conflict, and neither a cautious France nor a more helpful America would protest Britain's counteroffensive against Argentina. If they had a choice—as they did in this case—member states preferred not to be tightly bound, but rather to consider each emergency as it arose and depending on whether a permanent member was involved.

While this pragmatic policy looked weak-willed to convinced internationalists, it was probably a wise course to follow. Solidarity among the P5 was always a fragile platform, even after the ending of the Cold War. If a future crisis occurred in which a veto power opposed action, the Security Council would do little. If it occurred at a different (that is, lower) level of dispute, the Council would consider how to respond. Geography would often play as large a part as regard for international law—was the conflict close to home or far afield? After all, apart from the United States, none of the other permanent members, or large regional powers like India or Brazil that asserted claims to a permanent seat on the Council, had much of the "lift" or the firepower to operate successfully on the other side of the globe. Thus, if distant but sizable conflicts erupted, it would have been unwise to have insisted upon aggressive and extensive peace enforcement as a regular policy. If the conflict was a smaller-scale civil war, UN diplomats would be employed to negotiate a peace, and then perhaps blue helmet peacekeepers could play a role. But why commit blindly in advance?

Notwithstanding such cautions, the operation against Iraq had undoubtedly been a victory for the UN security system (especially in the eyes of Americans), for the image of the Security Council itself, for the creators of the Charter, and for the rule of law; even Saddam Hussein's retention of power in Baghdad for another decade could not detract from that. Had this been the end of peacekeeping and peace enforcement in the 1990s, the UN's officers and its outside supporters would have looked forward to the century's end with contentment. However, just as this classic case of Security Council resolve and purpose was drawing to a close, some very different and much more difficult challenges were emerging that were to shake the United Nations system to its roots and pose an even larger question about the world organization's ability to fulfill the Charter's lofty aims for humankind.

These challenges were the sheer explosion of civil wars, ethnic and religious violence, massive violations of human rights, breakdowns of authority, and humanitarian emergencies that occurred in the early 1990s. The practical and operational demands these many conflicts made upon the UN's peacekeeping capacities are for detailed discussion in the following chapter; what they meant for the Security Council and the secretary-general concerns us now. As Council members listened and learned in dismay about the unfolding tragedies in Yugoslavia, Haiti, Somalia, Central Africa, the Caucasus, and a dozen other hot spots, they could only reflect, ironically, that the recent Iraq crisis was really very simple by comparison.

Why did the multiple crises of the 1990s pose so serious a threat to the UN system? First, the sort of internal mayhem and collapse of social fabrics in places like Haiti and Somalia was simply not covered in the Charter at all. As we have seen, there had of course been certain earlier crises like the Congo in 1960 that offered guidelines for UN action, yet even that analogy could not help if there was literally *no* government at all for the world agencies to work with.

Second, there were simply too many appeals for UN help in too short a time. Understanding each crisis fully, therefore, and then deciding what to do with it, was virtually impossible when the Security Council faced one pressing issue—Cambodia, Rwanda, Mozambique, Haiti, Kosovo, and so on—immediately after another. Yet the urgency to do something was fueled by the crying needs of so many human beings and by the no less important fact that the world's media were bringing these tragedies to popular notice every day. For the Security Council to have understood and handled well one-quarter of these cases would have been an outstanding feat of organization; to handle them all, even moderately well, was inconceivable. But that is what they were bidden to do by the Charter and what parliamentarians, voters, and, of course, distraught communities expected them to carry out.

Third, the resources to implement the Security Council's many mandates were totally inadequate. It was, of course, welcome news that the Council was working closely together on a day-by-day basis, without the grinding clashes of the Cold War period. Only occasionally (for instance, regarding Russian unease at moves against Serbia in the early 1990s) did the prospect of a veto arise. And none of the Permanent Five now had ulterior motives in Africa, where the greatest tragedies were unfolding. Getting agreement to authorize a new UN operation was still a slow business, and the relief and peace enforcement contingents often arrived after the greatest damage was done; but most decisions caused little Great Power tensions. The problem was that with no effective Military Staff Committee and with no standing forces from member states, every deployment had to be put together from scratch. It was all very well for the Council to authorize a new operation in a certain part of the world. But it was left to the luckless secretary-general to go around to UN members, cap in hand, asking them to contribute soldiers, police forces, administrators, logistical support, and food supplies. Some members would contribute forces willingly for food distribution in Central Africa but decline to have their troops sitting between Serbs and Croats in Bosnia. Some countries might offer troops for peacekeeping but would balk at peace enforcement. Every mission involved a new and different combination of contributing nations—many themselves lacking real capacity and requiring military and financial assistance before they could play any role. Inevitably, this gap between promise and performance could only hurt the Security Council's reputation and give fresh ammunition to the critics of the UN's expanding activities.

Finally, there were the soaring costs of all this activity. The peacekeeping budget was always separate, and assessed differently, from the general UN budget. If it was hard enough to persuade all countries to pay the normal operating costs of the world organization, finding the necessary funds for every new peacekeeping action was a terrible challenge. By 1993, and for the first time ever, the peacekeeping costs were two to three times higher than the regular UN's annual budget for the whole organization. These additional burdens fell more heavily upon the shoulders of the Permanent Five than upon poorer and less privileged members*—as indeed was only proper, since it was chiefly they who authorized the missions to begin with. But not everyone saw it like that, and the problem became exacerbated by the shift to the right in the U.S. Congress in late 1994 and

---

*Although China and, after the collapse of the Soviet Union, an economically weakened Russia were assessed at a lesser rate because of their low gross domestic product (GDP) per capita.

the latter's demand that the American contribution (about 28 percent of the peacekeeping budget) be renegotiated. Whatever contemporaries felt about that demand—it had a fiscal logic, but the politicians who made the claim for readjustment displayed undue rudeness and scorn toward the world body—it left the Secretariat reeling, the UN's finances and capacities in shatters, and many other member states aghast and annoyed at the harshness of the Congress's display of power.

The result of all this was that by the mid-1990s, the United Nations was buckling under the strain.[9] There were some quiet successes in the midst of this multilayered crisis, as detailed later. But the blunt fact was that the world body had, by 1995 or 1996, exhausted itself. The happy "coalitions of the willing" that had readily joined the early peacekeeping missions were complaining of donor fatigue a few years later; paying for all these operations and, even more, supplying further contingents for each new crisis was straining the patience of even the most loyal of member states. And the triple disasters of Somalia, Rwanda-Burundi, and Bosnia during the mid-1990s had not only cast dark clouds over the UN's competence, but also raised awkward questions about sovereignty, accountability, and fairness. What should Security Council guidelines be when member states collapsed and the Charter offered no principles? Was it not overstepping its remit by authorizing so many interventions and then expecting non-Council nations, which had no part in the decision making, to respond repeatedly to the secretary-general's appeals for help? And if, say, a country like India contributed more than most nations to UN peacekeeping/enforcement missions, why shouldn't it have a permanent seat on the Security Council?

As the world body moved closer to its fiftieth anniversary, therefore, there were growing calls for reform and change. Amid these heated debates, none was more contentious than the issue of reforming the Security Council itself—its composition, its powers, its way of operating. And the hottest disagreements of all revolved around the twin issues of the veto and the five countries that had the right of wielding it.

It was good, and important, for the world body to reexamine its own structures now that fifty years had passed and the organization had changed so much; to many critics, it was well past time. Japan and Germany, the foes of the Grand Alliance a half-century ago (and still referred to in the Charter as "enemy states" in Article 53), were by now the second and third largest contributors to the UN's budget and felt they had claim to a permanent seat. But the greatest complaints about the existing situation came, rightly so, from developing world nations, particularly the larger ones like India, Brazil, and Mexico. That the five victor powers of 1945 should still possess their special privileges had long seemed to them an anachronism, especially given the reduced world position of Britain and France. This was less annoying when the Cold War had frozen the Security Council's ability to do very much, but now that the UN had moved into its post-1990 activism, the existing setup was far less tolerable. This was especially so because, apart from operations in the Balkans and the new, tentative missions into parts of the former USSR, all Security Council decisions about intervention (or nonintervention) concerned countries in the South. From the viewpoint of New Delhi or Brasília, the idea of adding further rich states like Japan and Germany to the Security Council, without any from the developing world, was simply a further insult. Unless things were altered, and dramatically, the Council's authority and respect in the minds of much of the world would be further weakened.

But how exactly was one to alter it? As we shall see when discussing Security Council reform in the last chapter of this book, all proposals for change lead immediately to substantial disagreements, even among those developing countries eager to alter the existing system. To have changed this structure in the most quiescent of times would have required a Solomonic judgment that was clever, persuasive, and acceptable to all parties. What that would be, even today, is hard to imagine; achieving structural reform during the UN's crisis of the mid-1990s was impossible. The world body was unique and irreplaceable, but it had been forged in circumstances that made it outmoded yet still central to the international system fifty years later. Worthy external commissions and newly created committees of the General Assembly toiled in vain.[10] Outside the walls, critics called for a "cleansing of the stables," and congressmen continued to refuse to vote appropriations for the United States' assessed share. Calls for "reform" mounted, but the word meant different things to different countries, NGOs, and individuals. Senator Jesse Helms's ideas about reducing the UN had little in common with the government of India's own drive to gain a permanent seat on the Security Council.

In short, the time was not right. Even more modest proposals, like adding a few more nonpermanent members to the Council, did not fly; nor did any ideas to resuscitate the Military Staff Committee or the even more striking proposal by Brian Urquhart and others to create a UN standing army responsible to the Council. Innovative funding proposals of the mid-1990s, like a small tax on international financial transactions to fund UN operations, fell by the wayside owing to Republican resistance. Within a matter of years, the hopes and schemes to empower the world body and bring it closer to the purposes of the Charter had faded, not entirely, but substantially. Perhaps this was not as terrible as internationalists thought at the time. To require the United Nations to alter its constitution in deep and important ways in the same period that it was grappling with eighteen peacekeeping and peace enforcement missions, undergoing a budgetary crisis, and in repeated quarrels with its most powerful member was, perhaps, inviting its disintegration and collapse. A breathing space and less ambitious and contentious measures were necessary.

This, surely, was the meaning of the replacement of Boutros Boutros-Ghali by Kofi Annan as secretary-general. Both men were devoted to the world body, but the latter appeared more politically astute and could get on with difficult American politicians, restore staff morale, and proceed at a less hectic pace. Acting together with the Security Council, his office wound up some missions and advanced only cautiously upon new ones; successes like managing the step-by-step transition to independence in East Timor after 1999 helped. Practical measures to anticipate and head off crises, and to improve postconflict rebuilding, made the UN look more competent. The American political mood became less openly hostile. The secretary-general was acutely aware of the awful and growing gap between the world's needs and its resources, and he recognized the tempered willingness of the richer member states to help. But he also saw no point in lecturing them; far better to go for a policy of quiet education. There were still many missions in the field, as well as those simmering interstate problems that refused to go away: the jagged Israeli-Palestinian peace process, India and Pakistan's perpetual quarrel over Kashmir, the continued threat of Saddam Hussein, and all the while the eruption of fresh African slaughters (Congo, Sierra Leone).

Thus, most members of the Security Council entered the twenty-first century in a cautious, not to say chastened, mood. The bigger ideas for change were no longer attractive, if they ever had been to the P5. The emphasis was upon practicality, not theory, which helped the U.S. government persuade the Congress to resume full funding of its share of the world body's expenses. There were differences of opinion and approach on the Council regarding, say, Palestine or how to handle Iraq, but in general it worked without bitterness. While, as mentioned previously, the UN still faced a substantial agenda of regional conflicts, their number and severity was down from the crisis days of the mid-1990s. Despite the other distractions, Annan seemed to be increasingly successful in steering attention to Africa, the continent facing the greatest concatenation of challenges, and in getting public opinion to recognize that efforts to help African societies must involve not only substantial resources, but above all cleverly shared work by all parts of the UN as well as by the NGOs, the churches, and international business. In this larger, holistic view of things, the Security Council is but one of the actors—a vital one, to be sure, for every community needs its nightwatchmen and policemen—but much else is also needed to make the world community content and prosperous.

Into this relatively calmer scene crashed the suicide pilots of al-Qaeda on September 11, 2001, and there quickly came the realization that the world had encountered, in a very serious way, a different form of security threat from that posed by aggressor states. Given the awfulness of the blow struck against New York City and the implication that no one was safe from something similar—on the morning of the attacks the United Nations building itself was evacuated, out of apprehension of further suicide planes—then of course both the Security Council and the General Assembly wished to affirm solidarity and combine in the struggle against terrorism.

The actions that followed al-Qaeda's assaults capture well the multidimensional nature of the international system at the beginning of the twenty-first century. Many of these were not necessarily the work of the world body itself, but they did suggest that there was such a thing as a global community. There was the impressive cooperation by central banks, police forces, and security services everywhere, in response to Washington's direct requests, to freeze all assets connected to terrorist organizations and to arrest local cells. Countries fighting their own domestic terrorists, or revolutionary movements using terror as one of their tools, realized that they had much more in common than they had thought earlier.

But these responses also produced more questionable consequences for the United Nations and a challenge to that holistic approach to the world's problems mentioned a few paragraphs earlier. Were the international body now to be refitted and refocused into a crusade against terrorism, wherever it lurked—a stunning addition to the remit of the original Charter—then any member state suppressing internal dissenters such as ethnic splinter groups could be tempted to justify its actions by describing the opposition under the same rubric. Taken too far, and used cynically, this would further weaken an international human rights regime already finding it difficult to handle the many current abuses and transgressions. Also worrying to UN advocates was the nature of the military mission against the Taliban and al-Qaeda forces in Afghanistan in the months following. Everyone could see—and the White House was happy to proclaim it—that this was overwhelmingly an American operation, more so even than the First Gulf War and Korean War had been; small contributions from other nations and the U.S. government's public rhetoric about the global alliance against terror could not conceal the fact that this was another operation run by the Pentagon in fulfillment of presidential orders. Since 1950, the vast majority of American military actions were either not sanctioned by the Security Council at all (Vietnam, Central America) or were "contracted out" operations where the Council felt it had no real purview (Korea, the First Gulf War, Mo-

gadishu, Afghanistan). Big powers are normally willful and demanding creatures, but it was not pleasant for liberal internationalists at
the dawn of the twenty-first century to consider that the UN's primary organ for security might be becoming merely a rubber stamp
for the world's largest and most assertive member—particularly since
the United States seems to be accumulating a list of rogue states and
evil regimes for possible future treatment.

A year later, those liberal fears were realized in the White House's
decision to topple Saddam Hussein, which could hardly be described
as an act of "self-defence" by any stretch of Article 51 of the Charter.
The Security Council quarrels over going to war with Iraq in 2002–3
showed, even more emphatically, the special problem of how and
whether the United States could and would fit into the system. To
anti-American critics in France, Germany, and many other parts of
the world, this seemed as big a problem as terrorism itself. How
could the parliament of man handle a single assertive nation that by
2003 was spending as much on armaments as the rest of the world
together? Ironically, the debate over the privileges of the Permanent
Five was now overshadowed by the intense international discussion
over America's unique and unipolar position in the system of states.
The challenge had been there as early as 1945—when the United
States came close to producing half of the world's total output—but
at that time America possessed a political leadership that was generally willing to restrain itself from unilateralism and placed great
hopes in a reformed international system. More than a half-century
later, the deadlock in the Security Council showed that these multi-
lateralist sentiments had ebbed, both within Washington and across
the American heartland. It also showed that the U.S. government, if
backed by the Congress, could do literally what it liked.

Yet in other ways, the Security Council's internal disputes over
Iraq were by no means novel to anyone familiar with the grinding
clashes of the 1960s and therefore should not have been regarded as
so surprising. France was insisting, once again, on its constitutional
right to veto unless Washington's proposed military action against
Iraq came under closer control by the Council; and the United States,
losing patience over the fact that Saddam Hussein had defied seven-

teen earlier resolutions, decided to go ahead without yet another specifically authorizing it. The tone of mutual disparagement in Paris and Washington was regrettable, often juvenile, but if anything it could be argued that the system *worked,* since the veto powers were always different from the rest. And the sight of Prime Minister Tony Blair flying back and forth across the Atlantic in strenuous efforts to broker a compromise reminded some of similar British policies in 1943–45 or during the Cuban missile crisis or the Vietnam War—trying to find a way to prevent America from bolting out of the tent altogether. Those who claimed at the time that the United Nations had "failed" miss the point. What had happened was that one of the breaker points (fuses) built into the 1945 system had been triggered. This is not to make light of the fury and prejudices of so many Americans at a time when they assumed, inaccurately, that they could expect global solidarity. Nor is it to dismiss the immense gloom, both in pro-UN circles and in many foreign governments, as they watched the disagreements in the Security Council worsen and then worried about the longer-term consequences. Ultimately, the world organization relies on the widespread trust of peoples and governments, both American and all others, that it can provide international public goods; should that faith waver, the urge to selfish solutions is bound to rise.

All this left the Security Council sitting athwart multiple crossroads and facing a very mixed agenda. As noted previously, it still had to deal with long-running international security concerns elsewhere in the Middle East, in South Asia, and in the Balkans. It was getting drawn into election-monitoring and observation duties in Central Asia and into an entire state-building process in a shattered Afghanistan. Further, enormous challenges were unfolding in West and Central Africa or simply smoldering away as in Sudan. This was a long list, yet its most powerful member was insisting that certain items—the war upon terror and the campaign in Iraq—must claim prior attention, or else Washington would engage only selectively with the UN. Each of these items gave cause for pause, and for very few of them could member states or the Secretary-General's Office look to the Charter for guidance. Some calls for action threatened to clash

with others, if not in a direct physical sense, then because they com-
peted for resources and attention—rising concern about massive
human rights abuses in Sudan, for example, could be overshadowed
by a hunt for al-Qaeda cells. Finally, the Iraq canker came back to
haunt, and weaken, the world organization in yet another way when
details emerged of the corruption generated by the "food for oil" program, itself authorized by the Security Council.

This was, then, a very different world from that which existed
when the Council first met in 1946. Yet apart from the increase in rotating members in 1966, there still existed the same old Security
Council in its outward form and in its privileged membership. Relating the Permanent Five in a satisfactory manner to the rest of the
membership remained a tricky matter, so tricky indeed that when the
issue of creating new veto powers was raised in the intergovernmental negotiations at the time of the UN's sixtieth anniversary (summer
and autumn of 2005), it was swiftly sidelined. All could recognize
that the Security Council, after six decades of grappling with challenges to international peace, and with a mixed record of success and
failure, had changed its methods and its approaches much more than
it had its structures. With the world still greatly ravaged by "the
scourge of war" and the threat of interstate and internal conflicts
turning into open hostilities, and with the Great Powers bound to
play the most prominent roles on the global stage, something like a
UN Security Council was still very much needed. Yet is the existing
Council, deep-frozen in time and so often fractured, the body to provide genuine international security for all? There are few who think
that. Yet can the 1945 system be amended absent great turbulence,
wars, and the remaking of the world order? There are few who think
that, either. Hence we all live, whether we like it or not, with this giant
conundrum. Everyone agrees that the present structure is flawed; but
a consensus on how to fix it remains out of reach.

CHAPTER 3

Peacekeeping and Warmaking

Of all the images and ideas we have about the United Nations, one surely is the most familiar: blue-helmeted soldiers patrolling a cease-fire zone, distributing food to displaced villagers, and guarding election centers. When it works well, and there are many examples of that, it is perhaps one of the highest expressions of our common humanity and a testimony to human progress. Despite mankind's dreadful deeds and follies over the past centuries, we have advanced. It is worth recalling, for example, that about four hundred years ago Swedish, Danish, Italian, and French soldiers (among many others) hacked and burned their way all over Europe; during the past fifty years they have instead been sending peacekeeping contingents everywhere from the Congo to the Middle East. To be sure, not every society today has their level of global conscience or could indeed offer contingents; but enough countries contribute regularly to peacekeeping to make this an important and new feature of our post-1945 international landscape.

Yet the most astonishing thing is that the UN Charter contains absolutely no mention of the word *peacekeeping* and offers no guidelines as to this form of collective action. Here is a prime example of flexibility and evolution in the story of how various governments and individuals interpreted—and reinvented—the original rules in the light of unforeseen and pressing events. It is a story, all too often, of horrific calamities and awful misjudgments, of failures both to anticipate and to respond in time, of overly ambitious doctrines and inadequate resources. But it is also a story of learning how to make the international organization work to head off conflict or, if that is not possible, to help embattled societies in their hour of need.[1]

The reasons peacekeeping, or at least our current notion of peace-keeping missions, is absent from the Charter are clear by now. In 1945, the term meant keeping the peace among nations and checking those that threatened their neighbors or countries further afield. The whole system was tilted to stop such transborder aggressions. It therefore had nothing to do with what happened within any member state, such as a certain part of a country striving for independence and perhaps seeking outside help, or civil wars between ethnic and religious groups. Intervention by the UN in the domestic matters of any state was not authorized, nor were members required to submit to such jurisdiction. It has been the safeguard of evil and embarrassed states ever since. It has probably also saved our international system from pushing certain Great Powers, criticized over their internal human rights abuses, to walk out of the fragile construct. Unsurprisingly, the tension remains: It is simply impossible for the world organization to provide for security and peace for all and yet not intervene against a sovereign state when those basic rights are infringed within its territories.

Recall that in 1945 there were only fifty states existing that could sign the Charter and play a role as members: The rest of the world consisted of conquered enemies, suspect neutrals (Spain, Ireland, and the like), clear neutrals (Switzerland), countries still in civil war (Greece), and, above all, the many European colonial possessions in Africa, Asia, the Pacific, and the Caribbean. The latter's condition and prospects were covered in those chapters of the Charter about trusteeship, which looked forward to the eventual independence of the colonized states. But with the exception of the Indian subcontinent and perhaps one or two other places, few of these were expected to engage in the dramatic decolonizations that would take place in the following twenty-five years. The British saw the strategic center of their eastern empire shifting from India into the Middle East and northeast Africa; the French were preoccupied in reasserting imperial rule; the Portuguese and Spanish colonies seemed moribund. Many contemporaries spoke of it being another century before Africa became independent.

Yet unlike 1918–23, when the global tremors that occurred were either calmed or suppressed, this time the world really had been transformed by war. The colonial powers were decidedly weaker and their publics turning to domestic matters; the impact of ideas about freedom and democracy had reached far deeper into dependent territories, often through the return of African and Caribbean soldiers from campaigning overseas. Yet despite the Charter's language about preparing the non-self-governing territories for their future independence, very little was done; or, more charitably, one could say that the resources allocated for economic development and political education were completely inadequate to meet real needs. And compounding all this was the undeniable fact that so many of these colonial territories possessed artificial boundaries that had both divided the same peoples and brought other ethnic groups together in contentious, mutually suspicious conglomerations. When these territorial units achieved formal independence, a number would be states with weak governance, inadequate human resources, and shaky boundaries and thus likely to burst at the seams. Ironically, then, decolonization created demand for a type of peacekeeping that had not really been anticipated. One had only to look at the slaughters of the India-Pakistan partition of 1947–48 or the massive displacement of Palestinians following the first Arab-Israeli war in the same period to get a harbinger of what was to come elsewhere.

The final twist was that, as noted in the previous chapter, neither the Military Staff Committee nor the proposal for UN bases had got off the ground. Perhaps both of them would have smacked so much of "First World" dominance or neocolonialism that newly developing countries would have regarded them with mistrust anyway. But the fact that the bases and their garrisons did not exist, and that the Military Staff Committee did not function as planned, meant that the Security Council and General Assembly had no tools at their disposal when the first challenges came.

Thus, the early efforts at peacekeeping by the world organization were limited, cursory, and exploratory. Given the constraints just described, they simply could not be anything other than ad hoc in nature. Indeed, some of the very early measures authorized by the UN were nothing more than temporary "peace observation" missions of the late 1940s, like those established by the General Assembly to deploy at Greece's borders during that country's civil war (but not within Greece, owing to the Soviet veto in the Security Council) or the observation group that monitored the withdrawal of Dutch forces from Indonesia.

Somewhat more substantial were the teams of military observers sent to monitor the truce that followed the Arab-Israeli war of 1948 (UNTSO)* and a parallel fact-finding and observation mission dispatched to Kashmir after the Indo-Pakistani cease-fire of 1949 (UNMOGIP). These were encouraging moves. Both the General Assembly and the Security Council were beginning to appreciate that such operations would be the concomitant to any UN mediation efforts between the parties in dispute and might last a long while. Moreover, these actions established the precedent of appointing a special representative of distinction and experience—in the case of the UN mission in the Middle East, the "mediator" was the remarkable Swedish diplomat Count Folke Bernadotte and then (after Bernadotte's assassination by the Stern Gang) Ralph Bunche himself. The countries contributing forces gained their first valuable experiences in this sort of work and developed an international cadre of peacekeepers for later crises.

However, the severe limitations of these early missions were painfully evident. The UN units were either unarmed or only lightly armed. They were not to use force, save in self-defense. Occasional attacks were made on their outposts and casualties taken. They could not prevent, say, a determined group of Palestinians from making a night attack on Jewish settlements or Israeli cross-border reprisals. Being blamed by both sides for favoring their foes was an all too common occurrence, whether for observer missions or full peacekeeping

---

*As this chapter unfolds, the UN's propensity for acronyms to refer to its offices and (especially) its peacekeeping missions will become more and more evident. UNTSO refers to the United Nations Truce Supervision Organization of 1948. Readers can enjoy guessing how and why the many other acronyms were coined.

operations. Very often the UN forces were reliant upon the host government for transport, supplies, and accommodations, putting them in a condition of dependency. And if the fighting resumed between the countries in the dispute, their task was to stand aside, not to try to prevent it. United Nations contingents in these areas therefore could not act as international policemen, warning the local pugilists to cease fighting or be locked up. This mildness of approach was different from the actions being pursued at the same time by the massive UN forces on the Korean peninsula. Indeed, it was hard to believe that both types of operations were, technically, authorized by the same world organization.

As we saw in the previous chapter, the intervention in Korea was indeed sui generis and would not be seen again until the 1991 Gulf War. Thus, it was from the other, smaller operations of mediation and cease-fire missions in disputed places that the panoply of what we generally understand to be United Nations peacekeeping was to grow. Within a decade they would take their modern form, in large part because of a pair of major international crises, the Suez conflict in 1956 and the Congo-Katanga secession struggle from 1960 to 1964.

The UN's precarious Truce Supervision Organization was already breaking down before the Suez crisis; in 1955, Egyptian and Israeli forces had clashed in the Gaza Strip, and Israel had attacked Syrian border positions. But the events of the following year—Gamal Abdel Nasser's nationalization of the Suez Canal, the Israeli invasion, the Anglo-French military intervention in Egypt—raised the temperature, and the stakes for the world organization, to much higher levels. They also demonstrated, even more bleakly, what the UN could and couldn't do. With two of the Permanent Five members centrally involved in the struggle and willing to use the veto whenever necessary, the Security Council was paralyzed. The General Assembly was certainly willing to play a role but knew that collective enforcement against P5 members could not work.

Thus, the Assembly's resolution—number 998 of November 4, 1956—was a landmark event. It placed immense responsibilities and powers upon Hammarskjöld's office by requesting him to set up an emergency UN peacekeeping force for the region. UNEF, as it was called, would be under the secretary-general's direction, and he would appoint a neutral military officer as commander in the field to whom the troops would report. Unlike earlier observation forces, UNEF would interpose substantial numbers of peacekeepers between the antagonists. Along the Egyptian-Israeli border and all around the Gaza Strip there would thus be a physical barrier between the parties. A new era had begun. Appropriately, this was the first time UN contingents wore the famous blue helmets.

This novel system was not without problems. The peacekeeping arrangements had to be both consensual and neutral. Without the agreement of the host governments and recent belligerents, UN forces could not take up station; and the same governments could insist on their departure, as Nasser rather foolishly did before the 1967 war. Should any incidents occur, the peacekeepers still could not take sides even if they witnessed one party doing wrong—unless, of course, they were given a new and very different mandate by the Security Council. This was to embarrass the world organization repeatedly in future conflicts, where their troops labored under these general instructions to stay out of things even as atrocities were being perpetrated before their eyes. In the Middle East struggles, it is doubtful that they could have done very much in any case; they were scattered, lightly armed units operating amid some of the most powerful armies and air forces in the world—a fate that many later missions would also endure.

Second, it surely was troubling that within eleven years of the San Francisco accords, such a relatively small role was assumed here by the Security Council, since it alone had enforcement powers and its permanent members were really the only countries possessing forces with clout. Given the poisonous gridlock of the Cold War, little could be done in the Council; and Resolution 998 was the best that could be achieved and a tribute to the General Assembly's initiative and sense of self. And the implementation of that resolution by Hammarskjöld and his key aides was truly impressive. Nevertheless, it would be fair to say that it was done chiefly with the tolerance and not the leadership of the Great Powers, a disturbing sign for the future.

As a result, the troop contributions to UNEF came not from the Permanent Five, but from neutral members—or at least from countries that were judged neutral in the Arab-Israeli conflict, since the host governments could and did object to soldiers from particular nations being stationed along the cease-fire lines. Luckily, there were plenty of governments willing to contribute, both to this mission and to others authorized in these years. The states that were agreeable to placing their military units under international authority usually came from Scandinavia and other European countries like Ireland, Poland, the Netherlands, and sometimes Italy. France would contribute troops to Lebanon and when African crises occurred, and Britain offered most of the peacekeeping forces in Cyprus. Latin American states like Brazil and Colombia were significant participants. Above all, forces came from British Commonwealth nations. Again and again, one notes peacekeepers from Canada, Australia, New Zealand, India, Fiji, Jamaica, Ghana, Pakistan, and Nigeria, suggesting that, having campaigned as part of a larger coalition army in the two world wars, they found it structurally and mentally easy to adapt to international peacekeeping. Thus, the image of blue-helmeted, lightly armed troops in observation posts or on border patrol became the accepted norm; peacekeeping had acquired its archetype.

On most occasions in the years following UNEF, this "soft mission" method was the norm. The chief exception here was the Congo crisis of 1960, yet its long, painful unfolding, as shall be argued shortly, actually reinforced the conviction about what sorts of interventions were possible. The disintegration of the Congo state challenged assumptions about how to achieve international security. This was not a conflict among member states but a bloody civil war. It also involved Africa—for the first time—a continent so underdeveloped and put so firmly "off the map" by its colonial rulers that when independence was rushed through in the late 1950s and 1960s, the successor states were heavily disadvantaged. The Congo was a particularly egregious case of neglect by its Belgian overlords, and then of overhasty colonial retreat, and then of Belgian reentry when the Congolese army mutinied and law and order collapsed. The Congo's largest and most prosperous province, Katanga, then declared itself independent with shady encouragement from white Rhodesia and South Africa.

With Belgian paratroopers returning to the Congo and the largest province breaking away, the beleaguered prime minister, Patrice Lumumba, was unequivocally right in his appeal to the UN that a member state's sovereignty was being violated. Getting the Belgians out as an international peacekeeping force came in was not so difficult. But there were two larger challenges. The first involved Security Council wrangling about interference in the domestic affairs of a member. The second was the practical task of bringing peace to a country as large as all of Western Europe. The latter fact alone meant that the peacekeeping mission (ONUC) was huge by peacekeeping standards of the time—at one stage almost twenty thousand peacekeepers were deployed—yet they were not enough to stop the slaughter of many civilians. It would have been kinder to the international organization had this first example of a "collapsed state" occurred in a much smaller place. But there was no such privilege of choice.

The next development was the use of force by United Nations troops—the first case of peace enforcement, not against a declared aggressor like North Korea or Iraq, but against the local thugs who were killing innocents of any race and also viciously attacking the peacekeepers themselves. In one particularly gruesome case in April 1961, forty-four Ghanaian troops were massacred; six months and many smaller incidents later, thirteen Italian air crew members were slaughtered. Congolese government forces, Katangese troops, and, in later stages, foreign mercenaries were causing sheer mayhem totally beyond anything conceived of by those rational planners at San Francisco. But this, along with Hammarskjöld's impassioned pleas and then his tragic death on the job, galvanized the usually inactive Security Council to respond, firmly and innovatively. Earlier resolutions asking all sides to cease fighting were replaced by directives to the ONUC forces to round up the foreign mercenaries, use military force to stop violence of any sort, and end the Katangese effort at independence. One can imagine the cheers of the disciplined but constrained Indian army battalions at the news that they could now do real soldiering! The result was not in question. The unity of the Congo was restored, and in June 1964 the last of the UN forces withdrew.

Yet there was also much debate about what this particularly difficult operation meant for the world body's future. On the positive side, the United Nations had responded, gradually but forcefully, to a member state's pleas for assistance and had returned that state to its integrity. It had shown it could enforce and not just observe the peace. The crisis had interested and involved the General Assembly in ways that had not previously been seen. It had also given its central offices, and the participating member nations, great experience, and the role of the Office of the Secretary-General as the operational center of peacekeeping and peace enforcement had become incontestable.

But the mission also stirred the feeling that the organization had gone too far and become too involved. Because it felt obliged to support the central government over the breakaway forces, it had certainly not been neutral and consensual, a fact that disturbed some member states in Europe and Latin America who preferred that the world body always play an impartial role. Moreover, what sort of example did it offer when the UN faced similar challenges? True, the peacekeepers had driven out the mercenaries and crushed Katanga's independence bid, but given the dreadful massacres all around, it could not be said to have been a great peacekeeping mission.

What was more, this messy record continued as the 1960s evolved into the 1970s.[2] How could it be otherwise, when the circumstances in each new crisis were so different from those in the last one? To begin with, there were the conflicts that did not come within United Nations purview at all, some of them among the greatest and bloodiest struggles of these decades. What the latter all had in common was that a permanent member was directly involved and would not let any criticism or hostile resolution advance in the Security Council— to the fury and frustration of developing-world members in the General Assembly, whose motions there were passed to little or no effect. There was no United Nations intervention in Algeria, for example, because of France. There was no role for the world body in the lengthy Vietnam War because of U.S. sensitivities, or in Cambodia because of China. By the 1970s, there were well over a hundred member states and more arriving by the year as former colonies became states. The "world community," if one could employ such a term, was now predominantly African, Asian, and Latin American, both in overall population and in General Assembly votes, yet any P5 member could still block their calls for intervention.

Yet perhaps the UN's incapacity to intervene in these disputes was something of a blessing in disguise. Both the Algerian and Vietnamese wars were extraordinarily violent, complex, and expensive. Even if there had been no threat of a veto, the idea that the Security Council might send in peacekeeping forces to either struggle, as it had done in the Congo, beggars the imagination; they would almost certainly have been blown away in the fighting. All that the world organization could reasonably do was offer its diplomatic "good offices," as it did many times during both wars. But if the belligerents didn't respond to the idea of mediation, little else could be done.

One gets a sense of how limited a UN role in the Algerian and Vietnamese struggles might have been by reflecting on the mixed success of the Security Council's policies in the other great and bloody conflict of this time, the Arab-Israeli wars. Here, too, were circumstances where deep ideological and ethnic and religious hatreds admitted of no compromise, where a history of betrayal and deceitfulness crushed a willingness to believe in the other side, and where out-of-control and radicalized forces became, essentially, unaccountable. Into this mayhem it would have been folly to dispatch contingents of lightly armed Norwegian and Brazilian peacekeepers with a Security Council mandate to sort things out.

That being said, the peacekeeping operations around Israel's borders—UNEF II, which reestablished cease-fire borders between Egypt and Israel (1973)*; UNDOF, which did the same on the Golan Heights between Israel and Syria (1978); UNIFIL, which was designed to aid the fading Lebanese government and bring peace to its southern border with Israel (1978); and the (non-UN) multinational force (MNF) that in certain parts took over that hopeless task after

---

*This led the UN Emergency Force of 1956–1967 to be labeled, retrospectively, UNEF I.

1982—did lead to strikingly different results, which give us a clue as to when mediation and peacekeeping might work and when it certainly won't. For the key, the one invariable and basic factor, was a political willingness to compromise by the parties in the fight.

UNEF II offers the best positive evidence. The Egyptian attacks upon Israel in October 1973 destroyed the precarious border of six years earlier and threw the whole future of the Middle East into question. This reckless action and its counterblows by a temporarily stunned and then aroused Israel inevitably brought in the two angry and supportive Cold War superpowers, until all parties—the initially successful and then battered Egyptians, the overwhelmed and then vengeful Israelis, and their twin backers—agreed to a Security Council resolution to halt the fighting and draw lines. United Nations troops established a temporary cease-fire line between Israeli and Egyptian forces and then created a wider buffer zone to calm the temperatures. The usual peacekeeping front players were again to the fore: Canada and Poland provided the largest contingents to UNEF II and thus in a way represented NATO and the Warsaw Pact alliances, then the other UN loyalists joined in—Finland, Ghana, Austria, Ireland, Sweden, and so on.

As such, it looked terribly familiar and therefore unpromising. But the real transformation was at the political level, in the bold decision of Egyptian president Anwar Sadat to fly to Israel and sign peace accords in 1977. This was historic for a whole number of reasons and one of the great personal acts of courage in the late twentieth century—akin, perhaps, to F. W. de Klerk's ending of apartheid in South Africa and Gorbachev's dismantling of the USSR. The chief import of the Camp David accords, in the region, was to show that an Arab state and Israel could make peace if the political will was there. But there was an even more general significance from the perspective of international peacekeeping and peacemaking. Drawing a line in the sand and agreeing to UN forces patrolling a demilitarized zone was one thing; it had happened elsewhere and surely was a lot better than active hostilities. But very few such arrangements had then been complemented by political resolution of the conflict itself, at least not until the 1990s. In UNEF II's case, the international troops could be pulled out as early as 1979, being replaced at a lower level by a multi-national force and observers (MFO) staffed chiefly by the United States, which had godfathered and subsidized the entire Egyptian-Israeli accords. Of course, this was a special case, driven by the U.S. government's strong desire to help Israel and to win Egypt over to the West. Yet the larger message was also important; agreeing to a cease-fire and a UN peacekeeping mission cannot of itself cause peace to happen if there is no political follow-up and mutual desire for a settlement.

Nothing stands in greater contrast with this success than the ill-fated efforts to make peace on Israel's northern borders, with Lebanon and Syria. The UN "interim" force in Lebanon (UNIFIL) was honestly meant but could do little because Palestinian fighters refused to stop fighting and terror bombing, Israeli military countermeasures (including repeated and large-scale sweeps into the north) were brutal but ineffective, and the various Lebanese ethnic-religious factions were tearing one another apart. The hapless international troops were insulted, disregarded, kidnapped, and shot at by all sides, taking many casualties, yet had neither the firepower nor the authority—as at the beginning in the Congo—to respond in force and subdue the awful mayhem. There was nothing in the Charter or in earlier experiences to give guidance; and the Security Council was bemused and dumbfounded. So even were the UN professionals. Brian Urquhart's memoirs of trying to deal with each of the unreasonable parties in this struggle are peppered with phrases such as "grisly and tragic," "ghastly," "even less promising," and "the real trouble had only just begun." They were, perhaps, understatements.[3]

Things were no better when, in 1982, the Western powers sought to head off another Arab-Israeli war by dispatching a multinational force into Beirut and southern Lebanon. At first sight it had promise; sending troops from three large nations, the United States, France, and Italy, to act as an interposition force and supervise the Palestinian Liberation Organization's departure from West Beirut, looked a lot more convincing than deploying the usual array of blue helmets from smaller, neutral countries. Yet just after the MNF had completed its task and withdrawn, the situation exploded again, with the assassination of Lebanese president Amin Gemayel, the Israeli army's illegal advance across its northern border, and the Christian militia-men's slaughters in the Palestinian refugee camps. All this pulled the three outside countries (now joined by Britain) back into the caul-dron, where they were swiftly forced to defend themselves. By the time the French and American compounds had been devastated by terrorist truck bombings, the West felt it was time to call it a day. Symbolically, the Reagan administration had ordered the massive battleship USS *New Jersey* to bombard the hills behind Beirut, rather as if the days of gunboat diplomacy had returned; but the West no longer had the temper of nineteenth-century imperialists, and the warship went home, along with the foreign troops, leaving Lebanese, Syrians, and Israelis entrenched in the rubble, glaring at one another across the Golan Heights while UNDOF, UNTSO, and UNIFIL units observed and observed, year after year.

United Nations peacekeeping generally works best when there is a physical buffer zone between warring parties who have agreed to a cease-fire. A classic case here was the world organization's re-sponse to the Cyprus conflict. This was another "not in the Charter" situation. Cyprus had become independent from Britain in 1960, with a Greek-Cypriot majority and a Turkish-Cypriot minority, each fearful and suspicious, each with an external and volatile patron. Communal strife finally caused the Security Council to establish an interna-tional peacekeeping force (UNFICYP) in 1964. Australian, Austrian, British, Canadian, Danish, Finnish, New Zealand, and Swedish troops and civilian police—doesn't the alphabetized list sound familiar?—ensured freedom of movement and supervised the cease-fire after the occasional outbreaks of fighting. But the 1974 military coup d'état against the Cyprus government, provoking the massive Turkish inva-sion of the northern parts of the island in response, changed all that. What were the lightly armed UN trip wire units to do when Turkish regiments poured ashore? Brian Urquhart's robust Scottish matter-of-factness on this dilemma says it all: "The arrival in its area of a large fighting army which it is neither equipped nor authorized to resist creates an impossible situation for a peacekeeping force."[4]

Fortunately, the Security Council insisted on a cease-fire before

Greece and Turkey themselves came to blows, and both sides on the island fell back, with the Turks, agreeably for them, in control of about 35 percent of Cyprus and the furious but divided Greek Cypriots unable to do anything about that. After negotiations, a demilitarized zone, a few miles wide at most, was set up along the entire 180-kilometer line that divided the two communities. The buffer troops within that zone were Australian, British, Canadian, and Danish.[5] Despite recent promising signs of a compromise, UNFICYP remains at work, almost forty years old and another confirmation that physical separation of the combatants is no guarantee that a real political solution is in sight. Still, if the participants cannot be reconciled, it probably is better that they are separated by a UN buffer zone rather than having the heavily armed rivals staring each other in the eyes, as in Kashmir.

By the 1980s, then, there had emerged a whole spectrum of possibilities with regard to the UN's capacity for peacekeeping and warmaking, with no single operation typifying the whole. At the very top of the spectrum was superpower conflict between East and West, with the threat of nuclear war. Here, because each side possessed the veto and the capacity to begin another world war, the UN had no constitutional powers—only "good offices" diplomacy by the secretary-general was at hand, if both sides wanted it.

The next category was medium-size regional conflict, as between India and Pakistan or in the Middle East. Here, clearly, the Security Council could authorize something, but only if the Permanent Five were in agreement, and during the Cold War they generally stood on one side or the other, protecting their belligerent client from critical resolutions in the Council. In any case, the Great Powers had no desire to get more involved in, say, Kashmir or Palestine than they already were.

Then there were possible breaches across international boundaries by rogue states (North Korea) or illegal and forcible attempts to change boundaries (Katanga)—both of which reminded statesmen of events of the 1930s and could be responded to with international force were the Security Council agreed upon such action. Occasionally, a Great Power itself might take action (for instance, the United

States in Grenada in 1983, the USSR in Afghanistan in 1979) where it felt its interests were under threat. But in general, under the shadow of mutually assured destruction, the P5 were cautious and simply wanted peace to be preserved.

Finally, and below that level—if "below" is the right term—there were conflicts caused by the internal failure of member states, chiefly in sub-Saharan Africa, bringing civil war and chaos, sometimes with radical groups unwilling to abide by peacekeeping resolutions. In many of these cases, diplomatic mediation, economic sanctions, and even peacekeeping itself proving inadequate, robust peace enforcement was required before the rebuilding of those shattered societies could commence.

Thus logically laid out (as they were soon to be in the secretary-general's An Agenda for Peace document of 1992), one might think that it would be relatively easy for those running the world organization to identify what type of conflict some new event was throwing up and, made wise by the earlier experiences, treat that case appropriately. As it transpired, however, things became much more complicated during the fifth decade of the UN's existence. Ironically, the world organization had scarcely finished its celebration of being awarded the 1988 Nobel Peace Prize, and the Cold War had scarcely been terminated, when the new, hoped-for international stability began to crumble.

The first indication of major troubles ahead lay in the sheer number of crises occurring in so short a time, combined with the Security Council's post–Cold War willingness, as we noted in the previous chapter, to authorize UN responses. In the forty years since the 1948 UNTSO decision, there had occurred only thirteen peace-keeping operations, and eight of those had been formally ended. In 1988 and 1989 alone, five new ones were set up to deal with the challenges posed by Afghanistan/Pakistan, the Iran-Iraq cease-fire, Angola, Namibia, and Central America. By the early 1990s, it was worse—Iraq-Kuwait, Angola (again), El Salvador, Western Sahara, Cambodia, Bosnia-Herzegovina, Serbia and Montenegro, Croatia, Macedonia, Somalia, Mozambique, Rwanda, Haiti, and Georgia. It was impossible for anyone to keep up with all this, even the expert officials at the Department of Peacekeeping Operations or respected academic authorities. What actually was the difference among UNTAC (regarding Cambodia), UNAMIR (regarding Rwanda), and UNOSOM and UNOSOM II (regarding Somalia)? The UN's own map of its peacekeeping operations across the globe, highly popular to teachers of international affairs in schools and colleges, had to be sent back to the printers again and again.

It was in the midst of this flurry of "new" peacekeeping initiatives that a very old-fashioned act of interstate aggression occurred when Iraq attacked Kuwait in 1990. The response by the international community was no standard blue helmet operation. The Security Council authorized member states cooperating with Kuwait to "use all necessary means," which was a carte blanche to do everything permitted under Chapters VI and VII of the Charter. This thus gave the U.S.-led counterassault against Iraq an international green light. The military force itself, however, was not established by the world body; rather, it was controlled by U.S. Central Command and thus had most of the features of the Korean War operation but without the UN flag. In contrast with those international peacekeeping actions usually distinguished by a lack of firepower and a striving to remain neutral, the Gulf operation involved massive deployments of aerial and ground forces against a clearly identified foe. American congressmen who usually muttered about the costs of the peacekeeping assessments said little about these far greater expenses. This was not good for the world body itself, for although the swift defeat of Saddam Hussein's forces was to be welcomed, the nature of this operation contributed to a widespread belief that UN operations were ineffective, whereas American military actions were decisive, efficient, and swift.

Of course, that comparison might not have been emphasized so much had it not been for the disasters that hit three of the most important peacekeeping efforts of the early 1990s—in Somalia, the former Yugoslavia, and Rwanda. Before trying to understand how they went wrong, however, it is worth noting the far longer list of United Nations mediation, peacekeeping, and even peace enforcement actions in this decade that were a success, fully or at least partly. The

Central American peace accords, and in particular the rescuing of El Salvador from its internal mayhem and strife, was a significant UN achievement. An international military observer group (UNIMOG) wound down the Iran-Iraq hostilities, and another (UNGOMAP) monitored the withdrawal of more than one hundred thousand Soviet troops from Afghanistan and handled all transition complaints. The world body also played a rather impressive role across southern Africa. The ending of apartheid, the holding of democratic elections in 1994, supervised by UN personnel, and the return of South Africa to a seat in the General Assembly were real advances. So important and weighty was this pivotal state for the entire region that its entry into the democratic fold had ripple effects elsewhere. A transition assistance group (UNTAG) successfully supervised Namibia's move to independence. With internal peace also coming to Mozambique, the Security Council could establish observers there (ONUMOZ) as the democratic process began.

Without it being proclaimed openly, the world body had now assumed a brand-new role in assisting transition states: that of election monitoring. It was one thing to have UN military observers confirming the withdrawal of the combatants' troops from disputed territories; it was altogether more positive to have international election officials and police forces confirming that a country's first ever democratic elections were generally free and fair. Indeed, many had thought earlier that a UN role such as this must conflict with the Charter's clause about noninterference in domestic affairs. Yet the first such UN election-monitoring mission—to Nicaragua (ONUVEN), set up by the secretary-general with the strong backing of the General Assembly and only the cautious "noting" of the process by the Security Council—was such a successful step for the democratic process that the earlier doubts about the wisdom of international interference chiefly vanished. If the parties in an internal conflict agreed on a monitored cease-fire and then requested election monitoring by the United Nations, was that not a strengthening of the country's real sovereignty rather than a weakening of it? This was an agreeable advance.

With similar transitions occurring across all of Eastern Europe, in Central Asia, in parts of Southeast Asia, and in Central America as well, there seemed much cause for optimism about international society in the early post–Cold War years. There were also, of course, serious setbacks. The early promising steps taken in the Angolan peace process—monitoring the withdrawal of Cuban troops by 1991 and the elections of the following year (UNAVEM I and II)—foundered on the refusal of the UNITA party to accept the results of voting that the UN special representative said was generally free and fair. The resumed civil war between 1992 and 1995 consumed another two hundred thousand lives before an uneasy political compromise was reached. Here was a case where ideological suspicions—especially U.S. dislike of the pro-Castro Angolan government and preference for UNITA—cast a baleful shadow; but in addition, the international missions in Angola were underfunded and underpowered and thus quite incapable of demobilizing the rebels. Nor could this distressed nation attract the worldwide attention that Somalia and Bosnia could claim.

Yet even when the United Nations committed much larger resources to a mission, that was no guarantee of an unchecked transition to peace and democracy, as the very considerable Cambodian operation (UNTAC) demonstrated. The goals were ambitious—getting Vietnamese troops out of Cambodia, ensuring free elections, and installing a new coalition government—and the world body invested heavily in them. A full fifteen thousand troops and seven thousand civilians, with a final bill of close to $3 billion, prepared for and then administered the May 1993 elections, which had a stunningly high turnout and seemed to most observers remarkably fair. But there was no Security Council mandate for heavy-duty action—that is, peace enforcement—against the two chief violators of the democratic process, the Khmer Rouge (still China's ally despite its horrible genocidal record) and the Cambodian People's Party (favored by Russia). Thus, when the UNTAC mission was wound up, with a lot of self-congratulation about the elections, the older rivals were still untamed. Technically, the twin mandates of establishing peace and instituting elections had been fulfilled. But Cambodia's peace was a precarious one and its government in reality very far from democratic.[6]

No setbacks in this necessarily painful learning process came close, however, to the three disasters that the international system suffered between 1993 and 1995 in Somalia, the former Yugoslavia, and Rwanda. The defeat of one of these UN operations, as Lady Bracknell might have said, would have been bad enough; to suffer all three tragedies in so short a time almost brought UN peacekeeping to its knees. The gap between the world body's high ideals and the good intentions of its policy makers on the one hand and the miserable effects in the field on the other could not have been wider.

Good intentions were certainly at the fore in the UN missions to Somalia, a country much plagued already by its colonial past, by the rival intrigues and arms sales of Moscow and Washington during the Cold War, and by its own incipient warlordism. When the disintegration of the Somali state in 1991–92 led to the internal displacement and starvation of millions of its citizens, the international community was shocked. It was also angered at the thought that the food relief workers and lightly armed UNOSOM I troops were prevented by the warlords from freely distributing the humanitarian supplies. Reversing its previous opposition to a broad United Nations mandate for action, but not wanting to be hampered by Security Council supervision, the U.S. government persuaded the Council to approve a large, American-led peace enforcement operation (UNITAF) involving as many as thirty thousand troops. This could be seen as a Chapter VII "enforcement action," which some experts now thought necessary in cases of internal violence and mayhem. Unfortuately, this meant that a mandate for strong military action now lay alongside earlier Council authorizations for a humanitarian relief operation, with every prospect that both missions would become entangled.

This confusion—was it still a traditional UN humanitarian relief operation under the old impartiality rules, or was it now an American-led coalition strike against defined enemies (like, say, Iraq), or was it a mixture of the two?—was at the root of the problem. Perhaps it could have been cleared up had the Security Council (especially the Permanent Five) sat down with the Secretariat with the honest intent of reexamining the Charter and measuring it against their own limited willpower and resources. But this never happened, and the Security Council and its more powerful members continued to follow their own courses. By spring 1993, UNITAF, although it had saved the lives of many Somalis, was clearly becoming unpopular among American politicians, and the Clinton administration decided to hand back the mission to the United Nations, though with the peacekeeping and peace enforcement missions horribly mixed up, the different ground forces pursuing different targets, and the lines of command confusing. Disaster for UNOSOM II, as it was now called, was just around the corner.

It came on the night of October 3, 1993, when American special forces under U.S. Central Command (and therefore headquartered in Florida) attempted an independent and secret raid on the Somali warlord General Muhammad Farrah Aideed that went badly astray. The eighteen American casualties in this Mogadishu battle were not large—certainly nothing compared with the numbers of Somalians dying each day from malnutrition—but the repeated showing on television of a dead American soldier being dragged through the streets of the lawless city was enough. Public revulsion in the United States forced a luckless Clinton administration to withdraw its troops within another few months, and UNOSOM II itself was terminated by March 1995, a horrible failure. Not only had the people of Somalia not been enabled to move forward to a state of democracy and justice and peace, which was surely the biggest failure, but the world body had suffered a heavy blow to its own reputation. Peacekeeping everywhere had been put under a cloud, with devastating consequences in Rwanda in the year following, as we shall see. And relations between the United Nations and its most powerful member plummeted to a new low. Angry congressmen stated that never again should "American boys" be placed under UN command, and they sought to embarrass their own government by withholding funds to the world body. Boutros-Ghali was never trusted by Washington again.

Somalia was bad, but the mission itself had been relatively simple in its outlines. The UNOSOM/UNITAF operations had been dealing with the increasingly familiar but hard-to-manage phenomenon of a collapsed state and had mixed up peacekeeping and peace enforcement missions thanks to a lack of clear mandates. There turned out to be far greater complexity in the case of the many operations and mandates associated with the UN's involvement in the former Yugoslavia. In fact, it is doubtful whether any of the great classical puzzles of diplomatic and military history—the War of the Spanish Succession, the Schleswig-Holstein Question, the Great Game in Asia—approached the complexity of the Balkan rivalries of the 1990s. The only one that comes close in five hundred years of international history is, ironically, the Balkan struggles and so-called Eastern Question in the decades before the First World War. That adroit statesman Otto von Bismarck sometimes cursed aloud at the way rivaling and murderous "Balkan sheep stealers" (his term) threatened the peace of Europe. He might not have been too surprised at what happened after the disintegration of Yugoslavia in 1991. But everyone else on this later occasion was surprised or just stunned at the unfolding of unbelievable events.

The ethnic and religious rivalries in this land went back to the early Middle Ages; here was the triple fault line between the Catholic West, the Slav-Orthodox world, and the northwest borderlands of the Muslim Empire. The hatreds had been papered over with the creation of the "south Slav" state of Yugoslavia in 1919 and were again disguised with the creation of Josip Tito's federated Communist regime after 1945. But during the Second World War itself, they had exploded into cruelties that took even the Nazi invaders by surprise. If there was one place left in Europe where genocide was possible, even at the end of the twentieth century, it was probably here. The unraveling of the Soviet Empire and the dramatic political and territorial changes elsewhere excited nationalist movements within Yugoslavia and put unbearable pressures on the federation, pressures exacerbated by the premature decision of Germany to recognize Slovenia and Croatia as independent states. With the Serb-dominated union breaking apart, minorities and majorities of Muslims, Croats, and Serbs everywhere took up arms and sought to fix borders along ethnic lines, driving out the "other" lest they be driven out themselves.

It would burst the bounds of this chapter to give a blow-by-blow account of all that went wrong in the years following 1992, and which involved what were to become no fewer than eight peacekeeping missions (if the later Kosovo operation is included). The road to this particular hell was paved with good intentions, and many outstandingly intelligent and courageous individuals gave their best to contain war and restore peace. But time and again, well-meaning bodies that sought to play a role—the UN itself, NATO, the European Union, the Organization for Security and Cooperation in Europe (OSCE)—were stopped by the blunt fact that peacekeeping is impossible if there exist powerful angry forces who prefer fighting to compromise.

Four aspects of this sad tale deserve special note: the lack of unity among the major powers; the confusion about the mandates; the gap between operational aims and the resources provided; and the intermittent but powerful role of public opinion and domestic politics. For the major European nations, especially Britain, France, Italy, and Germany, this matter was much, much closer to home than anything in Central Africa—and closer not just in an obviously geographic sense and out of fear of spillover of this violence and enforced migration across the Adriatic and into Central Europe, but also because the mutual slaughters so completely contradicted their fondest hopes of a united, harmonious Europe. It therefore made a lot of sense for the Europeans to take the lead in any peacekeeping or further steps. This was readily agreed to by the outgoing Bush and incoming Clinton administrations, the latter of which had enough on its plate elsewhere and was soon to be badly bruised by events in Somalia.

But the problem was that none of the European armed services, not even the French and the British, had the logistical and military power to carry out the mission (UNPROFOR) in the face of rising local recalcitrance and violence. By 1994, the United States was pushing for serious air strikes to deter the Serbs, but the Europeans were bitterly opposed to that idea, because it was their lightly armed peacekeepers who were on the ground, surrounded by murderous, heavily armed belligerents, whereas the Americans adamantly refused to commit troops. Finally, resolutions and actions that were deemed too strongly tilted against Serbia were blocked by Russia, whose government was struggling with its own post-USSR domestic problems but felt committed to its traditional role of protector of Slav interests in the Balkans. At Security Council meetings, the permanent members were rarely in agreement on this issue.

As with the Congo and Somalia operations, the crucial distinction between peacekeeping and peace enforcement was repeatedly blurred. Perhaps that is because the borderline between the two is by its nature a very thin one and easily crossed; both options are, after all, offered in Chapter VII of the Charter. But in this case, the confusion reached an all-time high. Sometimes it simply was not possible to maintain the impartiality and "soft" stance of a peacekeeping mission, trying to keep supply routes open, protect refugees, and answer all the other claims on UNPROFOR's services when UN contingents themselves came under serious attack. Thus, the language of the Security Council's resolutions became stronger as the atrocities increased and made more open reference to Chapter VII enforcement, but those decrees were not accompanied by the necessary strengthening of the military forces. Member states were genuinely and bitterly divided among themselves between a soft and a hard policy. And the UN's most important player, the United States, badly burned by Somalia and not happy about Balkan involvement—though increasingly pressed at home and abroad to act—was wary of placing American troops under any international controls and so insisted in 1998 that measures against the Serbs that included U.S. troops be conducted by NATO, where of course it had the dominant hand. Yet the authority to order retaliatory strikes (usually against Serb shellings) involved a so-called dual-key system that required the agreement of the special representative of the secretary-general and the NATO commanders. "Contracting out" to a regional organization did not flout the Charter—it was provided for in Chapter VIII—but in this case it clearly was a judgment on the world organization's own military weaknesses.

Sometimes the mandate ad hoc–ism worked fine. UNPROFOR was also tasked with patrolling Macedonia's border with Serbia to prevent raids by each side; this was probably the first deployment of peacekeeping forces as a preventive or deterrent measure, something suggested by Boutros-Ghali in An Agenda for Peace. Interestingly, it did contain American forces, and in a curious way this may have helped to keep things stable, since any deaths of U.S. troops in this Macedonian mission (later UNPREDEP) might well have provoked the powerful air strikes of the sort that were at last occurring around Sarajevo. Years later, in 1999, a Security Council resolution placed the southern Serb but Albanian-dominated province of Kosovo under UN administration to enforce the peace and rebuild the country. Yet in actual fact, the mission (UNMIK) shared that effort with the OSCE and with a NATO force (KFOR) that included Russian troops. Coalitions of the willing had come back onstage, and no one complained about it. What works, works.

But the lessons learned had been hard and the costs steep. The gap between the strong language of certain UN mandates and the weakness of actual peacekeeping forces on the ground was blatant—and recognized and exploited by the Bosnian Serbs and, less systematically, by the Croatian and Muslim forces. Most of the early Security Council resolutions merely called upon the parties to cease firing and work together. When that route was obviously not being taken, later resolutions cautiously increased the UN presence on the ground, but the contingents were small and their powers to act, except in self-defense, very constrained. Little wonder their home contributing governments feared that their contingents were hostages to fortune. Repeatedly the secretary-general advised against bolder resolutions, not because they seemed wrong in themselves, but because he was well aware that contributions to effect such plans would not be forthcoming. The most egregious example of this refusal to face reality came with the Security Council's passing of Resolution 836, demanding the enforcement of the "safe areas" (UNPAs) that had been set up earlier in Bosnia but were being threatened from all sides. To ensure "full respect" for the sanctity of those areas would require an additional 34,000 UN troops, reported the Secretariat. Worse than that, none of the co-sponsors of Resolution 836 themselves would contribute additional forces. To ease consciences, the secretary-general also indicated that there was a "light option" of 7,600 troops, which he thought was a more realistic figure given member states' reluctance.

However, it was completely unrealistic to suppose that a few more lightly armed units would deter embittered Bosnian Serbs intent upon ethnic cleansing. When the latter shelled the outskirts of Sarajevo in May 1994 and UNPROFOR called in NATO air strikes, the reaction was fierce and humiliating to the UN; its peacekeepers were taken hostage, tied up, and placed as human shields near possible air targets. Only a couple of months later, Bosnian Serbs overran the "safe" area of Srebrenica and massacred thousands of Muslims within, while the peacekeepers could do nothing. Then, at last, the worm turned. A rapid reaction force (RRF) from Britain, France, and the Netherlands, consisting of heavily armed, mobile battalions, was moved into the region. NATO air strikes intensified to drive the Bosnian Serbs out of the safe areas and compel them into agreeing to the Dayton Peace Accords. When Croatia began the same sort of ethnic cleansing of Serbs in its safe zones, the Security Council mandates were firm and the peace enforcement units of five thousand (UNCRO) were both competent and considerable. Finally, the scandal of the Srebrenica slaughter led to the replacement of the ill-named UNPROFOR by an enormous NATO-led enforcement mission of fifty thousand troops, with substantial American participation and significant Russian units. Even the Bosnian Serbs saw little point in resisting the daunting stabilization force (IFOR), and a battered land, partitioned roughly and cruelly along ethnic lines, gained some respite at last.

The final element in this bruising tale was that of public opinion, whose winds and currents buffeted the UN ship from all sides. The passions and fears within the various parts of the former Yugoslavia were supreme; local leaders who suggested compromise and working with the world body were considered traitors. The secretary-general's various special envoys found that deals and agreements were breached within weeks and counted for nothing if it appeared too much had been surrendered. European publics anguished between a fear of their forces being sucked into a bloodbath and shame that such atrocities could still be occurring on their continent; many states had regarded the end of the Cold War as the signal to slash defense spending and had few trained troops available and no means wherewith to send and sustain them. Strongly felt pro-Serb voices and mutterings within the Russian army made Moscow's cooperation with the West over Bosnia a great difficulty. And U.S. public opinion was perhaps the most volatile of all. Contempt for European weakness and mishandling of things in 1993, and recoil at its own troop losses in Somalia (and, perhaps more distantly, in Vietnam), made it leery of any commitments on the ground; yet the genocides in Srebrenica and elsewhere made it demand that the American government get involved. This was not a happy chapter in the life of any of the players who participated.

The Rwanda crisis of 1992–95 had simpler historic roots, but the tally of human casualties was fifteen or twenty times higher than that of all Balkan slaughters—indeed, it reached genocidal proportions not seen since Cambodia. The ingredients for major internal strife in Rwanda were familiar ones: a polity that had been distorted by Belgian colonial administrators, who had always favored the Tutsi minority over the 85 percent Hutu majority; the turning of the tables following the unplanned and unprovided-for independence in 1961, and then three decades of Hutu suppression of the Tutsi, many of whom fled to nearby Uganda, from where they launched guerrilla attacks that were the pretext for more discrimination within Rwanda. Add to this a ruined economy and the fastest-growing population in the world, with hundreds of thousands of young unemployed males gathered into ethnic gangs. Small arms were common and, when carbines were lacking, there were machetes. In August 1993, the three Western Great Powers and the Organization of African Unity pushed each party into the Arushi agreement, which optimistically called for power sharing, free elections, and an integrated army, all supervised by a UN assistance mission (UNAMIR). This was no longer a negative policy of keeping the peace, but nation building with a vengeance, positive, progressive, and democratic, though the original plans recognized that there would have to be some element of Chapter VII enforcement to neutralize the armed gangs and protect civilians.

Then the project collapsed dramatically, not in the Rwandan capital, Kigali, but 1,100 miles to the northeast, in Mogadishu. The

UN authorizing vote for UNAMIR came before the Security Council as planned on October 5, which turned out to be two days after the American raid upon Aideed had gone badly wrong. In confusion and under immense internal criticism for that failure, the U.S. government blocked a strong mandate for the Rwandan operation and sought to reduce the troop size to a minimum; at one stage the State Department proposed a mere 100 peacekeeping troops, while UN officials on the spot were begging for up to 8,000. When the compromise total of 2,500 was agreed upon, it was hard to get contributions from member states, most of whom did not know the difference between Hutus and Tutsis and in any case were reeling from the "donor fatigue" of supplying major missions in Somalia, Cambodia, and the former Yugoslavia. The international units arrived in Rwanda in driblets, underarmed, underfunded, and possessing only an observer force mandate. With the air still hot in New York, Washington, and Geneva about whether the UN had failed in Somalia because it had interfered too much, the insistence upon neutrality is understandable, at least during the early stages of this unfolding catastrophe. But the unwillingness to act was clearly affected by domestic politics and turned out to be the single worst decision the United Nations ever made.

It is difficult to write about the massacres that followed without feelings of grief, fury, and shame. A one-hundred-day extermination campaign by the Hutus, sparked off by the plane crash (by shooting) of both Rwandan and Burundi presidents on April 4, 1994, led to the slaughter of some eight hundred thousand souls; Tutsi bodies, tossed into the rivers, floated downstream in vast, slow-moving packs, jammed like logs drifting to the sawmills. Hutu militias also assaulted the detested Belgian UNAMIR troop contingent, which rapidly left the country. The militias then marched into UN compounds to wipe out Tutsi refugees, encouraged, so it was said, by the American pullout from Somalia, which they took as evidence that the West could not endure casualties among its own troops. The UN's role here—by which is meant, deliberately, the Security Council's role, for it is no use blaming the general body when only the Council had power to act—was shameful and miserable. The international observer troops under the Canadian general Roméo Dallaire, who had repeatedly warned that extermination was coming and begged in vain for more men and a mandate to intervene, were so shocked by the slaughters that many of them continue to suffer nightmares today, a decade and more later. But their harm was psychological only; the Rwandans' loss was total.

The confusion and lack of purpose continued. With African member states complaining that the Security Council preferred to devote resources to Northern crises like the former Yugoslavia but brush off far worse Southern calamities, and with the UN Secretariat begging for a change of policy, the Council slowly—and the U.S. government very reluctantly—agreed to a larger UNAMIR II contingent, but it did not go into action until mid-July, after the main massacres had ceased. Shortly before, a frustrated France had received approval to send in troops to establish a humanitarian protection zone and of course oversee its own political interests in an area of the world it regarded as special to itself. But by this time the regrouped Tutsi armies, who always regarded French motives with mistrust, had organized themselves and turned for vengeance on the Hutus in the so-called protection zone. When more than a million Hutus fled over the border into Zaire, the civil strife moved into and destabilized the far larger state, leading to the collapse of the Mobutu government and thus to further massive refugee crises. Malnutrition, lack of clean water, and rampant diseases added to the catastrophe. Although UNAMIR II was pulled out of Rwanda at the end of 1995 with the Tutsi back in power and claiming to be the legitimate government, it would be only a few years later that the Security Council felt compelled to authorize a new peacekeeping operation—for the Congo itself. Apart from a few courageous UN officials and soldiers like General Dallaire, it is hard to see that anyone emerged with credit from this terrible Rwandan tragedy.

This was the lowest point in the UN's history, and the finger-pointing on the one hand, the search for practical reforms on the other, and the drumbeat of calls for the whole organization to be shaken up became a cacophony. It was a crisis not at a single level, but at virtually all levels and at the same time. The basic cause was clear: There was simply too much chaos in the world, and the United Nations was being asked to do too much. As the 1995 Yale–Ford Foundation report on the world organization noted, "Of the nearly 100 armed conflicts in the world since 1989, all but five were, or are, internal." One doubts if the resources of the Churchill-Roosevelt-Stalin Grand Alliance—even if its leaders could have accepted these totally new circumstances—could have borne the strain. But angry Republican congressmen, shocked human rights organizations, and disgusted African governments were not in the mood for such comparisons and rationales. And no amount of pointing to the world body's successes, in peacekeeping and elsewhere, stemmed their criticisms. It was hardly surprising that when the United Nations met for its fiftieth anniversary in San Francisco in June 1995, it had a subdued air to it.

How can one rank the list of exposed weaknesses? To begin with, the United Nations was becoming financially bankrupt, trapped between the twin pressures of rising operational costs and the unwillingness or inability of major states such as Russia, Japan, and the United States to pay their dues on time. Developing countries rightly complained that as more moneys went to conflict prevention and humanitarian relief, less was available for investments in education and infrastructure among poorer nations far from the conflicts. Rightwingers wanted the UN stables cleansed, the bureaucracy cut, the budgets—regular and peacekeeping—drastically slashed. They were in no mood for generosity. What was the point of the Secretariat urging large and decisive operations, and the Security Council agreeing, when both knew that member states would not pay?

Driving the cash crisis was the overstretch in peacekeeping and peace enforcement operations—their number had tripled within a few years, and in place of earlier UN observation forces of one thousand to five thousand men, certain newer operations had totals of twenty thousand or even fifty thousand. What was more, in some missions the quality of the peacekeeping troops diminished as the deployments went up and as relatively new member states were pressed to contribute forces as well. It was one thing to insert a battalion of Gurkhas or Royal Marine commandos into a country ravaged by youthful gangs and see the public violence shrink when the heavy men came in. But to expect ill-equipped and scarcely trained units from many newer nations to perform under pressure far from home was too much to hope for; some of their governments had contributed troops simply so that they would get the foreign currency for themselves (since governments were remunerated for each soldier at the same high, Western daily rate). Lack of expertise, lack of coordination, and lack of sheer fighting competence diminished a UN mission's capacity to get the job done. All too often, a volunteered unit had no means of getting to the operation unless it was airlifted in by a resentful United States, which had sworn not to get directly involved and sometimes demanded compensation. Far too many arrived late, as in Rwanda, to find the massacres finished. Failures in the field thus frustrated the completely overworked Department of Peacekeeping Operations.

Above all, there was the lack of clarity about the mandates for so many missions. The fault here clearly lay at the door of the Security Council. As we saw in the previous chapter, many of their authorizations and resolutions had been too vague, or too restrictive, or too rash. But this failure needs to be understood in the pressing, confused circumstances of the time. Reports from the field were unclear or contradictory. Council members who pressed for firmer action would be cautioned privately by others that the proposal would not get a majority or would be vetoed; so they withdrew their motion. Events from a previous and totally different mission ricocheted into the next one, as with Somalia's tragic impact upon the Rwanda crisis.

It was scarcely surprising, then, that the Secretariat came under fire from all sides. Some voices accused the secretary-general of being too weak and not standing up to the Permanent Five as Hammarskjöld was said to have done. Developing nations said the office was too obsessed with peacekeeping, to the neglect of the UN's many social and economic functions. Conservatives in the United States accused the world body of arrogating too much power to itself and of threatening the sovereignty of member states. Brian Urquhart's proposal that it might be worthwhile considering some form of standing UN army, trained, coordinated, and located in select bases to respond to a new Security Council mandate, was screamed down as yet another insidious effort by the world body to become a sovereign state itself. Clearly, those critics were ignorant of the original ideas for UN bases, but then ignorance was rife at this time. As a result, the secretary-general's own office became more pessimistic and less capable of suggesting major reforms. Its job, said the critics, was to shake up and reduce its own morale-battered staff still further, not to invent new tasks or advance new agendas. But how was that negative advice to help the deteriorating situation in the eastern Congo or in Sierra Leone?[7]

It was not the end of the world, but it was just a thoroughly stressful time for the outgoing Boutros Boutros-Ghali and the incoming Kofi Annan. The difficulty of trying to steer a way forward for the UN that would genuinely assist nations in dire need, while responding to the donor countries' diminution of faith and goodwill, was compounded by the convulsions within American domestic politics in the later years of the Clinton administration. All this made absolutely compelling the case for having a "breather." Some of the larger peacekeeping and peace enforcement operations were expiring as they reached their natural conclusion or were wound down rather abruptly out of political necessity; by the end of the century, Somalia and Cambodia and Rwanda no longer existed as UN missions. The numbers of authorized international troops shrank accordingly. The secretary-general's internal reforms (for instance, developing better accounting methods, cutting staff, reducing overlap), along with an agreed reduction in America's assessed contribution, gradually untethered the funds withheld by the U.S. Congress. The crisis in the former Yugoslavia continued to cause constant anxiety and effort, but regarded as a whole, the peacekeeping "overstretch" of the mid-1990s had been much reduced.

In addition, there were incremental improvements at the practical level. The quashing of the idea of a UN army on political grounds did not stop the military staffs of many "willing" states from improving their training of specialist peacekeeping and peace-building capacities, in anticipation of future calls for help from the secretary-general. The Department of Peacekeeping Operations received more resources, more personnel, and more respect. The previous peacekeeping failures—and successes—were analyzed carefully and helped to establish new ground rules. Standardization of military resources—hardware, communications, language, command structures—improved apace.

There was also a marked increase in what one can only term the judgment levels concerning new requests for international action. No one needed reminding that too timid resolutions led to disaster (Rwanda) and that too bold authorizations were perilous (Mogadishu). Finding the golden mean was to remain much easier said than done. But by this time a lot of experience had been accumulated and a lot of hard lessons learned. Which was just as well, because unfortunately, by the very late 1990s a new slew of internally generated crises arrived at the Security Council's table—East Timor, Congo, Sierra Leone, Ethiopia/Eritrea, and Kosovo (again) now headed the agenda. Again, all these were the sort of conflict that had not been thought about in 1944–45; all were like foundlings dropped off at the UN's door in the middle of the night. But this time the response was more calibrated and more promising, despite early disasters and the still common failure to understand how seriously a conflict was unfolding. The foundling hospice was more used to its charge.

Consider, for example, the emergence of a type of mission that combines the "hard" face of Chapter VII peace enforcement operations with the "soft" elements of mediation and state rebuilding that one might find in parts of Chapters VI and IX–XII of the Charter. The best examples recently have been in East Timor and in Sierra Leone. Both were initially disasters of the first order, rather like the Congo; huge numbers of innocents lost their lives, and the world community was slow to act. But both countries were eventually given resources, military and civilian, to quell the discords, protect the cease-fire, and restore the civil fabric—in line with the Brahimi Report of 2000, which asked for more robust actions if one party to a dispute was clearly involved in wrongdoing. Security measures had to come first (as is evident, latterly, in both Iraq and Afghanistan), before civilian improvements. Only by forcefully stopping banditry, warlordism, and ethnic cleansing could efforts begin to create, or re-create, a normal and democratic way of life. This, surely, is uncontentious. What was different, and better, was a growing willingness to tolerate different approaches to achieving those larger goals.

Thus, in Sierra Leone, Royal Marine commandos were eventually sent in by the U.K. government to stop rampaging, limb-chopping criminals and drive them away; in East Timor, Australian troops enforced the peace and protected the subsequent elections. Decisive actions against atrocities did work provided competent member states were willing to take them. This was hardly a matter for congratulation. The UN's previous turning of a blind eye toward Indonesian mischief in East Timor, and the vacillations over years in dealing with those gangsters Foday Sankoh in Sierra Leone and Charles Taylor in Liberia, showed that the world organization still responded too slowly to large transgressions of human rights and had a tendency to seek compromises with leaders determined not to share power. The central UN security system, deliberately kept weak by its owners, was therefore likely to be less effective in stemming gross violations of human rights than a few robust nation-states.

The insertion of British troops into Sierra Leone and Australian soldiers into East Timor seemed to some critics neocolonial operations, but the fact was that no other effective force was on offer. The early West African peacekeeping forces in Liberia (ECOMOG) were underpaid, ill fed, and unwilling to fight the bloodied rebels; the units from African countries sent into Sierra Leone in 1999 (UNAMSIL) were humiliated and sometimes taken hostage until the British marines arrived. Moreover, a lead country, having engaged itself in the military task at hand, as with Australia in East Timor, was also likely to contribute much to the postconflict rebuilding, the holding of elections, and the ebbing of the fears of a people much ravaged by war, as if to show to itself and the world that its military operations were not in vain.

In addition, although they might not have the military muscle of a large, well-equipped power, an increasing number of contributing states were stepping forward to offer aid to distressed regions, in the form of small garrisons, police units, and election teams, all closer to desired international standards. Thus, of the forty-seven thousand "military personnel and civilian police" serving in the fifteen UN peacekeeping operations in September 2001, the list of contributing countries was a staggering eighty-eight. Many of these units, as previously remarked, were very small in their numbers and certainly could not contribute to peace enforcement. But when one thinks back to the limited array of willing and able peacekeeping states a quarter-century or half-century earlier, this was indeed a change.

Yet as the United Nations moved into the twenty-first century, not even its most ardent supporters could claim that its performance in the areas of peacekeeping and enforcement since 1945 constituted a great success story. Glaring failures had not only accompanied the UN's many achievements, they overshadowed them. It will take a long time, and many more future successes in peacekeeping by the world body, before the catastrophes in Bosnia and Rwanda are placed in a perspective that recognizes the UN's potential and successes as well as its limitations. Perhaps that recognition is coming: A very recent report by the Canada-based Human Security Centre claims that armed conflicts are declining, genocides and human rights abuses are tumbling, and deaths in battle are falling fast—and attributes these remarkable advances to the surge in recent years of UN conflict prevention and peace-building efforts.[8] It would be nice to think that that claim was right, and that these trends will continue, one day also bringing peace and stability across Africa and the Middle East. The sixty-year record of UN peacekeeping points, to this author, to a more muted conclusion: that while there were many (often unsung) successes, international operations so often stumbled because of the severe weights placed on the camel's back. Above all, one can conclude that the practice of announcing (through a Security Council resolution) a new peacekeeping mission without ensuring that sufficient armed forces will be available has usually proven to be a recipe for humiliation and disaster. If the major powers can learn that lesson, a great gain will have occurred.

Nevertheless, one also comes away from this tale struck by the sheer range of ways in which conflicts have been resolved. Sometimes it has been by diplomacy, as in the Central American peace process or the accord over Namibia in the early 1990s. Sometimes it has involved a long-lasting UN intervention mission, as in Cyprus, with the result unsettled. Sometimes it has called for a massive deployment of force under Security Council direction, as in the Congo. Sometimes it has involved peace enforcement tasks being subcontracted to other bodies, as with the IFOR in the Balkans and the NATO operation in Afghanistan. No single model fits all cases, and in retrospect we can see that the Security Council should have recognized this fact much earlier and thus have had a better chance to be much clearer in its mandates when authorizing the many but varied missions.[9]

What this implies, however, is a weakening of the assumption by the UN's more fervent supporters that there would and should be a standard pattern for international peacekeeping and enforcement. Having NATO run Afghanistan (however sensible in military terms) was a diminution of the world body's authority. Letting Britain move unilaterally into Sierra Leone to crush the gangster mobs, or watching France do much the same in Côte d'Ivoire, put the UN further on the sidelines. Of course, the ending of the slaughters in Sierra Leone was completely desirable, but it came at the cost of a further slipping of the world organization's position or, to put it another way, of further illustrating its weaknesses in this field.

The same conclusion about the world body's ineffectiveness could be drawn about the American government's decision to go to war against Iraq in 2002–3 and its refusal to return to the Security Council for specific approval of military action. Politicians, historians, and legal scholars will long debate the wisdom and validity of this American war. While some regard President George Bush's action as illegal, others point to the disregard by Saddam Hussein's brutal regime of seventeen successive Security Council resolutions as overwhelming justification for the intervention. But the blunt fact was that a Great Power, indeed the strongest nation of all, could not be constrained from unilateral action by international organization and opinion; it therefore could do things that other, lesser powers could not, a further confirmation that not all member states were equal—as if they ever had been. The United Nations will never be in a position to block "warmaking" by a determined Great Power, not, that is, without the strong chance of another great war.

What all this tells us is that the forms the world community possesses of resolving conflict and securing peace, while many and most flexible, never have been, and never will be, uniform. It takes no genius to recognize that demographic, socioeconomic, and religious pressures upon internal and international stability are building up across Africa, the Middle East, Central Asia, and the Far East. The next cases for Security Council attention are already in the pipeline. But how the United Nations will respond to future calls for peacekeeping and peace enforcement will depend on the political and geographic circumstances of a specific crisis; on whether publics are willing to sustain the burdens and losses that international peacekeeping endeavors may demand; and, especially, on whether the Great Powers will approve an operation and even play a role in it themselves.

CHAPTER 4

Economic Agendas, North and South

To promote social progress and better standards of life in larger freedom"; and, for those ends, "to employ international machinery for . . . the economic and social advancement of all peoples," the United Nations "shall promote higher standards of living, full employment, and conditions of economic and social progress and development." These, it will be recalled, are the bold and assertive words of the Preamble and of Article 55 of the United Nations Charter.

Sixty years later, humankind is a very long way from achieving those goals, and there is probably a majority of opinion—North and South, right and left—that feels the world organization's record here is a poor one. Many would employ harsher terms, with conservatives regarding the whole enterprise of a world organization charged with pursuing higher standards of living as a fraud and a chimera, and liberals feeling that this one never had enough power, resources, and political commitment to get off the ground. The failures in this field are therefore substantial, and although there has been an impressive growth of the world economy since 1945, even the warmest friend of the United Nations could not claim that this (uneven) spread of prosperity should be attributed to its actions and insights. All this admitted, one could fall into the equal error of writing off the world body's economic policies as an entire failure and, perhaps an even greater mistake, ignoring the chance to understand what worked well and what didn't.

The economic "agendas" that are referred to in this chapter's title should be seen as interdependent with the two other elements of the UN Charter's larger purpose, the international security and peace-keeping provisions discussed earlier and the social and cultural agendas that are discussed in the following chapter.

The relationship between economic distress and political violence that the UN planners often referred to was easy to appreciate. While Fascism and Communism possessed strong psychological appeals, both had flourished in the seedbeds of economic despair—unemployment, malnutrition, poverty, poor health, and vast social inequalities. Those of our present generation who regard the world organization as having only "security" functions need this constant reminder that, to some of the UN's founders, the application of force by the world body was regarded as a reactive measure to be employed only when aggression had occurred. By contrast, the more successful the cooperative steps toward global prosperity, the less likely the need for recourse to military action by the world community. Thus, the inclusion in the Charter of the goals of higher standards of living and full employment was no mere verbiage.

Admittedly, it is hard to think that Stalin and Molotov felt strongly about these aims, and there were practical-minded officials in the British Treasury who worried that promoting "full employment," if taken literally, would cause great inflation. Yet this language, as we saw in Chapter One, was drafted by people committed to Roosevelt's New Deal policies at home and, in the British case, to establishing a postwar welfare state. What could be more natural than to carry thoughts about the domestic agenda into the international arena? It is quite common for those who believe that institutions can play a major role in improving society at home also to have a high regard for international governance, whereas opponents of "big government" domestically are often profoundly suspicious of global organizations.

Without being completely cynical about the motives of the Great Powers, then, it is obvious that their governments really did not regard the Economic and Social Council as a principal organ that was a full equivalent to the Security Council. All of them were heavily invested in international security matters, as they showed by putting themselves at the heart of the new system through their permanent membership and veto powers.

By contrast, decisions within ECOSOC were to be made by majority vote, where no countries had any special status or privileges; if the Great Powers had thought vital interests were involved, they would have insisted on some form of veto. Moreover, as the economist Kenneth Dadzie has observed, the language used in the Charter with respect to development was fragile and ambiguous "compared with the purposeful and direct language" used with respect to peace. Members were *bound* to work for international security, but only encouraged to cooperate for global prosperity.[1]

Institutionally, there was the problem of overlap and confusion among the many UN bodies that already dealt with, or were newly created to deal with, economic and social affairs. Readers who come to this topic for the first time must be daunted by helpful authors who warn, "Organizationally, the United Nations is highly complex. Within the system there are commissions, agencies, funds, centers, unions, conferences, councils, institutes, offices, departments, programmes, boards and other bodies, all set, according to official organizational charts, in a neat structure centred around the General Assembly. In practice [however] . . ."[2] What could be simpler! Unfortunately, it is to this key deficit that we shall have to return time and again in both the present and later chapters.

One major example of the diffusion of powers is the curious tale of the "distancing" of the powerful Bretton Woods organs from the United Nations family. Although the language of the Charter is delicate here, it is not unreasonable to assume that the various specialized agencies—and not just the International Monetary Fund and the World Bank, but also the longer-standing International Labour Organization, the Universal Postal Union (UPU), and the rest—were in some way or other to be coordinated by the ECOSOC itself. According to the text, all these agencies were, through negotiation, to be "brought into relationship" with the United Nations. The latter was to make recommendations "for the coordination of the policies and activities of the specialized agencies" and take appropriate steps to get regular reports from them (Articles 57, 58, 63, 64). Yet one gets the sense that this was rushed, almost evasive language. How exactly (or why) does one relate the International Maritime Organization to the ECOSOC? It was going to do its work, establishing regularity and safety at sea, in any case.

Thus, it was well-known that many of these technical agencies, having been established by intergovernmental agreements that specified their powers, were touchy about their autonomy, which explains why the Charter language uses "may" as much as it does "shall." On the other hand, it simply didn't make sense to declare lofty general aims in the Charter for solving the world's economic and social problems through international organization and not try to set up regular and coordinated structures to achieve those ends—or not to have those structures report and relate to the member states themselves through the General Assembly and its ECOSOC.

This created an obvious tension, not so much with the technical agencies, but between the General Assembly's membership and the Bretton Woods institutions. The IMF and the World Bank, as mentioned earlier, are not democratic in their decision-making structures, being much closer to the makeup of the Security Council itself. Voting power in the IMF depends upon the size of a nation's quota of funds, and its Executive Board, which determines all regular business and policies, has to contain representatives from the world's five largest economies. Similarly, of the World Bank's twenty-four executive directors, five are automatically from countries holding the largest number of loan shares, while the other nineteen are elected every two years from the rest of the world.[3] This was purposefully done so that the biggest economies would retain "the power of the purse" in dispensing loans and aid and not have their resources taken over by a majority of poorer countries. Understandable as that is— one could hardly imagine the U.S. Congress or other national parliaments agreeing to surrender budgetary power altogether—it meant that the chief task of the UN in this field was to reconcile the richer countries' incumbent control with the broader global ambitions of the Charter. Hence, in part, the setting up of the ECOSOC with its coordinating responsibilities in the first place.

But Article IV, Section 10, of the World Bank's own charter prohibits interference in the political affairs of any member, which means that its directors can, if they so choose, render assistance to countries regardless of whether or not they are in violation of the United Nations resolutions and ideals—as was to happen on many occasions in the decades to come. Furthermore, in 1947 the Bank negotiated an agreement with the UN that permitted it to keep confidential all information that might interfere with its "orderly conduct" of business. As the Bank's general counsel at the time argued, it had always been intended as a "financial and economic agency and not a political one." All the specialized agencies would thus stand some distance from the more "political" agendas and desires of the General Assembly and the ECOSOC—in other words, be aloof from the will of the majority of its national shareholders. Consultations and cautious cooperation with the rest of the world organization was one thing; being "coordinated," or being "brought into relationships" they didn't like, was quite another. Here was a huge disagreement within the UN system that would grow larger over time and last to the present day.

In the early postwar years, however, this seemed less important a matter, owing to more pressing political and economic conditions. A full one-third of the world or more (certainly by the time of China's change of regime in 1949) was in the Communist fold and thus had little relationship to the UN's economic decision-making process, and certainly not to the World Bank and IMF, lest they become tainted by a capitalist system they wanted to see buried. Stalin's refusal to allow the Central and Eastern European nations to apply for Marshall Plan aid in 1948 had already indicated that Communist societies would follow their own economic path. Another quarter of the globe was still under European colonial rule, and although the first tentative steps toward development were being taken in the British territories, there was little movement in French, Spanish, and Portuguese possessions. Tied into a tight tariff system by their metropolis, they were either exploited for their raw materials by the colonial power or neglected on the excuse that it would be unwise, even unfair, to change traditional societies too swiftly.

Thus, the only regions that could fully be part of the Bretton

Woods "system" were the United States and Canada, non-Communist Europe, Australasia, Japan, Latin America, and (after 1947) the Indian subcontinent. Despite the size and population of the latter two regions, the focus was upon the rebuilding of societies in the North that were shattered by the Second World War, partly because the need was so close and so evident and partly out of American fears that the desperate peoples of Europe and the Far East might swing toward Communism. But the figures regarding reconstruction aid and loans speak for themselves: "By 1953 the Bank had lent only a total of $1.75 billion (of which $497 million was for reconstruction), while the Marshall Plan had transferred $41.3 billion." So even in the North, the Bretton Woods institutions were minor players now that the Cold War set the international agenda. In the South, their roles were even smaller; the IMF hardly considered the developing world until the late 1960s, while the World Bank, bemoaning the lack of projects, had dispersed only $100 million to poorer countries by 1950.[4]

Moreover, in pursuing their recovery, many of the national parliaments and administrations of Europe and the Far East chose to grapple with significant structural reforms (nationalizing certain industries, establishing a central bank, creating a welfare state, building new infrastructure), so that little time and energy were left for thinking about significant international economic cooperation between developed and developing countries. Despite the noble language of the Charter, member states were concentrating not upon North-South growth, but upon internal choices. They debated whether to run their economies on American free market lines, try the new and impressive West German "social market" model, or adopt the socialist economic system. Whichever of the three paths were taken, there was material progress. The United States in Truman's and Eisenhower's time was enjoying its long, consumer-led growth. A revived Germany and Japan were soon to be leading their neighbors to remarkable regional recoveries. If the Communist states' standards of living still lagged far behind, they were nonetheless growing. Perhaps simply the ending of total, exhausting war meant that recovery was foreordained to some degree. But in narrow economic terms, the UN played only a minor role.

It is therefore unsurprising that when, around 1950, the first thoughts by officials in these international bodies were given to development policies in the colonies—or lands soon to become independent—the emphasis was upon ways to improve internal structures, or what was coyly termed "measures requiring domestic action."[5] The richer parts of the world were doing just fine. All that a newly independent Asian or African state needed to do, therefore, was to join the club and obey the club's rules: Buy and sell on the world market and don't go Communist; and build up local infrastructure, education, and society. Ghana's peanuts would buy Britain's trucks. Indonesian timber would buy American kitchenware. All would be well. Naturally, Communist and socialist states saw things differently, yet in fact they, too, had a set of club rules of their own. The newer, radical thinking about "development" was yet to come.

This period was not totally barren concerning progress toward international economic cooperation. An observer during the 1950s would have been struck by the sheer amount of activity and the large number of very busy bodies in this field. Some, like the ILO, were continuing the work they had been doing before the war, and with renewed vigor. Others, like the new Food and Agriculture Organization (FAO), were working hard amid the postwar devastations. The newly established regional economic commissions—in Europe (ECE) and Asia and the Far East (ECAFE), then Latin America (ECLA), much later in Africa (ECA)—appeared to be particularly active and rather successful in persuading governments to think in a broader, nonparochial way. Most probably this was because they had a focus and common regional challenges that their parent body, the ECOSOC, could never possess and compelling physical needs (for instance, improving railway infrastructure) that tended to make them think and act as a bloc.

Closer inspection would have revealed that the situation was unsatisfactory in other ways, particularly in the splintered and overlapping nature of the system that had emerged. The specialized autonomous agencies with their chiefly technical functions were both the easiest to understand and the least controversial or political— everyone could agree on the continued need for the Universal Postal

Union, for example, and be happy with its simple governing structures. Then there were the IMF and World Bank, in a league of their
own and, some critics even then felt, in a world of their own. Finally,
there was that large cluster of bodies that did indeed report to the
ECOSOC and get supervision from it; these ranged from the Council's main committees, concerned chiefly with coordinating all this
agency business, to its many functional commissions (on transport
and communications, the status of women, narcotics), to the regional
economic commissions, to certain special organizations like UNICEF
and the Office of the UN High Commissioner for Refugees (UNHCR).
Concerned in part by what it saw as unmet needs and frustrated by
its own restricted powers, the General Assembly was already developing the habit of creating newer bodies that would report to it, even
if this created policy overlap and bureaucratic overload. Moreover, at
least two of the Assembly's own main committees—the Second Committee (economic and financial) and the Third Committee (social)—
already could not resist the temptation to move from being broad
framers of policy to making executive recommendations in those domains and thus duplicating the ECOSOC. All were in danger of chok-
ing the system.

In contrast with the assumptions of the more idealist and statist
wartime planners, UN economic policies preferred to follow laissez-
faire assumptions. The IMF and World Bank "offered a hand," so to
speak, in assisting specific countries in their recovery, under agreed
conditions. The General Agreement on Tariffs and Trade (GATT),
which came into being in 1947, held the ring for international commerce, at least for industrial goods; but its very purpose of liberaliz-
ing trade through the reduction of tariffs and other barriers was a
negative one, very much based on a free market belief that the international system was essentially benign, within which all would flourish if their economic energies were not artificially restrained. More
interventionist policies and proactive bodies for the global arena did
not seem necessary, nor was there much debate upon the political
structures of power and wealth, domestically or internationally.
When W. Arthur Lewis, the redoubtable West Indian proponent of
human equality (later recipient of a knighthood and the Nobel Prize

in Economics), published *The Theory of Economic Growth* in 1954, he could assert, "First it should be noted that our subject matter is growth, and not distribution."[6] Such advances as were achieved in the field of development—development in the South, that is—were to be in the form of technical assistance in agriculture, medicine, education, and training, perhaps also Bank advice on macroeconomic policies. It was a form of aid that offered expert advisers, but very little in the way of capital resources. Second, and also very useful over the longer term, a great number of the UN and specialized agencies began to gather and analyze comparative economic and social statistics, the absolute sine qua non for future policy and administrative decisions. But these were relatively quiet times.

It is difficult to recapture the seismic shifts that occurred, in thinking and policy and eventually in institutions, when about a decade later the so-called Third World arrived on the center of the policy stage. This was in its way as massive a change in attitudes and practices as was also occurring in the realm of peacekeeping during the 1960s—which was no accident, since both were the result of the unexpectedly swift collapse of the European colonial empires and the emergence within a few decades of around one hundred new members of the United Nations. In the 1960s alone, forty ex-colonial states were admitted to the General Assembly. The old UN system (only fifteen to twenty years old, of course), with its majority of votes in the North, would never be the same again.

For centuries, as we have seen, the future coming together of humankind into a parliament of man had been proclaimed by European and American prophets and declarations—by Smith and Kant, by Gladstone and Wilson, in the Fourteen Points, the Atlantic Charter, and the United Nations Charter itself. Now, at last, as the newly established governments of more and more peoples of the world arrived in New York City to claim their seats in the General Assembly and other bodies, those visions seemed realized—not completely, perhaps, but approximately. The Assembly itself was much more visible than before and a much more exciting place to be, partly because the Security Council was frozen by the Cold War for much of the time, but chiefly because most new members wanted to put international economic matters at the forefront of UN politics and relegate security issues to a secondary place.

Along with this zest for change came anger and frustration at the existing system, and especially at the existing power balances. Much of this feeling was natural. Many of the leaders of the newly independent states had been imprisoned for years or had fled into exile; all had been witnesses to foreign rule, which was rarely without exploitation. The West might now be welcoming them into the club, but sometimes with condescension and self-congratulation and a too swift forgetting of the damage that had been inflicted. More important than that, the older and richer members of the club seemed to have found ways to preserve their privileged position—in the Security Council, in the World Bank and IMF (whose chiefs were almost by tradition an American and a European), in their technical domination of the specialized agencies. No wonder the new Group of 77 developing countries (G-77) attached such importance to the General Assembly, its main committees, and such bodies as the ECOSOC and UNESCO, for not only did small and poor countries have votes there equal to the large and rich, but it was where their agendas on development, structural changes, and cultural issues could be pushed.

The South's greatest frustration, however, was based upon the increasing evidence that the gaps between richer and poorer countries were simply not closing (with the exception of a few small East Asian economies). On the contrary, they were widening steadily, decade after decade. In 1947, average income per head was $1,300 in the United States, between $500 and $750 in Western Europe, and around $100 in most underdeveloped countries—thus, a thirteen-to-one disparity between the top and bottom. A full forty years later, as the World Bank recorded in its 1991 Development Report, the disparity was around sixty to one—richer countries enjoyed per capita incomes of more than $20,000 each year; the poorest nations struggled with not much more than $300 per annum,[7] a trend that was already evident by the 1960s and 1970s and provoked the anger. Development economists have many technical explanations for this sad story: The newly independent states chiefly produced raw materials and foodstuffs whose prices were low, but needed to import much more costly

manufactures and services; the Northern economies had large resources of educational, institutional, infrastructural, and financial
capital with which to grow further and of which there was little or
nothing in the South; many of the UN investments made in developing countries were unwisely chosen and poorly administered; and
so on.

To developing countries, this was an evasion. In their eyes, they
had at last entered the world community only to find that the "playing field" of supposed sovereign equality was badly tilted against
them. Not only had centuries or decades of colonial dependency
prevented them from being able to compete with the modern world,
but the present structures conspired to restrain them further. The
terms of trade—raw materials versus manufactures and services—
were daunting. Capital was expensive. Loans came attached with difficult conditions. "Conditionality" (that is, requiring countries that
accepted international loans to meet certain economic, social, and human
rights conditions) itself was humiliating to many governments: Were
you "sovereign" or not? Agricultural lobbies in richer countries kept
food tariffs high. Far from being free and self-standing economies,
the newer nations were still in a condition of dependency; "neocolonialism," the Ghanaian leader Kwame Nkrumah called it. Most annoying of all, the greater part of the export enterprises operating after
decolonization—mines, vegetable oil plantations, rubber companies,
fruit growers, petroleum and natural gas giants, banking and ship-
ping services—remained with foreign firms that usually took their
profits out of the country. Seen from this view, the North's undemocratic multinational corporations were global capitalism's tools to
keep the South in a subject condition.

These complaints were echoed and magnified by voices from two
other fields, the Communist world and Western radicals. By the
1960s, Stalin's sullen paranoia about the rest of the world had given
way to Nikita Khrushchev's enthusiasms. Not only did the USSR
and the Warsaw Pact states play more of a role in the General Assembly and the ECOSOC, but Moscow embraced a global strategy for
the first time, and most optimistically. Arms sales to the developing
world shot up, military advisers were lent to Communist-leaning

regimes, and barter arrangements proliferated (neither the Soviet bloc nor developing countries had much in the way of foreign currency reserves). This was clearly intended to bring as many new countries as possible into the Socialist camp, and in key regions—Central America, Southern Africa, Egypt, Southeast Asia—the ideological and internal political struggle would last for years, sometimes decades, and involve a number of regime changes and violent civil wars. And it was accompanied, inevitably enough, by a barrage of attacks upon Western capitalism for having "underdeveloped" the South. By the 1970s, this propaganda had its bizarre side when the People's Republic of China, having broken with Moscow, also entered the development assistance game, accusing both the West and the USSR of malevolent policies toward the former colonies.

This criticism of the 1945 world order, and thus of the economic policies and institutions that supported that order, was joined by radicals and leftist liberals in the West. If one looks back at the 1960s and 1970s, it seems there was no existing idea, practice, policy-making structure, or cultural habit that was not under attack as being either irrelevant or a dangerous obstacle to "progress." This was a violent swing of the pendulum and probably could not last; but at the time, it appeared that much of the developed world was also heading leftward and demanding changes in the status quo both internally and internationally. Interest in the developing world surged on campuses and in the media and made its way into many a labor or socialist government in Europe. Finally, this intellectual revolution had its equivalent in the former colonies themselves, many of whose leaders had been educated at institutions in the West (the Sorbonne, the London School of Economics) that were critical of laissez-faire capitalism and advocated a large state sector and Fabian-style economic planning.

UN institutions and personnel were not ready for all this. The privileging of the Permanent Five, the priority given to security matters (even when frozen), the autonomous powers of the specialized agencies, and the general assumptions about following club rules and overall market forces made natural targets for the advocates of a new international economic order, outraged at the general unfairness of it all. It was the World Bank that took most of the criticism, since after the reconstruction of Europe and Japan, it had refocused its attention and resources upon the newly independent world—something that made a lot of sense, since that kept its role distinct from the IMF's mission of assisting any national economy in trouble. The Bank had also decided upon the reasonable strategy of giving priority to projects that one could not expect private shareholder capital to invest in: basic infrastructure, for example, or training programs. It was the visible face of the North in the South. But, as we shall see, the actual implementation of this strategy was to be much criticized in the years to come—for its preference for large-scale projects over simpler grassroots improvements, its failure to understand that change might need to come slowly and take account of local inputs and conditions, its naïve belief that what worked in one country could be equally well pursued in another, and its less than perfect control of spending.

But those were operational and accounting failures and could be corrected by the application of proper business methods, transparency, and an empathetic approach to local and regional needs. The proponents of the new international economic order were advancing a much larger criticism, that the world economic system as a whole was so flawed that merely firing its managers and changing its daily operations was irrelevant. Put crudely, the "have-nots" (the South), encouraged by the socialist bloc and First World radicals, were challenging the "haves" (the North and its institutions) about the existing balance of economic power. Distribution, not growth, was back on the agenda. Here again, the domestic and international agendas marched to the music of the same drummer. If you were intent upon changing the "unfair" and privileged socioeconomic system inside, say, West Germany or California or Brazil, you also sought to alter the 1945 international socioeconomic order.

What did this sea change in ideas mean in terms of the complex, multilayered, multiempowered United Nations system operating in the economic arena? It would be silly to suggest that everything was turned upside down. The Bretton Woods institutions were responsive only to the extent that their major shareholders wanted them to be. Much of the technical, specialized agency work (negotiating slots on the international airwaves) went on as before. So did many specific and already funded projects, whether they were training programs, the setting up of agricultural research centers, the remarkable efforts to eliminate tropical diseases, or other grassroots activities. Few of these important UN roles, like the steady elimination of polio, caught the headlines, just as they remain chiefly unnoticed today. The seismic shifts were therefore best measured at the upper, political level of the world organization, reflecting the G-77's numerical domination of the General Assembly and the ECOSOC.

Probably the largest and most easily agreed innovation was the creation of the UN Development Programme (UNDP), founded in 1965 through the merger of two existing bodies, a program of technical assistance and the so-called UN Special Fund. This consolidation signified a number of things: that a more holistic approach would be taken to development—indeed, the UNDP's approach was to consider the needs of a recipient country as a whole rather than a specific project; that there would now exist a General Assembly organ that, while not a declared rival to the World Bank, might undertake ventures that the Bank would decline on commercial grounds; and that to recognize this change, the resources available—from voluntary contributions by some of the richer UN members—would be increased, as indeed they were, though never enough. Regrettably, many of the UNDP-supported projects were to exhibit the same weaknesses regarding accountability, quality control, and focus that plagued some of the Bank's investments, but its very existence was a significant step forward, not just symbolically or as another source of funds, but as a challenge to more traditional views about economic growth and development.

Even more important, in the view of developing nations and their economic advisers, was the first United Nations Conference on Trade and Development (UNCTAD), which took place in 1964 and was to initiate a succession of such global conferences as well as being made a special standing organ of the General Assembly itself. Although the work of UNCTAD was to be overwhelmingly technical in nature, the ideas that drove it were not. In fact, they came from political disenchantment, especially among South American governments and intellectuals and the Economic Commission for Latin America itself, at the condition of *Dependencia* to which they were subjected by the existing global power structures. Far from believing that the international economy was essentially benign if only its weaker parts could be strengthened, the new ideology assumed the contrary. "Persistent divergence between North and South was seen as the natural order. If these tendencies were to be corrected, deliberate policy actions would have to be taken, and thus international policy negotiations would become a special and continuing responsibility of the UN."[8] The result was an almost dizzying array of international agreements and codifications, the subjects ranging from restrictive business practices to debt rescheduling to commodity (cocoa, tropical timber) arrangements.

The existence of UNCTAD and the convening of fairly regular global conferences often lost significance in the eyes of the world because of its bureaucratic processes, its technical focus, and its terrible jargon. Even a true believer in global justice could hardly get excited at reading that in March 1995, UNCTAD's own Trade and Development Board "adopted the agenda and programme of work for the High-Level Intergovernmental Meeting on the Mid-Term Global Review of the Implementation of the Programme of Action for the Least Developed Countries for the 1990s."[9] Yet the true significance is buried in that ludicrously elaborate title. There was a deep concern for the least developed countries and a profound mistrust in the early years of UNCTAD that market forces alone would help them to their feet—on the contrary, a belief prevailed that market forces would keep them pinned to the ground and that national governments (especially in the North) should therefore agree to adjust economic policies to support the Third World.

This ideological assault upon the 1945 system was accompanied and reinforced by the rise of new UN bodies in the social, gender, and environmental fields, which will be covered in the following chapter. There was the explosion in international conferences, in improved business practices, in agreements that were intended to create a more even commercial and legal playing field. There was a surge in funding for development and from many different contributors: from the World Bank and the regional development banks, from the funds flowing through the UNDP and other ECOSOC agencies, from the churches, from giant foundations like Ford and Rockefeller and Carnegie, from bilateral aid of both East and West, including, massively, from the Kennedy administration (though this last with its own political agenda and with funds that would soon evaporate). If there was a lot of anger at the existing power structures, and at continued colonialism and apartheid, there was also a lot of confidence that those structures would be overthrown, or at least drastically amended. There was also, tragically, Vietnam, which led to further radicalization. Watching the willpower of the world's leading capitalist power being broken by Vietnamese peasant-soldiers was both a rallying call for radicals and a confirmation that the old system was rotten. Thus, when the General Assembly passed its famous Declaration on the Establishment of a New International Order on May 1 (World Labor Day), 1974, it looked as though a historic watershed had been crossed. Fairness and global equity (meaning the dissolution of the Northern-dominated world order) would now obtain. And many believed this.

This was not just the rhetoric of "have-nots" punching their fists into the air against the "haves." Just a year before, and in the wake of the 1973 Arab-Israeli war, the Organization of Petroleum Exporting Countries (OPEC) used their near monopoly to quadruple the price of crude oil. The result was a powerful confirmation of how dependent the modern world, both North and South, had become upon a single commodity; and the resultant political and economic repercussions were both immense and inseparable. At a stroke and in the years following, enormous capital resources were transferred to the oil-producing nations in the Arab world, plus outlier OPEC countries like Venezuela and Nigeria. There was much euphoria initially in the G-77; if this massive switch in wealth could be brought about by raising the price of petroleum, why not do the same in the global markets for copper or coffee? Primary producers would at last get their day in the sun.

Unfortunately, for most nations producing raw materials, the sun never appeared. There simply was no other product close to the value and strategic significance of petroleum and thus the capacity for creating a reverse dependency between South and North. Modern life without petroleum was paralysis; without fruit, or cocoa, or even bauxite, it was inconvenience. Besides, there wasn't a chance of forging a cartel like OPEC in other material fields: The more newly independent countries that entered the world community, the faster they sought to produce their own coffee, vegetable oils, and textiles, which further depressed their prices, the added value of which was minuscule compared with that of machinery or armaments imported from the North. In fact, perhaps the largest consequence of the OPEC price hikes was to divide the developing world between those that had oil and those, the great majority, that did not. From this time onward, the term *Third World*—arrogant but convenient in the early to middle stages of the Cold War in describing countries that were neither Western capitalist nor Eastern Communist—became ever less useful. What did oil-rich Kuwait have in common with poverty-stricken Mozambique? Of what use to the United Arab Emirates was the World Bank's new loan program when its chief economic problem was to recycle excess petrodollars? By the 1970s, in fact, Arab states were being approached by the international financial agencies to provide an "oil facility" for their less fortunate brethren.[10]

As that decade unfolded, things got worse rather than better. Even the least developed nation had come to rely upon trucks and automobiles and thus upon imported petroleum; when prices quadrupled, there was no way it could pay for such imports. As its balance of payments worsened, it also could not return the interest on its borrowings from commercial banks or from the international agencies, chief of which was the World Bank. This was the crisis foreseen a quarter-century earlier by U.S. senator Robert Taft, when he expressed doubts about the Bretton Woods agreements. If a bank's debtors could not repay, even after generous extensions of the debt terms—if they could never repay—then was this really a bank or a permanent transfer mechanism for nonreturnable capital? And if that was ever admitted, would the World Bank itself ever be able to borrow again from the capital markets? Was its creation a mistake?

For many countries in the South, the situation by 1970 or so was grim. Many of them, in Latin America and Africa, were under au-

thoritarian and even dictatorial regimes, where whatever wealth remained in the country (and was not siphoned off to bank accounts
in the North) was in the hands of a small kleptocracy and where
human rights abuses were commonplace, thus provoking indigenous
revolutionary movements. Others were dictatorships of the parties
of the Left, once again lacking any tolerance or decency. A few were
full democracies, like India or Costa Rica or most Caribbean island-
states. Regardless of their politics, though, all were badly damaged by
the further worsening of the terms of trade. Instead of overall improvements in their social structures, there was stasis, in many cases
decay; and since this was a period in which virtually all countries in
the developing world were experiencing a major surge in population
growth, they were caught in a double trap of stagnation and rapid
demographic growth. To radical intellectuals and politicians, this called
not for dialogue with the existing order, but for confrontation.

Confrontation there was, chiefly in the form of civil wars across
Latin America, Africa, and Asia and politically in the North-South
debates. Yet the system held together. The UNCTAD conferences, for
example, never gave up, either in their pursuit of technical harmo-
nization or in their deeper pressure for more equity in the global trading and commercial world. But that world itself was clearly out of
joint, even in the richer countries. The 1973 oil "shock" had slowed
economic growth everywhere. Whether caused by it or by some
cyclical/structural domestic change, the fabulous U.S. productivity
growth slowed to a crawl after 1973 and would not really take off
again until the 1990s. And Europe was also far less vibrant than it
had been in the 1950s and 1960s. Only in parts of the Far East was
the economic outlook rosier, but that seemed merely to offer a special
regional exception to the general trends.

Inevitably, then, the leading capitalist nations felt less capable than
before of generous policies, simply because of their own slower
growth rates and altered domestic agendas. With incomes stalling
and unemployment rising in the OECD (Organization for Economic
Cooperation and Development) countries, it was not possible to
maintain the levels of international aid that had only recently been

promised. In 1977, the richer countries committed themselves to working toward an annual allocation of 0.7 percent of GDP for aid. Technically, that was not an impossible target. But politically, it was much more difficult now that so many OECD countries were wincing under their own widening budget deficits, and in fact none of them (apart from a few virtuous Scandinavian countries and the Netherlands) ever met it. On the contrary, in the United States and Britain in particular, there was a growing conservative resentment at always being pilloried by their own Left and by the Third World and a feeling that charity began at home. They had new spending agendas, for the new Cold War was heating up again and NATO and Warsaw Pact defense spending was spiraling, and they were furious not only at the ingratitude of aid-receiving nations, but also at the increasing evidence that UN development assistance had been mismanaged on the ground, if not outright stolen by corrupt governments and their bureaucrats. Foreign aid in the future would be strategic, targeted toward countries friendly to the West, and conditioned by the laws of transparency and accountability.

And where had the International Monetary Fund, the World Bank's more austere sister, been during this period of the South's new assertiveness and then its weakening? Since its inception, it had been doing its Keynes-appointed job, buttressing global financial and currency exchanges, heading off 1930s-type protectionism, and offering loans to rescue national economies in short- to medium-term trouble. Its concerns were all in the North—convertibility, devaluations, reserves, the gold standard—and with making the global capitalist engine stay on the tracks. It was helped by the general economic recovery in the 1950s, by the system of fixed exchange rates, by the agreement that an ounce of gold be traded at $35. But it was then challenged by successive British economic crises and the collapse of sterling as a reserve currency, and even more by the enormous post-1971 dollar crisis, leading to the United States' eventual abandonment of the gold standard and fixed exchange rates. One might think, therefore, that the IMF had enough on its plate just to stop the First World from economic convulsion, and it is true that in all of the histories of its first twenty-five to thirty years, there is scarcely any mention of the developing world. By the time of the oil shocks, however, keeping the advanced economies out of trouble was not enough.

The catalyst here was the ballooning of the international indebtedness of the non-OPEC countries in the South, for all the reasons given earlier—weak demand for their products in the North, the catastrophically high price of oil, the easy borrowing from cash-surplus lenders that then backfired when interest rates soared, the horrible global recession of 1981–82. Developing countries' total indebtedness, which was around $100 billion in 1972, soared to $250 billion in 1977 and was to peak at $1 trillion in 1985, when debt repayments to the banks and the oil states and the international institutions, had they been made, would have amounted to $130 billion in that year alone—a "reverse flow" that made a nonsense of the entire North-South cooperation. The system was close to collapse. And in August 1982, Mexico announced that it could not meet its payments, something that shocked the international bodies, especially the IMF, since it had assumed that as an oil producer and relatively liberalized economy itself, Mexico was less likely to default than other developing countries.[11]

This forced a rescue package for Mexico, organized at first by the usually quiet and technical Bank of International Settlements and then increasingly under IMF direction because of the dire political implications to the global financial system. Those organizations worked closely with the U.S. Treasury under the Baker Plan and negotiated an amended repayments schedule with the commercial banks. By 1983, the IMF had been forced to do the same for Brazil, whose indebtedness was almost as severe. At the end of 1984, the IMF estimated that it had loaned some $22 billion in support of adjustment programs for sixty-six countries. Essentially, it had also turned itself into the issuer of "good housekeeping" certificates and would remain as such when the world recession ended and trade and capital flows expanded again in the mid-1980s. A few years later, the IMF's geographic reach expanded eastward when it began extending special drawing rights to former Warsaw Pact countries like Poland and Hungary. In 1992, the IMF and the World Bank, working with

Western governments and commercial banks, assembled a colossal $24 billion package for the former USSR to help it in its critical restructuring. All of these were to bring their problems and much excited debate at the time (causing Africa and the other poor regions to slip further off the radar screen), yet decision makers felt they had no alternative if they were to avoid a 1930s-type collapse of the international monetary and banking order, which would have been a supreme irony forty or fifty years after the Bretton Woods institutions were established.[12]

One casualty of the repeated oil shocks and worldwide slowdown in growth was the assertiveness of the South in its demands for a new international economic order. To be sure, actual needs were just as great as fifteen years earlier, and the turbulences confirmed the old saying that the countries hurt most in a recession would always be the poorest ones. But the overall atmosphere had changed. As the North sought to deal with its own economic problems through stiff anti-inflationary monetary and fiscal policies, it was in no mood for financial laxity in the South. The governments of Margaret Thatcher and Ronald Reagan believed that any new loans should have strict housekeeping rules attached to them, and the commercial bankers, and the IMF, could not have agreed more. Moreover, by the 1980s the intellectual pendulum among economists was swinging back to a belief in market forces and away from "welfare statism" whether at home or abroad. These sentiments were reinforced by the virtual abolition of capital and currency controls by the Anglo-Saxon countries, followed more reluctantly by other members of the OECD. The resultant surge in international capital flows was far larger than any moneys going through the Bretton Woods institutions and quite eclipsed any resources raised by UN agencies themselves. Attracting that capital into one's domestic market—or, negatively, taking market-friendly measures to avoid capital flight—was the key consideration for countries both rich and poor. Unsurprisingly, that hot money was much more likely to go to Singapore or China than to Dahomey or Yemen.

Finally, the astonishing success of the East Asian "tigers" sent a further, though mixed, message into the debate over development. Japan's economic success had now been followed by those of the smaller economies in the region, South Korea and Taiwan as well as Hong Kong and Singapore, then the larger states like Malaysia and Thailand and Indonesia, and then—after Deng Xiaoping's internal reforms—a vast swath of coastal China, in many cases with amazing double-digit annual growth rates and thus soaring prosperity. Ironically, this Oriental success story meant that the so-called South was now split into at least three camps: the (chiefly Arab) oil producers, the East Asian miracle states, and the poorer countries of South Asia, Africa, and Latin America. Coordination among them was still happening, in terms of ECOSOC and General Assembly declarations; but at the more technical level, in UNCTAD committees, they were seeing the world economy in different ways. The self-development of East Asia was making "development" an old-fashioned word. And it was lifting many more millions of people out of poverty than did any World Bank program in Chad.

This was not to say the swing to more conservative economic and political philosophies was uncontested; it was in fact very bitterly opposed by most developing governments and by sympathetic and anti-laissez-faire voices in the North. Statist administrations in, for example, the France of President François Mitterrand harbored deep suspicions of the new trends because they threatened their own internal spending policies and the traditional ways of life of their own political supporters. Apprehensions about globalization were growing, year by year, among all who felt threatened by the newer economic trends, by the increased volatility and competitiveness. Yet for all this discontent, in practical terms governments that found themselves in trouble economically and turned outside for help had to agree to a reform "program" that usually contained a large degree of fiscal discipline and thus controls on state spending. This was a central part of the Baker Plan that offered the lifeline to Mexico. At the important UNCTAD VIII meeting in Cartagena, Colombia, in 1992, there was agreement that good stewardship of the domestic economy counted, that North-South confrontation was destructive, and that the division of the globe into rival trading blocs was not the way to go.

As a result, when the term *structural reforms* was used, that increasingly meant reform of domestic structures *within* a country seeking help rather than alterations in the international power order. And the accompanying slogan *level playing fields* was in effect a defeat for the earlier argument that developing countries needed special consideration and should not necessarily be tied to the principles of the market. In other words, if the 1990s saw some institutional compromises in the North-South debate, it was chiefly because a weakened South felt forced to make concessions. This becomes clear from Secretary-General Boutros-Ghali's 1994 An Agenda for Development. It had been requested by the General Assembly as a document coequal to the 1992 An Agenda for Peace and intended to remind the Great Powers that security was not the only, or even the major, issue for the world organization. But following its forty draftings and revisions, and in its contorted references to "finding the right blend" of encouraging private enterprise and aiding government direction of the economy, the new document fell between stools. While preserving much of the rhetoric of the new international economic order, An Agenda for Development showed that the Left had been forced off the high ground by changing pressures and the "discipline" of market forces.

These changes in mood did not make things any easier for the IMF or World Bank. Extreme conservatives were now deeply suspicious of both institutions and called for their abolition. When major IMF rescue operations failed, or when a country receiving vast sums of aid still found itself in trouble (Mexico, Russia, and Brazil were obvious and very large examples), the IMF was bitterly attacked for misjudgment, for loaning too recklessly to governments that were corrupt and inefficient, and generally for wasting other people's money. But it was criticized perhaps even more harshly by the Left, which always disliked the principle of "conditionality" and accused the IMF of compelling home governments to impose austerity programs that hurt the poor. "Conditionality" is, of course, the hallmark of bankers everywhere; no financial body loans money without asking for some safeguards. The real question was, what sorts of conditions should be asked for? After all, by the 1990s both the UN and the specialized agencies were suggesting a newer array of internal conditions—the end of human rights abuses, transparency in government, democratic

elections, advancing the status of women—that Western liberals
rather liked, even if most developing countries still protested in vain
against this practice.

The World Bank was caught in this two-flanked criticism even
more than its sister organization. This was probably because the IMF
was far less visible to the public, operating as it did through confidential meetings with recipient governments, which themselves had to
implement the hoped-for recovery programs, whereas the Bank functioned on the ground, funding and supervising projects that were distinctly in the public eye and which, if they were deemed to have gone
wrong, had visible signs of the failure. The Bank's record had long
been under attack. It had been denounced by liberals, for example,
for continuing to grant loans to South Africa well after apartheid had
become unacceptable to the civilized world; and denounced by conservatives for raising any moneys for aid ("welfare") at all, especially
when so much of it couldn't be repaid. But it was the failures of specific Bank projects, and the news that they were having unforeseen
but clearly detrimental side effects upon local communities and environments, that really got it into trouble.[13]

It should be said that many of these disasters were not the fault of
the Bretton Woods institutions—at least, not directly. To respect national sovereignty, loans were negotiated with governments themselves, but what if the latter did not or could not fulfill the plan, or
decided to reverse policies, or even collapsed, as many African governments did in the 1970s? Local agencies and corrupt administrations could misuse funds, carry out programs in a clumsy way, or pay
no attention to environmental matters. Moneys given in conjunction
with other UN agencies to support, for example, the cleanup of the
Mediterranean were attractive on paper but failed because of continued illegal pollution and inadequate policing by local authorities.
Other projects were straightforwardly misconceived. The early preferences for large-scale power plants and infrastructure investments
were overambitious, placed lots of money in the wrong hands, and
were not pitched at the right level. Some independently funded projects clashed in their purposes with others. There was often little local
input or transfer of technical knowledge and a general assumption

that the same operational and managerial methods could be applied from one country to another. There was ignorance about the environmental consequences of some of the Bank's projects. Many of the dedicated and intelligent officials of the Bank, the UNDP, and other agencies working in the field realized those failings very quickly, but it was not so easy to convey that back to Washington, New York, and Geneva.

The negative publicity was brutal, heavy, and relentless. Local activists were combining with Western anthropologists, NGOs, church groups, and the media to draw attention to highways that blasted their way through tropical forests, dislodged indigenous peoples, worsened the atmosphere and rivers, and benefited the unscrupulous few. The same was true of many dam projects. In all cases, the intention was good—improving communications, increasing power and water supplies—and the Bank and the UNDP were fulfilling their stated purposes of giving financial aid to poorer countries. But things were not going well on the ground, and that was what attracted the most attention from the Left. Conservatives, on the other hand, felt confirmed in their belief that giving international aid was likely throwing money down the drain.

Ironically, the criticisms pointed to newer trends that would help enhance the UN's development record in the longer term. As various later reports on development hinted, it probably had been necessary for the world organization and its members to go through the financial and political crises of the 1970s and 1980s—including the backlash—because it helped agencies and governments to see what worked and what didn't, what was politically feasible and what was not. A financial crisis, whether in Britain or Mexico, tested the IMF and often led to improved responses and instruments. Heavy criticism of a World Bank project gone wrong—not unlike similar criticism of a peacekeeping operation gone wrong—had the potential to stimulate better, more realistic policies next time. A lurch to the left in the North-South debate, ignoring the fact that one group of nations was asking the democratically elected governments of another group to transfer resources, simply had to be replaced by more subtle and appropriate ways of achieving greater global cooperation, such as microcredit lending schemes, which we discuss in the following chapter. This, on the whole, was gradually being done. Agencies and governments, like human beings themselves, are all capable of learning from errors. But by their many early mistakes, the world's financial and development agencies left an impression of misuse and incompetence that would be hard to shake off.

Any summing up of the efforts made and progress reached by humankind collectively in the economic spheres during more than the half-century after 1945 is bound to be a mixed one. The greatest lesson that emerges, surely, is that domestic policies rather than international help counted most in a country's rise to prosperity—from West Germany's Wirtschaftswunder to Silicon Valley's high-tech boom to Singapore's entry into the camp of rich nations, the message was that there was no substitute for wise internal policy measures or the encouragement of enterprise. Only a few fortunate oil-rich countries bucked that trend, yet even here the evidence suggests that over the longer term, good governance and prudent policies are a better national resource than gas in the ground. But it would be a misreading of history to move from that economic truism to the conclusion that the United Nations system, its own agencies and the specialized agencies, and all the other associated institutions had had no effect on economic developments in these five or so decades.

By the year 2000, the UN agencies had come a long way in improving themselves and thus being in a better position to help those whom they were designed to serve. The change was noted most visibly in the activities and ideas advanced by an invigorated UNDP, and just how that body and its sister ECOSOC institutions like UNEP, UNESCO, UNICEF, UNFPA, and others worked to become more effective and accountable will be told in the following chapter. Although much still needed to be done, considerable streamlining of activity, improved interagency cooperation, and a more exact understanding of where and how each body was most (and least) effective made for little-known but significant progress all around. There was also more cooperation between UN agencies, the World Bank, and the UN Regional Banks, especially on particular projects in the field and where technical assistance was the first priority. The Africa Capacity Building Initiative, for example, involved cooperation between the World Bank, the African Development Bank, the UNDP, and other UN agencies, plus bilateral sources of income. The New Partnership for Africa's Development agreement of 2001 committed African leaders to full transparency and accountability in governance, following which donor countries, reciprocally, would give additional development aid. This was starting to get things moving on the ground, and with local actors to the fore.

Thus, while the heated political debate about the global economy continued unabated, capacity building was going ahead in many places. Even a world-weary cynic would have to acknowledge that individual cases of improvement did count. A triple grant (World Bank, UNDP, UNEP) to a small village on the slopes of Mount Kenya to help control water and generate electricity was transforming a society that for generations had lived close to disaster. A UNDP loan to small farmers in Kyrgyzstan was giving its recipients their first chance ever to build a future and become prosperous. Here were small success stories of which the UN agencies were proud; they certainly deserve as much of a hearing as the tales of mismanagement and waste.[14]

Yet it remains true that the UN's own development agencies cannot answer two larger charges: namely, that (1) they have not had the capacity to assist the truly poor, lowest one billion people of this world, despite their best efforts; and that (2) they have had little role, if any, in the story of the amazing rise in the standards of living of hundreds of millions of families worldwide, but chiefly in Asia. It's a fair thought that both occurrences might be beyond the reach of global agencies ever to affect their downward or upward spirals. Perhaps, then, UN agencies can operate only at the margins or in specific, favorable contexts.

The same might be said about the IMF and the World Bank. A lot of the agitation to change or abolish the Bretton Woods institutions at the time of their fiftieth anniversary—"Fifty Years Is Enough!" was a characteristic slogan and movement—was impractical, but the very fact that there was severe criticism, together with the exigencies of the 1990s, led to a rethinking of missions and refinement of policies.

The two sisters were returning to their separate responsibilities, with the IMF being point guard and fireman for rescuing countries in financial trouble and the World Bank concentrating more upon long-term help to the poorest of the poor. But it was a separation that recognized that on many occasions they would work hand in hand, since an economic and social crisis in a developing nation or a faltering emerging market country might sensibly call for a multilevel response and a wise division of labor. Both continued to be powerfully challenged—the IMF by Latin American fiscal crises, the needs of the former Soviet republics, and the unexpected East Asian financial meltdown of the late 1990s; the World Bank by the call to meet Africa's growing needs—and things could, and did, go badly awry in both dimensions and thus kept their critics busy.[15] On examining some of these failures, one comes away with the impression that the IMF in particular could not win: If it granted a large loan to, say, Russia or Brazil and attached banker's conditions to that loan, it would be criticized for its austerity. But if it did nothing, it would be attacked for failing to head off a global financial crisis. Perhaps the best that can be said is that, had the IMF and World Bank not existed and played the roles required of them, the world financial and currency system as a whole would most probably be in worse shape than it is today.

The same might be said for the advances made in the critical field of world trade arrangements, which generated controversies and attacks more violent than any launched on the Bretton Woods duo. The establishment in 1995 of the World Trade Organization (WTO) in place of the GATT marked the conclusion of the arduous Uruguay Round negotiations and, seen in longer-term perspective, the realization at last of the idea of an international trade organization proposed much earlier as the "third leg" of the Bretton Woods system—and now a body, like them, independent of the ECOSOC. The WTO had much more teeth than the GATT, which alone made it a more important and controversial body, and its remit to police the rules regarding trade without discrimination challenged the protectionist habits of rich and poor countries alike; it also dealt with many more goods and services than industrial products. Much of its energy was to go into sorting out quarrels between the United States and the European Union regarding hidden subsidies, the favoring of farmers, steel duties, and the like—often a thankless task, given the way governments on each side buckled to powerful domestic lobbies before being induced to compromise at the international table. Yet compromise and fudging was better than a 1930s breakdown.

But the biggest controversy about the international trading order that the WTO policies and UNCTAD resolutions sought to promote was whether, by its open market principles, they inherently favored the powerful over the weak. This debate must appear as a dialogue of the deaf. Advocates of the level playing field held that good governance and encouragement of trade will attract foreign investment, increase incomes, and improve the quality of life in all countries without the need to distort market principles or grant special treatment. Critics in the South complained and continue to complain that unrestricted globalization is tilted against developing countries, which have inadequate resources to negotiate WTO accords (which are done behind closed doors), have no control over the inflow and outflow of capital, are far too dependent upon a few export commodities, and therefore have no chance of handling giant corporations possessing much greater powers. Liberals in the North protest that the push for globalization and modernization everywhere is threatening individual cultures and ways of life and that it can only create further pressures upon damaged environments on land, at sea, and in the air. Union leaders fear that a totally free market system hurts the living standards of Northern workers, whose labor could not compete with the far cheaper costs of enterprises in the South.[16]

Any belief that these were not serious concerns was swept away during the angry demonstrations outside the WTO's ministerial meeting in Seattle in late 1999, for the sheer heterogeneity of the protesters—environmentalists, trade unionists, anarchists, human rights advocates, spokesmen from the South—showed clearly that the 1980s/1990s "shift" away from managing the global economy back to a liberal, market-oriented order was unacceptable to millions. A much more empathetic and poverty-focused World Bank under James Wolfensohn, or an imaginative and vigorous UNDP under Gustav

Speth, might have then been instituting appropriate, holistic development programs; but to their critics they still represented the old order, merely clothed in more fetching garb. The tension between the lofty rhetoric and high egalitarian principles of the UN Charter and the actual distributions of wealth, power, and influence in the world economy remained unchanged as the human community entered the twenty-first century.

Here, then, was the greatest reproof of all upon collective endeavors to improve humankind's condition—namely, that there remains shocking evidence of mass poverty in Darfur and Myanmar and so many other parts of the globe, even at the same time that many other millions in Bangalore and Shanghai are rising into the middle classes. Depending upon which statistics one uses, there are still between one billion and two billion people (one-third of humanity) existing on $2 or less a day. Malnutrition, lack of clean water, lack of health care, and lack of education and employment afflict many a land. Diseases old and new stalk entire societies. Desperation is driving communities to damage their environments, even toward ecocide. "Collapsed states" in many parts of Africa are the ultimate expression of our failure to render help in time; and given the buildup of demographic and environmental pressures, more collapses are possible, indeed likely. Outside of Africa, especially perhaps in Latin America, countries that began to climb from their poverty in the past two decades have found their gains fragile or short-lived when financial crises erupt, capital flees abroad, and new austerity measures are introduced—as if they had not known enough austerity already. In the North, battered former socialist economies are in better shape but still struggling to survive the new competitiveness. And many a socioeconomic group even in the richer countries feels job insecurity and concern about the future. This is, as we said at the beginning of the chapter, a disappointing record. Even if a greater part of humanity enjoys higher standards of living today than was the case in 1945, the deficiencies that remain are so large that there is no room for congratulation. The task is still incomplete, and by a large margin.

CHAPTER 5

The Softer Face of the UN's Mission

The military and economic tasks entrusted to the United Nations by its own Charter are often regarded as the "hard" edges of global cooperation; they imply strength, purpose, practicality. They suggest a man's world. By contrast, the agendas covered in this chapter are sometimes described, condescendingly, as the UN's "soft" purposes—feminine agendas—women and children, international public health, population issues, care for the environment, respecting and encouraging cultural diversity, pursuing social freedoms. As such, they are regarded as being of secondary import. They have, after all, no powerful body like the Security Council, the International Monetary Fund, or the World Bank to advance their purposes. Instead, there is a plethora of less well-known and less influential entities (that is, various UN programs, commissions, funds, offices) whose sheer variety of names, as we noted earlier, suggests confusion, overlap, and only modest influence on the world stage.

This impression is true enough, on first encounter. UNICEF is not the Security Council, and the United Nations Population Commission is not the World Bank. Their budgets do not come close to those of Microsoft or Exxon. Their staff is less than that of the Chicago Police Department. Yet all these traditional ways of measuring things fail to capture the truly revolutionary nature of the soft agendas in the sweep of world history. In no way are those matters of secondary import to the future of humankind.

Behind the UN structure as a whole is a troika of converging thoughts: security, prosperity, and understanding. To prevent war and aggression, the founding fathers thought there needed to be set in place robust security and military mechanisms, a reactive system controlled by the Security Council. And to stop states being driven into conflict by despair, there should be more positive and proactive economic policies, aimed at creating commercial and financial integration, and shared prosperity. Yet the founders of 1945 didn't stop at proposing military and economic instruments. They also thought that instability, jealousy, nationalism, and aggression were affected by massive cultural, religious, and ethnic prejudices. So they tried to put in place an apparatus to advance the social and cultural aspirations that were embedded in the language of the original Charter. In the early years, it should be stressed, these were little more than aspirations. Perhaps the important point was simply that the lofty aims had been declared and publicly agreed to.

What also had been decided upon was the institutional location of most of the agencies that would pursue those aims. This was to be an arena for action that above all concerned the General Assembly and its ECOSOC.[1] Since the Security Council arrogated to itself authority in affairs of war and peace, and the Bretton Woods institutions were the biggest operators in economics and finance, the General Assembly viewed the UN's social and cultural agendas as playing fields where they could be the leaders. Moreover, to the Scandinavian and South American members and to newer UN countries from the developing world like India, these policy areas—rather than military matters—were the agenda items that counted, because in one way or the other they focused upon "the people without history," those who did not enjoy the military and economic and media influence of the traditional power elites. The Great Powers would usually pay serious attention to these agendas only when they seemed to affect their national interests and prestige. It is significant that many of the soft agencies have their headquarters in Geneva, Vienna, Paris, Rome, Tokyo, and Nairobi, whereas the Bretton Woods institutions were deliberately located in Washington, D.C., and the UN headquarters placed firmly in New York City.

Not all UN bodies operating in the fields of social, environmental, and cultural policies are direct subsidiaries of the ECOSOC. The system, as the reader might guess by now, is not that clean-cut. A specialized agency like the World Health Organization, for example, works closely with its sister organizations, but it remains an intergovernmental body—that is to say, governments join it, and it is thus constitutionally different from the United Nations Environment Programme (UNEP), which was established by an express vote of the General Assembly and reports back to the Assembly via the ECOSOC twice a year. Anyone coming to this field for the first time is entitled to be breathless and bewildered at learning of the sheer number of overlapping, agenda-sharing, and rival agencies within the world organization.[2] What, for example, is the relationship between the ECOSOC's Commission on the Status of Women, the UN Development Fund for Women, the General Assembly's Committee on the Elimination of Discrimination Against Women, and the ECOSOC's International Research and Training Institute for the Advancement of Women? Surely conservative critics have a case when they call for a streamlining of this overelaborate but loosely constructed edifice?

We will try to address such issues in the following pages, but it is clear that a chapter—or even a full book—on the UN's social, environmental, and cultural policies could swiftly dissolve into an "alphabet soup" of describing a long list of entities, rather than looking at this phenomenon as a whole. There simply is not space in this work to talk about the UN Group of Experts on Geographical Names or the International Union for the Protection of New Varieties of Plants, or even the World Tourism Organization, or to spend time querying their existence. Instead, we shall focus on a cluster of transcendent and related issues that have seized the attention of the world organization: environmental matters; social matters relating to health, population, women, and children; and cultural and intellectual affairs. There are, obviously, certain overlaps with the economic agendas covered in the preceding chapter and with the human rights agendas dealt with in the following chapter; but the themes treated here can stand by themselves.[3]

Immediately after the Second World War, member states were passionately keen to rebuild international society and were not yet convulsed by East-West tensions. With retrospective knowledge of how those dreams were to be swept away, or at least greatly curbed, one is struck by the ambition and optimism of the time. Already in 1945 the world body had created its Educational, Scientific, and Cultural Organization (UNESCO) to push a remarkably wide cultural agenda. A year later, there was an amazing burst of institution building. It was the foundation year for the UN International Children's Emergency Fund, which, originally intended to give help to children in war-ravaged societies in Europe, was later reconstituted to provide child health and welfare services to poorer, developing countries while keeping its original acronym (UNICEF). The ECOSOC established in that same year the Commission on Population and Development, an early stab at those major and looming issues; it also set up its Commission for Social Development (CSD) to advise in those fields. In addition, it created its Commission on the Status of Women (CSW) and then—what would become a perennial favorite of world bodies—founded the Commission on Narcotic Drugs (the UN may have more bodies dealing with drugs than with any issue apart from disarmament and weapons inspections).

All of these new creations sat alongside some of the older special-ized agencies—literally and physically: Certain streets in Paris, Geneva, Rome, and Vienna have UN offices and specialized agencies cheek by jowl with one another, as also happens near the East River in Man-hattan. As noted earlier, some of the agencies were older, like the In-ternational Labour Organization and the Universal Postal Union. But the nations of the world were also setting up new, autonomous, inter-governmental organizations at the same time they were allowing the General Assembly and the ECOSOC to create subsidiary bodies. The World Health Organization—whose proclaimed objective is "the attainment by all peoples of the highest possible levels of health"—is, as noted previously, also a creature of 1946. The equally important Food and Agriculture Organization, designed to respond to world hunger and sustain global agriculture, was born a year earlier. Thus, bodies established by intergovernmental treaties emerged at the same time as entities created by the General Assembly, but it didn't seem to matter at the time. These were heady days, and it is not surprising to learn that numerous individuals, emerging from wartime service, sought to dedicate themselves to working for international organizations in order to make their personal commitment toward a better world in peacetime. Few of them became household names, although one might note among them that redoubtable former British paratrooper Brian Urquhart, the great development economist from the West Indies W. Arthur Lewis, the renowned black American diplomat Ralph Bunche, and the influential French international lawyer René Cassin, all of whom appear in this text. In Urquhart's recollection, "We were all optimists and regarded the occasional cynic or 'realist' with contempt."[4]

As it happened, however, implementing the social and cultural policies of the United Nations soon slowed, because too many other fields claimed prior attention. The Cold War obviously hurt those early hopes. It was hard to generate appreciation for cultural diversity in the midst of the Berlin, Korean, Suez, and Hungarian crises. The greater part of the resources of UN bodies and the specialized agencies went to the absolutely necessary task of rebuilding nations and economies shattered by the Second World War. When that was accomplished, the world organization faced the sheer press of decolonization and the trebling of its membership—and the focus shifted to meeting the needs of economic development, as was noted in the previous chapter. Since it was assumed that little or nothing could be advanced in the social and cultural domains without achieving economic growth and prosperity, the soft items took second place.

Perhaps the most significant practical achievement in these early years—which parallels the story of the economic agencies—was the work of some relatively modest UN institutions, the statistical commissions and the groups of economic and scientific advisers. For the first time in history, the nations of the world had declared through the UN Charter that they were intent upon improving all of humankind, but this could not be done without proper knowledge of social, economic, and demographic facts. Given the disruptions of the Second World War, the UN's founders felt they were groping in the dark, so it is not surprising that as early as February 1946, the ECOSOC set up a Statistical Commission. Assembling statistics, studying how to

define what is an equitable "standard of living," measuring population growth and fertility rates, and studying plant loss or climate
change may seem arcane scientific procedures. But they would ultimately provide the data that would accompany major international
actions and legislation, particularly as regards the developing world.
Indeed, by 1971 the ECOSOC had ordered its Statistical Commission
to pay "special regard to the requirement of reviewing and appraising
economic and social progress, taking into account the needs of the
developing countries." This, more than anything else, was to be
the direction in which the General Assembly, the ECOSOC, and all
the subsidiary bodies and associated agencies would go.

The change of emphasis—from restoring war-torn societies in the
North to assisting social development in the South—can be seen
in the composition of UN bodies themselves. As the number of member states in the world organization increased, so did the constituted
members of all the offices previously mentioned. Thus, the original
membership of the ECOSOC, a mere eighteen in 1945, was increased
to twenty-seven in 1963 and had shot up to fifty-four by 1971.
Its own Commission for Social Development went from eighteen
(1946) to twenty-one (1961) to thirty-two (1966). Given the worries about international drug trading, the Commission on Narcotic
Drugs leapt from fifteen members in its original (1946) state to fifty-
three by 1991. In almost all cases, the memberships were specified
by what is called "equitable geographical distribution"—that is, so
many members are from Africa, so many from Asia, so many from
Latin America/the Caribbean, so many from Europe, Eurasia, North
America, and Australasia. There were fewer and fewer references to
the need for experience and competence, for who, after all, would
measure national nominees against such criteria?

The political implications of this were clear. The General Assembly, the ECOSOC and all its bodies, and even some of the specialized
agencies were becoming more democratic or, perhaps better put, at
least more representative of the world's overall population. They desired, and demanded, a new socioeconomic order. They felt they were
on the move despite the fact that the Security Council and Bretton
Woods institutions were remaining unchanged from the power rela-

tionships of 1945. This was a troubling disjuncture, one that would disappoint the boldly proclaimed social, environmental, and cultural visions of those early years and of all those who sought to recover those visions in later decades.

In the first decade, those who ran the new social and cultural agencies had little time to consider this disjuncture, for the work at hand was overwhelming. As one author puts it, at the time the UN Charter was being signed, "bread, milk, meat, sugar, and fats and oils were being rationed in many countries. There were also severe shortages of other essential foodstuffs. The demand for coal, steel, timber, and electric power far exceeded the available supply. Countless homes in Europe and Asia had been destroyed or made uninhabitable, and the remaining dwellings—inadequate before the war—had become dangerously overcrowded in most of the larger cities. Vast numbers of refugees were unable to return to their homelands. Railways, highways, bridges, ports, and factories awaited repair and reconstruction. The prewar network of international trade and payments was disrupted. A welter of problems, long-term and short-term, needed attention."[5] The refugee problem alone stretched the UN's limited resources. The eight million displaced persons in Europe in May 1945 were soon joined by another eight million "expellees" from the East, by Cossacks and Ukrainians striving to avoid Soviet revenge, by Jews attempting to get to Palestine. Millions of others, facing malnutrition and unemployment, would clearly try to migrate to the "New World" at the first chance possible.

Thus, a large number of these early UN agencies were created not by careful planning and negotiation in the cool foothills of Bretton Woods, but in immediate response to gigantic human tragedy: The UNRRA for immediate refugees, UNICEF itself, and the FAO all had to go to work immediately. Most of them were expected to fade into oblivion once the post–World War II emergencies were over, though alas hardly any of them were permitted to do so. As noted earlier, UNICEF remained, keeping the word *Emergency* in its title, while the UNRRA became the International Refugee Organization (IRO) and then, in 1951, the Office of the UN High Commissioner for Refugees. The latter was much reduced in its powers compared with the IRO, but that was because the Cold War was already intruding and making the lofty human goals proclaimed in the Charter less realizable. The Soviet Union maintained that only refugees from Fascism should be supported by the UNHCR, that it wished to have no part in the U.S.-dominated FAO, and that it saw UNESCO as an ideological battlefield. In so doing, of course, it made sure that the rest of the Warsaw Pact nations kept their distance as well—scientific socialism, it asserted, would much more easily provide for people's needs than would capitalist materialism.

But the biggest disappointment was that the human tragedies of war and displacement were also now occurring far outside Europe's battered lands. In fact, within a decade of 1945 the old continent had made immense strides in economic recovery and in social investments, but disasters were now accumulating elsewhere, in the poorer parts of the world. The dreadful "struggle at birth" between India and Pakistan in 1947 had resulted in 9 million Muslim refugees fleeing the former country and 5 million Hindu refugees moving out of the latter. The war in Korea created 4.5 million refugees in the South. At least in those cases, the fleeing migrants were being taken in by their own countrymen, so there were reasonable chances of absorption and integration for many families, as there were for East Germans resettling in the Federal Republic.

This was not true for those 1 million Palestinian Arabs who had fled or been driven across the boundaries of the newly established state of Israel in 1948, chiefly into Jordan. So dire was their plight—they were virtually destitute, their presence dragged down local living standards, and diseases were easily transmitted—that within another year the General Assembly felt compelled to set up what would soon be the UN Relief and Works Agency for Palestine Refugees in the Near East.[6] Here again, perhaps with the improving situation in Western Europe in mind, the planners thought they were dealing with a temporary problem; the documents talk optimistically about the right to return to one's property (or get full compensation) or about "reintegration projects" in the countries of resettlement. But the obstructionism of the host governments toward UNRWA workers and their resistance to domestic integration programs for the refugees (preferring to keep the Palestinians in camps) has been matched only by the intransigence of successive Israeli governments against the idea of the Arabs returning to their family lands. With the numbers increased by the Arab defeat in the 1967 war, and with the demographic explosion in the refugee camps—by 1994 the UNRWA was providing essential services to more than three million people—the General Assembly has had the unhappy task of renewing the agency's work every few years, with no end in sight. This incapacity to deal with the hapless, desperate victims of war was a harbinger of much to come, especially across Africa, Asia, and the Balkans.

In the mid-1950s, scholars at the Brookings Institution in Washington, D.C., came together to produce a large study entitled "The United Nations and Economic and Social Cooperation," a sophisticated balance sheet of what had been achieved in those fields during the first ten years of the UN's existence and of what had still to be done or had not been done well. Its conclusions were important but unsurprising. Social and economic progress in some parts of the world (Europe) had been good in that decade, some results were only fair (Latin America), and some were disappointing (Asia). Because of continued colonialism, Africa was scarcely mentioned.

The report also noted tensions between two or more desirable goods. For example, programs and agencies that were technical by nature made more progress and were less contentious than those affected by politics, but if UN bodies became purely technical, they would forfeit the politicians' (that is, their paymasters') interest. Rival economic philosophies ran against the universalist aspirations of the Charter: The Communist bloc stayed mainly aloof, and there were already significant differences between those European countries favoring a larger role for governments and American suspicions of a statist approach. Some programs found it difficult to work out whether their main aim was to achieve broad improvements (for example, raising nutrition levels for all) or to assist targeted groups (refugees, children), especially when financial resources were insufficient for all needs. Some intended short-term programs (UNRWA, UNICEF) were becoming longer-term and required a rethink.

UNESCO was already identified as attempting too much and dissipating its energies. In sum, the Brookings report concluded, the UN's record here "left much to be desired"; but given the extraordinary dislocations caused by the war, later regional struggles, and the "paralyzing effect" of East-West strife, what was achieved during the previous decade "should afford a basis for qualified optimism about the future." This would not be the last time in the UN's history that such cautious, approbatory language would be used.[7]

The most significant trend the report noticed was how, even by 1955, "the special problems of the undeveloped countries [were becoming], so to speak, the stock in trade of United Nations economic and social programs." Some attention had been paid even in earlier days. Labor standards and social security provision (or lack thereof) in colonies and poorer countries had concerned the ILO in the interwar years. And the worldwide food shortages of 1945–48 stimulated the FAO into giving assistance to non-Western countries shortly after its own creation. But the really large shift of attention came from the 1950s onward, partly because decolonization was gathering pace and partly because newly available statistical data were revealing for the first time the full dimensions of social issues—poverty, malnutrition, population explosions—within poorer nations. Finally, of course, the Cold War itself was expanding out of its European arena, and East and West were beginning to compete for the support of influential regional leaders like India, Egypt, Brazil, and others.

The UN's social and cultural agendas were never separate from the realities of international politics and economics—in fact, they interacted constantly with those realities. Given the growing movements for political change in the 1960s and 1970s, it was no surprise that there also occurred an explosion of efforts to alter the social agenda, manifested most clearly by a series of ambitious UN world conferences, the first of which is generally regarded as being the United Nations Conference on the Human Environment, held in Stockholm in 1972. Then came the reaction. The next phase, lasting roughly throughout the 1980s, was influenced by the revival of free market economics and political conservatism in many developed countries, especially the United States. UN world conferences continued to be held but now met under the cloud of fiscal austerity, skepticism about their motives, and disappointment about their results. The third phase was attended not only by the termination of the Cold War after 1989, but also by a widespread belief that renewed efforts were needed to meet the world's increasingly serious social and environmental challenges. This led to a plethora of attention-catching and important world conferences throughout the 1990s, which in turn petered out gradually, partly from exhaustion (could one really have a major UN world conference every year?) and partly from a need to take stock—considerations that still prevail.

To avoid turning this into a mere catalog of UN conferences—the political scientist Michael Schechter's admirable study counts thirty-two between 1972 (Stockholm) and 1996 (Rome), and there have been others since then—our focus will be on the three areas identified earlier: (1) environmental matters; (2) social matters relating to health, population, women, and children; and (3) cultural and intellectual affairs.[8]

A few general remarks are in order here. First, the vast majority of these soft conference agendas were also those of the South—the exceptions being the 1993 Human Rights Conference (Vienna), the first few early conferences on women's rights, and the several conferences on the law of the sea. Some were explicitly so, like the Paris UN conferences (1981, 1990) on the least developed countries; and others were potentially universal but were then given this focus, like the World Conference on Science and Technology for Development (Vienna, 1979). The South's aspirations at these meetings were almost always supported enthusiastically by what one might term "the concerned North," such as the Scandinavian countries, the Netherlands, Canada, and a few others. Those conferences usually avoided meeting in a Great Power locale: None were held in London, or in Moscow, or in Beijing (until the 1995 World Conference on Women); the only conference held in New York City was that on the quasi-"hard" topic of disarmament and development in 1987, plus the World Summit on the Child in 1990. Paris was something of an exception here, because it contained so many UN agencies and preparatory secretariats (perhaps also because delegates liked visiting Paris). What emerges clearly from the public statements following these conferences is, predictably, that most of the countries of the South and the concerned North were strongly in favor of intergovernmental action and structures, whereas delegates representing more conservative governments were wary of or hostile to this tendency, being also opposed to a large role for government at home.

A second general aspect of the UN conferences was their popular nature. Very few, if any, meetings were held behind closed doors, as was commonplace with the Security Council and the agencies dealing with finance and trade; rather, they were held in the full glare of world publicity. At the UN Conference on Environment and Development—the "Earth Summit" held in Rio in 1992—the proceedings were covered daily by CNN television, by the press agencies, and by the world's newspapers. No fewer than 108 heads of state or government flew to Rio make a statement, an indication that this was the place to be. But equally interesting was the presence at the conference of 2,400 representatives of more than 650 NGOs, while some 17,000 people took part in NGO forum activities. Also there were the powerful and liberal American philanthropic foundations such as Ford, Rockefeller, MacArthur, Pew, and Carnegie, which funded many of the study groups, workshops, and publications surrounding the conference. We shall look at this phenomenon more closely in Chapter Seven, but one cannot write about the pursuit of the UN's social and cultural agendas without remarking on this development.

Third, the world conferences focused strongly on "follow-up." It was not enough to have the secretariats labor, often for years in advance, if nothing was to come out of these international meetings at their close. Thus, nearly all the conferences ended with a solemn declaration, many of them led to a new UN convention, and several were soon followed by a new institution that was to monitor the agreements and help member states carry them out. For example, the World Food Conference in Rome in 1974 led almost immediately to the creation of the World Food Council (WFC) and the International Fund for Agricultural Development (IFAD), while the 1975 World Conference on Women in Mexico City led to a flurry of new ventures—the UN Development Fund for Women (UNIFEM), the International Research and Training Institute for the Advancement of Women (INSTRAW), the UN declaration of "the Decade of Women," and, a few years later, the General Assembly's adoption of the Convention on the Elimination of All Forms of Discrimination Against Women. Very often the delegates to a world conference voted for midterm, or five-year, assessments (and conferences!) on how their resolutions were being observed and implemented and asked for annual reports from the newly established bodies.

It is easy in retrospect to see the pitfalls that this burst of international legislating, regulating, standard setting, and agency creating would encounter. It was making the structures of the world organization ever more elaborate and overlapping, though rarely providing resources for increases in staff, unless of course a rich country showed a particular desire to support a new body—as Japan does with the United Nations University, which just happens to be located in Tokyo. The agencies themselves were rarely subject to external scrutiny or their staff to tough hiring and firing criteria. Not only was the workload spiraling for the General Assembly and ECOSOC committees as well as for the existing or newly created bodies, but greater demands were also being placed upon the home civil services of all member states to provide data, collect statistics, write reports, and monitor treaty legislation. The poorest and most war-torn countries could not possibly meet these demands, while the world's most powerful country became increasingly frustrated at what seemed to be the creation of overambitious, overlapping, and underperforming institutions— the scene was thus set for conservatives to complain all through the 1980s and 1990s that much of the UN represented a waste of money. And although this agitation against "bloated bureaucracies" was often exaggerated, it was sometimes closer to the mark than liberal defenders of the world organization would admit.

Finally, there was the tricky issue of "compellence" versus states' sovereignty, by which is meant the use of international protocols and agency monitoring to get member states to carry out actions that they suspect are against their national interests. This should not have come as a surprise. If sovereign states are sensitive about UN interfer-

ence in matters affecting their security needs, they will probably also
be wary about agreements that affect their own economic, social, cultural, environmental, and civil rights domains. This had already been
seen in the economic field in the fierce disagreements over UNCTAD,
or the role of the Bretton Woods institutions, where the 1970s pressures of developing and concerned Northern nations for a new international economic order had caused a backlash in the 1980s from
some of the richer industrial nations. But such a backlash was also
to be predicted when UN conferences voted on "targets for compliance" regarding global emissions or set overly ambitious levels for
annual transfer contributions from North to South for development
aid. Perhaps the mutual anger of liberals and conservatives could
have been reduced had less confrontationist language been used—
certainly those running the conferences strove as best they could to
avoid breakdowns and walkouts. Or perhaps, since the quarrels reflected basic ideological differences and political frustrations, they
were unavoidable. Certainly they showed the difficulty of turning the
lofty wording of the UN Charter into practice in a world of 190 sovereign states where the gap between rich and poor countries was so
large.

International agreements and policies relating to the environment are
a very late agenda item in this story, yet their relatively brief evolution
tells us so much about the process of groping toward common goals
that it will be treated as the first and most detailed of our case studies. This tale also serves as a perfect example of both the potential
and the difficulty of reaching that Tennysonian vision of a truly
global commonweal.

To begin with, the environmental debate illustrates how new international concerns arise and then snowball into a larger movement. As
one scholar reminds us, "The UN Charter makes no mention of environmental protection. It does not specifically refer in setting out its
objects and principles to the aims of preventing pollution, conserv-
ing resources, or to the need for sustainable development." This was
hardly surprising, she continues, since the perceived need in 1945
was to remedy the League of Nations' deficiencies in deterring aggres-

sion, protecting human rights, and creating prosperity.[9] Besides, the greatest postwar desire—apart from avoiding an outright East-West conflict—was to pursue economic growth, whether it took the form of rebuilding shattered industries in Europe and the Far East or ensuring that modernization came to the former colonial territories. What was urgently needed, as the Brookings report quoted earlier had said, was more coal, more gas, more timber, more bricks and water, more iron and steel, more agricultural produce, more fish and poultry and animal products. During the fuel crisis that paralyzed Europe in the winter of 1947, people shivered as they gazed at immobile trains and quiet factories—what gave hope was to witness locomotives, power plants, and factory chimneys emitting smoke and trace gases! Apart from legislation that protected endangered species and established national parks (something that went back to the 1900s), little else was happening in the environmental field.

The first changes in thinking occurred in the North and were provoked by increasing evidence that human economic activities were damaging environments, other species, and *Homo sapiens* himself. The great London "smog" of December 1952, a combination of damp weather conditions and appalling levels of industrial pollution, caused thousands of deaths due to respiratory illness yet in turn led to the U.K. Clean Air Act of 1956, a major step in curbing emissions. Legislation also appeared for the cleaning up of the rivers of Europe and North America by banning the discharge of heavy metals, oil, and other effluents into the water. People began to become concerned that acid rain was ruining historic buildings and treasured woodlands alike. Then, a little later, there were the pathbreaking, disturbing books. Rachel Carson's *Silent Spring* (1962), for example, argued that DDT and other agricultural chemicals had dire effects upon small wildlife, birds, and insects. The evidence and the responses were at first local and regional, as, for example, when liberal U.S. states like California, Wisconsin, and Massachusetts began to demand environmental controls, whereas states more reliant upon heavy industry such as Ohio and Indiana were correspondingly more reluctant. The closeness of Western European countries to one another also made for some early coordinated actions—it was useless for the Netherlands

to ban industrial discharges into the Rhine if the nations upriver did
not: Common standards had to be adopted by all littoral states.

But once people became concerned about polluted air and water
locally, or about overfishing in the waters offshore, it was not too
large a step to think more broadly and to wonder about damage to
the globe as a whole. Why bother to eliminate DDT on the western
plains of the United States to protect the graceful Swainson's hawks if
the pesticide was to be heavily used on the Argentine pampas, where
those same hawks wintered and fed upon locally infected insects and
mammals? What was the point of Sweden and Finland having tough
clean air acts when the southerly winds carried brown coal emissions
from East Germany's inefficient factories across the Baltic and ruined
their forests? What was the point of the British and Irish governments
limiting their own fishermen's catches in offshore waters if fish stocks
were being reduced by Spanish and Polish trawlers? Moreover, the
newer literature upon human pressures on the planet was also assuming a global scope, as well as an apocalyptic tone. The book titles
were purposefully suggestive. In 1971, Richard Falk published his
study *This Endangered Planet,* and a year later Dennis Meadows and
his colleagues brought out their Club of Rome study called *Limits
to Growth*—an obvious challenge to all of the orthodox economic
growth literature that ruled the field. Even earlier, in 1968, Paul
Ehrlich published his scary bestseller, *The Population Bomb,* and introduced a new concern: Not only were the economic activities of the
existing (say) 3.5 billion humans hurting the planet, but the doubling
of populations in poorer countries over the next decades would destroy their environments and be a further restraint upon escaping
from poverty.

A second noticeable feature of the environmentalist movement
was the involvement of civil society—that is, of self-mobilized groups
(chiefly in the North, chiefly middle class) that were often suspicious
of big business and government and wanted concerned citizens to
play a more active part in deciding society's fate. It was no coincidence that the emergence of these groups occurred at the same time
as the civil rights movement in the United States, the women's movement in the West generally, and the student protests of the 1960s—all

were challenges to the established order and to traditional thinking about how to arrange affairs. There were, of course, older, genteel bodies like the Sierra Club and the Audubon Society, but they were now joined by more radical and activist organizations such as Friends of the Earth, the World Wildlife Fund, and Greenpeace. Some of their campaigns were single-minded ("Save the Whales," for example), but they all brought new energy and focus to the issue of what man was doing to his planet. And certain groups, with Greenpeace to the fore, were determined to draw even more attention to this issue by spectacular demonstrations and protests. Whether one approved of their stunts or not, they clearly had an effect. Parliaments, under pressure from their own "green" movements or "green parties," began to set up environmental subcommittees to question governments and offer reports, governments themselves created Ministries of the Environment or Environmental Protection Agencies and allocated increased funds, and new national legislation was drawn up to reduce pollution or to preserve endangered species or ecosystems.

With the historical UN Conference on the Human Environment (UNCHE) in Stockholm in 1972, this movement went fully global.[10] Four years earlier, the ECOSOC had asked for such a world conference, which Sweden offered to host. The dynamic secretary-general of UNCHE, Maurice Strong, consulted experts, prepared drafts, invited interested NGOs to attend, and in many other ways set the scene for all future UN world conferences. Once again, the language was lofty and ambitious. The preamble to the Stockholm declaration proclaimed that "man has the fundamental right to freedom, equality, and adequate conditions of life, in an environment of a quality that permits a life of dignity and well-being." Now, at last, environmentalists felt, the soft agendas had come to the center of the world's stage. By contrast, the famous conferences of earlier times (at Westphalia, Vienna, Versailles, Potsdam) seemed narrow in membership and limited in scope.

But it soon became clear that the environmental concerns of many Northern nations were matched, if not exceeded, by the deep suspicions of Southern governments that their plans for economic and industrial development might be throttled. An earnest Canadian's worry about the destruction of the tropical rain forests was countered by anger from Brazilian and Malaysian delegates at possible interference in the use of their domestic resources. The "Limits to Growth" report, timed to appear for the Stockholm conference, was seen as threatening not only by corporations (especially in extractive and heavy-manufacturing industries) and by conservative free market economists in the North (to whom economic growth was the holy grail and who derided the notion of "limits"), but also by governments in Asia and Latin America. Of course, both positions had sense. If development and growth could not be pursued, there was no chance of lifting billions of people out of poverty; but if they were pursued without regard to the environment, that might threaten the sustainability of humankind itself.

The result, as so often with UN and other international conferences, was a compromise in the concept of "sustainable development."[11] The emphasis would be placed upon using new technologies and other ingenious approaches that would both allow the exploitation of natural resources and reduce environmental damage. Growth would continue, but it would be much more sensitive and sophisticated, aided by the transfer of resources (capital, technology, scientific expertise) from the richer to the poorer countries. All this was easier said than done and would soon be followed by disappointing setbacks. Yet the Stockholm conference of 1972 had significant consequences, many more than its critics allowed.

The first was the establishment of the UN Environment Programme to be the focal point of the world body's efforts to grapple with environmental matters and to be a coordinator and stimulator to the other parts of the system. Significantly, its secretariat headquarters was to be in Nairobi. The Governing Council of UNEP consisted of fifty-eight states elected triennially by the General Assembly, thereby making enough room for sensitive member countries to feel they had some control of this new, radical body and emphasizing its democratic nature. Under a series of very vigorous executive directors, UNEP was to push its agendas to the forefront of the UN's nonmilitary concerns by monitoring the state of the planet, prodding other agencies, acting as a database, and pushing for many improvements in, for example, international environment law and standards. In addition, the mobilization of the NGO movement at the Stockholm conference was the unleashing of a genie that could never be put back into the bottle; all future UN global conferences were to a large degree modeled on this one, and in particular on the need to relate to international civic society. Governments, parliaments, national ministries, and even the specialized agencies were going to be much more in the public eye with respect to their environmental record, as both UNEP itself and the NGOs sought to monitor follow-up of the many resolutions and protocols that emanated from UNCHE.

Yet two decades later, concerned governments, NGOs, and individuals were calling for another major global conference—this was to be the Rio Earth Summit of 1992—to deal with the disappointing record of the intervening years. What had happened to the early promise? The first thing, surely, was that the Stockholm conference had been too ambitious; it had staked out wonderful desires and ambitions for the improvement of the globe that, alas, the crooked and frail condition of humanity could not match. Nation-states, East and West, North and South, all sensitive to their domestic worries, all jealous of ceding sovereignty, could not follow through the high intentions. One scholar notes that the Stockholm declaration "laid down twenty-six disparate principles: two proclaimed rights; four related to conservation of resources; two to pollution; eight to development; nine to general topics; one called for acceptance of state responsibility for environmental damage."

But how could a country like Mozambique, in civil war and with a per capita income of $100 per annum, fulfill those aims? How was it possible to check that late-Maoist China was complying? How could the rather weak and amiable governments like those of Greece or Italy or Uruguay enforce all those provisions? How could a U.S. administration, having to share powers with the Congress and pressed internally by the right-wing foes of international governance and accountability, ever agree to external regulations? Of course, a few Nordic or British Commonwealth countries like Denmark and New Zealand complied with virtually everything, but that simply pointed to the problem—it was much easier to fulfill international environmental accords if you were a homogeneous, rich, democratic, liberal, and educated (and non-American) society than if you were not. Three decades after the Stockholm conference, this blunt fact remains unaltered.

There was, therefore, little fulfillment of the intended aims of the Stockholm accord. On the other hand, there was all too much evidence of humankind's increasing and damaging impact upon the environment. Satellite photography or compelling articles in (say) *National Geographic* magazine revealed that the tropical rain forests were succumbing to ever more slash-and-burn assaults. Fishermen everywhere complained of diminished stocks, though they rarely considered their own role in that trend. Industrial emissions in India, China, and Brazil greatly increased deaths due to respiratory diseases. In June 1988, the chief scientist to the U.S. Environmental Protection Agency told dismayed senators that "global warming" existed and was growing.

Following the recommendations of the Brundtland report (1987), "Our Common Future," which offered the same concerned views of the future, there took place the second major UN Conference on the Environment and Development, in Rio in 1992. The amazing world publicity given to this event, and the astonishing attendance of governments and NGOs, were mentioned earlier. We should also note some other features. The first was that it was held in the South; twenty years after Stockholm, the locus of the UN's environmental agendas had moved to below the equator. The second was that it was probably the most acrimonious global conference ever. That is hardly detectable in the summaries and "briefing notes" of the world organization's Department of Public Information (DPI), which felt it had to tread lightly to avoid offending powerful member states. Instead, it emphasized the positive aspects of such events: the attendance of a record number of heads of government at any international meeting ever; the many representatives from NGOs at the conference and the even larger attendance at the parallel NGO forum; the ten thousand attending journalists (can that really be true?); the Rio declaration on the environment; the accord on the preservation of forests; the Convention on Climate Change; and the creation of various high-level and interagency committees and advisory boards. All of which produced the self-contented language, as, for example, in the following summary of the Rio conference: "Governments recognized the need to redirect international and national plans and policies to ensure that all economic decisions fully took into account any environmental impact. And the message has produced results, making eco-efficiency a guiding principle for business and governments alike."[12]

The Earth Summit was not a total breakdown and disaster, but it was marred by quarrels that showed how "disunited" the international system had become almost a half-century after World War II and a quarter-century after decolonization. The disputes were, once again, chiefly of a North-South nature. Developing countries were frustrated, indeed outright angry, at the continued (and, in many cases, increasing) gaps between the richer one-fifth of the world and the poorer four-fifths. Brazil, India, and Malaysia vocally expressed resentment at Northern concerns about their deforestation, dirty industrialization, global warming, and loss of species, charging that the proposed environmental control measures were simply means to prevent the South from catching up. How, for example, could Americans declare concern about burned-out Brazilian rain forests and Chinese industrial smog when the United States itself was the largest contributor to global trace gases? And if the richer countries were so worried, how much would they pay as compensation for the reining in of Southern industrialization?

As usual, the moderate and anxious Nordic countries were willing to offer additional funds, but the 1980s Thatcher-Reagan turn against "welfarism," whether domestic or international, meant that these complaints and concerns were essentially dismissed by other governments in the North. Intellectual property rights or, rather, the virtual monopoly that Northern private capitalist firms had over such property also turned out to be a real minefield. In consequence, the United States' delegation to the Earth Summit had a particularly tough time, partly because of its opposition to internationally imposed controls, but also because of President George Herbert Walker Bush's decision not to attend.

The array of resolutions, declarations, and "principles" enunciated at Rio thus meant less than might appear. The Statement on Forest Principles (preserving tropical rain forests) ended up as nonbinding, chiefly because of Malaysia's insistence that logging one's forests was an internal matter. The final text of the Convention on Climate Change (the UNFCCC), as two analysts noted politely, "is typical of many of the Rio agreements, where a highly politicized discussion led to weakened texts."[13] Follow-up negotiations on environmental targets and rules, like the Montreal (1987) and Kyoto (1997) protocols, annoyed American conservatives who hated any restrictions on how and what their businesses could do and who also challenged the special treatment given to countries like China. But the U.S. walkaway from the Kyoto accords in turn annoyed Europe, Canada, and other nations eager to relieve pressures upon the planet's environment.

The result of these measures was more than what existed in 1945 but much less than what internationalists and environmentalists desired for our planet. Meanwhile, the pressures continued. The industrial decay of Russia and the Ukraine led to further environmental damage in those countries. Slash-and-burn agriculture in Brazil, Central America, India, Indonesia, and Africa hastened global warming, as did (and does) China's "dirty" industrial growth. The U.S. government and powerful business interests continued to oppose most limits on fuel use. The "Blue Plan" for cleaning up the Mediterranean is in trouble owing to overpopulation and uncontrolled pollution. Ice caps and glaciers melt with increasing rapidity, from Antarctica to the Swiss Alps, the oceans grow warmer, and on current evidence, hurricanes and other storm systems intensify in strength. With the world's population soaring from its present six billion to eight or nine billion around 2050, how can the social fabric and the ecosystems hold?

What has improved, then? First of all, we are definitely a lot more aware of the impact of human action upon our planet than we were in 1945. The coverage of environmental issues by the media; the emergence of NGOs, church groups, and foundations; the use of the Internet; and the creation of environmental protection agencies are all indicators of public awareness that continued work is needed in this domain. Second, there are many examples of a higher regard for our ecosystems, the creation of more and more protected parks and forests and wetlands, the growth of institutions like the World Wildlife Fund, or the amazing development of "ecotourism" in countries such as Costa Rica, in place of diminishing banana production and burned-out forests.

Finally, there is the international cooperative architecture itself, almost all under the United Nations system. It took the world organization—or, rather, its member states—a long time to recognize that preserving and sustaining the planet was part of its remit; and many governments still do not commit to that responsibility. Impoverishment, dire social need, and dreadful religious and ethnic conflicts that blind people from admitting their common humanity retard the process. Scorn for international efforts by some richer nations make difficult agreement on common global arrangements to improve environments and help the poorest of the poor. And the UN has sometimes been its own worst enemy. The location of UNEP headquarters in Nairobi has proved to be a mistake and an embarrassment that lasts until today. The weaknesses of the host government make it an uninviting place, high-quality international staff cannot be tempted there, and it is grossly underfunded.

Nonetheless, the global community has moved forward, recognizing its common future. True, it has often been upset and pushed back by crises, failed states, and fresh evidence of increasingly damaged environments. The move toward an improved world environment has frequently been hurt by negligent or even hostile governments and weakened by the all too obvious gap between proclaimed aims and moderate accomplishments. So the many lapses are evident, yet international civil society, whether NGOs, foundations, or concerned societies, appears committed to pushing for further improvements. Whether the globe can ever really be protected from our capacity to damage it remains an open question. Taken overall, the post-1945 record is not an encouraging one.

Much the same assessment can be made, in a briefer way, of the world organization's journey toward improved rights for women and children and for families in general. As noted earlier, the Charter had affirmed faith "in the dignity and worth of the human person [and] in the equal rights of men and women." Unlike the environment, then, this was not an issue that had to be discovered—but it was one that had to be truly implemented rather than remaining just words. In 1945, about half of the nations that signed the Charter still had some restrictions upon a woman's right to vote or hold office, and in the colonial dependencies the discriminations regarding gender were often worse. Moreover, as we have noted many times thus far, the political and economic conditions during the first decades after the Second World War pointed to other priorities, regarded as more pressing at the time—reconstructing industries and infrastructure, creating new alliance structures (for instance, NATO), kick-starting economies, and building a welfare state. It is true that the latter two aims would assist the condition of women, but there was nothing gender-specific about them.

By contrast, there was a very early recognition of the special social and health care and educational needs of the child. This was natural enough—protecting young children from harm knows no political or ideological differences, and legislating to that end went back to the early Factory Acts of the nineteenth century. Then there was the additional concern, in the immediate aftermath of World War II, about the severe plight of so many children in Europe who were badly affected by malnutrition, rickets, polio, smallpox, and tuberculosis—and all too often without parents. Creating UNICEF as an emergency administering body to handle this human crisis was seen by all as absolutely necessary.

By 1953, it had become clear that the needs of children were global in dimension, causing the General Assembly to give UNICEF permanent status and charging it to focus particular attention on the developing world, which is also reflected in the fact that for many years now, the majority of its thirty-six-member Executive Board have been from Asia, Africa, and Latin America. Thanks to a succession of superb senior administrators, UNICEF has probably had the most successful track record of all the UN agencies, as is witnessed by the amounts of privately generated contributions to the fund each year. Governments, private foundations, local fund-raising efforts, and even airlines are all keen to show their support for this best of good causes.[14]

All this was topped off by the World Summit for Children, held in New York City in 1990. It was, as usual, overelaborate: There were "ten major goals and seventeen supporting targets, set for the year 2000, with 'stepping-stone' goals for 1995," all contained in the World Declaration on the Survival, Protection, and Development of Children. Then there was the important and solemn Convention on the Rights of the Child, to be ratified by all governments as they took steps to meeting these international targets. (The only countries that did not ratify the convention were the United States and Somalia.) It hardly needs saying that such declarations and treaties were not enough; with the world's population still growing fast, all steps forward (immunization programs, freshwater plants, prenatal care centers) in some parts of the globe were accompanied by fresh pressures from the vast numbers of hungry and sick newborns, especially across most of Africa. Perhaps the best that can be said is that the protection of children had at least been written into international agreement, that governments ratifying the convention were now to be held to high standards, and that in UNICEF there was a world body of unequaled vigor and commitment.[15]

By contrast, the campaign to improve women's rights was always more controversial and gained ground much more slowly. It did not take off until the women's movement of the 1960s in America and Europe, which then had spillover effects in much of the rest of the world (though not in the Soviet bloc or in China, both of which maintained that they'd always had gender equality). If you were pushing for changes in divorce laws, reproductive rights and access, and equality of opportunity in California or Copenhagen, it was also compelling to push for similar opportunities in Calcutta and Capetown, regardless of cultural differences. This agenda was no longer local, but global. It fitted in with the radicalization of the General Assembly's political agendas, with the pressures for a new international economic order, with the heightened awareness about the environment, and with the general assault upon the traditional loci of power. White, uncaring, capitalist men in the North were now to concede influence and affluence to nonwhite/Southern, environmentalist, pro-government, and feminist movements. Although a bit of a caricature—the liberal and feminist agendas were also supported by many governments and male politicians in richer countries, like Pierre Trudeau of Canada—it has a ring of truth to it.

This may then be why the story of the UN women's agenda seems to imitate that told earlier of the efforts to achieve global economic equity. The 1975 conference in Mexico City on the rights of women did indeed create measures for advancement in the international field, paralleling domestic improvements in gender equity within societies— hence the UN's Development Fund for Women, the training institute, and then the General Assembly's 1979 adoption of the Convention on the Elimination of All Forms of Discrimination Against Women. But it is doubtful whether the publicized "Decade for Women" (1975–86) really did all that much, as measured against the genuine needs and hopes of womankind. Indeed, the Mexico City decisions may have marked a high tide, soon to be followed by a waning of energies and pledged resources.

There were various reasons for this gap between intentions and achievements. The 1973 oil "shock" ushered in many years of slow growth, except in a few East Asian economies, and tight spending that correspondingly reduced moneys for virtually all international programs. Since, for example, UNIFEM operated on voluntary contributions, it limped along on a minuscule budget—as late as 1994, it received only $14 million from outside sources for its operations. The training institute (INSTRAW, in the Dominican Republic) was similarly constrained. Nor was this helped by the conservative backlash in the North at the end of the 1970s. Mrs. Thatcher's government in Britain, soon to be joined by President Reagan's administration in the United States, had little fondness for the feminist global agenda, especially if it involved the transfer of taxpayers' funds that subsequently might be used to support reproductive health programs (including contraception and abortion) that offended their political backers and their own beliefs.

But all that political controversy, institutional underfunding, and sclerosis paled in comparison with the relentless demographic and economic pressures upon women in the developing world for whom these various programs were intended. The planet was adding another 140 million new humans each year during the 1980s, chiefly in Asia, Africa, the Middle East, and Latin America. Drought, famine, and internal conflict were widespread and usually affected women and children most. Legal rights for women were disregarded in many countries and societies, from Arabia to Central Africa—so much for universal norms. A decaying Soviet Empire brought with it deteriorating health care levels for all its population except its elites. Two-thirds of all the world's illiterates in 1985 were women.

Yet as the tide could wane, so also could it wax. By the early 1990s, the Cold War was over, the Thatcher-Reagan tendency was replaced by kinder, gentler policies, the notion of "human security" was being pushed by the UNDP and the World Bank, and the facts about the failure to close the gender gap were becoming ever clearer. The World Bank's chief economist at that time, Larry Summers, went on record as saying that the single best measure to improve conditions in the developing world would be to increase the access of girls and young women to education—a sweeping claim, but one entirely convincing to those who worked and observed in that field. The campaign for gender advancement may have stagnated for a while, but it was time to push again.

So, twenty years after Mexico City, the United Nations assembled its most ambitious global conference ever, that on women and development, held in Beijing in September 1995. By this stage, the world organization was on a roll, for this event followed conferences on the child (1990), the environment (1992), human rights (1993), and population (1994) and preceded that on habitat and cities (1996). Moreover, the supporters of these successive events were now arguing that they all fit together. The UN's own notes about the Beijing conference told readers that this global momentum had profound effects:

> From the Children's Summit in New York, where the special needs of the girl-child were emphasized; to Rio, where the Earth Summit articulated the pressing need for recognition of women's central role in sustainable development; to Vienna, where special emphasis was put on the equal rights of women; to Copenhagen, which underscored the central role that women have to play in

combating poverty; and to Cairo and, later, Istanbul, where women's right to control over decisions affecting their health, families and homes was affirmed. All of these Conferences prepared the way for the Beijing Conference, helping to break new ground in the struggle for equal rights and a central role for women in decision-making at all levels of society.[16]

As such, the conference had all the by now standard features—189 governments participated, 2,100 NGOs were in attendance, 30,000 individuals gathered at a parallel "fringe" conference, and the whole event was covered by 5,000 media representatives. The resulting document was the Beijing Declaration and Platform for Action. It asserted women's rights to equality and more specifically declared that women had a "right to inherit." It condemned rape as a war crime. To please the feminists, it asked nations to reconsider laws against illegal abortion; to please the Vatican, other conservative Christians, and the Muslim world, it affirmed the "social significance of maternity, motherhood and the role of parents in the family and in the upbringing of children." It called for follow-up to be supervised by the ECOSOC and requested all the UN bodies—INSTRAW, UNIFEM, CEDAW, and the rest—to become better coordinated and more focused. And it asked member states consciously to commit to the Platform for Action.

Some of them did just that. For example, India promised to increase investment in education, with a major focus on women and girls; it also established a commissioner for women's rights to act as a public defender in that area. The United States set up a White House Council on Women and pledged to fight domestic violence against women. Mauritius ordered a review of all laws that might discriminate against women. Did these declarations make a real difference? It is hard to say. It is worth noting that at about the same time (the 1990s), and probably more important than all of those state-centered measures, there were many examples of women taking the initiative, founding their own microbusinesses in, for instance, India and East Africa (often with help from the World Bank, the UNDP, and U.S. philanthropic organizations), and thus becoming economically independent. These were real on-the-ground advances, as opposed to official declarations.

Yet progress was painfully slow in many parts of the world and nonexistent in others. The triumphalist language about the successes of these global conferences made no reference to the fact that they coincided with some of the most severe setbacks to UN peacekeeping efforts across the world. The conference organizers had not yet woken up to the fact that the post–Cold War world was a messy place. It is hard to imagine how women's rights could be advanced in war-torn places like Kosovo, southern Sudan, Liberia, and Sierra Leone. There was and is little sign of equality to inherit in, say, Oman or Saudi Arabia. Countries that execute women for adultery are hardly living up to the 1995 protocols, nor are tribal leaders who allow mass rapes of defeated enemies. Some Indian provinces are remarkably progressive, but in many of the poorer Indian villages the old prejudices remain. Female infanticide is still common across Asia—the gender-balance statistics simply give it away.[17] Even in the immensely rich United States, women represent a disproportionate share of those living in poverty.

The best indicators of this gap between proclamation and achievement come from the UN's own statistics, which are remarkably unvarnished and thorough. The clumsily named CEDAW (that is, the UN Committee on the Elimination of All Forms of Discrimination Against Women) produces regular and chilling reports of mass rapes, torture, and sexual enslavement in various parts of the world. UNIFEM statistics show the awful socioeconomic regression for women and girls in the poorest regions. The Human Rights Watch annual report on women's rights, summarizing a UNIFEM report that assessed the condition of women five years after the 1995 conference, bleakly observed:

Despite the pledges made by governments at Beijing, the situation for women is getting worse in certain areas. For example, the number of rural women living in absolute poverty, i.e. life-threatening poverty, has risen by 50 percent over the last two decades as opposed to 30 percent for men. . . . Although women work two-thirds of all hours worked, they earn one-tenth of all income and own less than one-tenth of the world's property. . . . Two-thirds of the 110 million children who are not receiving an education are girls.[18]

Other accounts, from, say, the UNDP's Human Development Index would suggest that those are conservative estimates.

Here, then, is the problem. The women's agenda has certainly advanced since 1945, but it has done so in a very disproportionate manner. It has been most visible in places that hardly need UN assistance, like Stockholm and San Francisco, but is scarcely noticeable in Somalia and Senegal. Ancient gender prejudices account for much of this, but so (perhaps even more) does poverty. For the past decade, the number of people living on less than $1 or $2 a day has barely moved, and in sub-Saharan Africa the numbers are increasing absolutely. And poor women suffer the most. No matter how many UN agencies and commissions are created for women's issues, and no matter how many other international bodies from the World Bank to the ECOSOC show concern, this remains a signal failure in our human condition.

If UNICEF is virtually everyone's favorite UN agency, the candidate for the most controversial—and in some conservative circles most unpopular—would probably be UNESCO. This is immensely ironic. It was founded to reduce cultural and ideological misunderstandings and to bridge prejudices rather than increase them. It does not possess the immense political power of the Security Council or the IMF, so one might wonder why what it does gets so much attention. And, in any case, much of its work is nonpolitical and welcomed by all. So why has it attracted controversy?

Perhaps its constitutional remit was too ambitious—"to contribute to peace and security by promoting collaboration among the nations through education, science and culture in order to further universal respect for justice, for the rule of law, and for the human rights and fundamental freedoms which are affirmed for the peoples of the world, without distinction of race, sex, language or religion, by the Charter of the United Nations." Those are lofty and vague goals, especially for a body that now has a rotating Executive Board of fifty-eight representatives, meets only twice a year, and has no legislative authority at all. Perhaps, too, it attempts to work in too many fields—world heritage sites, return of stolen cultural properties, sport, the oceans, the biosphere; even when those activities are farmed out to particular intergovernmental committees, the results and recommendations return to burden UNESCO's shoulders. It is too heavy a load, yet little of what it does in those cultural fields attracts sustained attention from the powerful member states.

The real reason the organization caused controversy was that it became *the* venue for the venting of ideological and racial prejudices—exactly the opposite of the founders' intentions. Ideas are never neutral, and during the Cold War in particular there was indeed a struggle for the minds of men—especially for the minds of those in the Third World. Already during the Korean War, U.S. conservatives had expressed anger that UNESCO had not come out on the side of the West. By 1954, the USSR, which had declined membership a decade earlier out of the (justified) suspicion that its purpose was to advance free market liberalism, decided to join, as did various other Communist states. Membership also came, of course, to all the newly decolonized nations. Because of tensions elsewhere—especially over the North-South economic "order"—and because more powerful UN organs were either in the hands of the wealthy countries or frozen by the Cold War, UNESCO became the venue for expressing anti-Western sentiments. Much of this ideological boxing arose from strong differences about "statism." Because so many of the newer governments were engaged in state building, they were much more in favor of active governmental intervention and redistribution of resources than were laissez-faire Americans. These differences surfaced in many places, including UNESCO's programs for revising school curricula (especially history textbooks), which had seemed a good idea for reconciling French and German mistrust after 1945 but was less attractive to conservatives if the teachings called for a new international economic order.

The two issues that most aroused the wrath of America, Britain, and some other Northern nations were UNESCO's stance toward Israel and its push for a "new world information order." Its 1974 General Conference denied Israel membership of any regional grouping, condemned Israel's alteration of historical buildings in Jerusalem, and asked UNESCO's director-general to take over the educational system in the occupied Arab territories—an impossible proposition without the agreement of the Israeli authorities. Clearly, these measures were driven by dislike of the occupation of East Jerusalem, the Gaza Strip, and the West Bank, but those were explicitly political controversies that should have been fought out at the Security Council and the General Assembly. The result was to make many U.S. politicians suspicious not just of UNESCO, but of the world organization in general. The atmosphere only became worse when Arab states managed a year later to persuade the General Assembly to pass a resolution that equated Zionism with racism.

At about the same time, a fresh dispute arose over pressures by developing countries for a new world information and communications order. This had its origins in discontent at the prominence of organs like the BBC, Reuters, CBS, and other media, which, radicals charged, pushed a Western free market view of the world and distorted what was going on elsewhere. Like the issue of historical restoration in Jerusalem, the health and fairness of the world's press was, technically, within UNESCO's remit. Yet the 1978 UNESCO Declaration on the Media, calling for restraints on free press and broadcasting, was a minefield into which the organization should not have attempted to tread. To be sure, the dominance of the Western media in world news, though perhaps exaggerated then and now, means that the playing field between richer and poorer countries is uneven. And as with the ideological debate over the role of the state and of international governance, there can be legitimate differences of opinion. But to try to alter that imbalance through a political resolution by UNESCO—including, among other ideas, the state licensing of journalists—was clumsy and impractical and gave critics fresh ammunition.

All this was compounded by the growing evidence that UNESCO was badly run at the top. A large proportion of its staff worked in the expensive new building at 7, place de Fontenoy, in Paris; in fact, 80 percent of personnel were not in developing countries at all. About 60 percent of its budget went to salaries, a disturbingly high figure. The director-general, Dr. Amadou-Mahtar M'Bow, was widely regarded in the West as incompetent, favoring cronies and anti-Western staff appointments, creating too many personal advisers, and straying into overly political matters. By 1984, both Britain and the United States had had enough and withdrew from UNESCO, which not only deprived it of their contributions (the United States had paid around 25 percent of its budget), but also put a large question mark over its legitimacy. Of course, pro-UNESCO governments spoke in its defense, but there was no denying that widespread damage had been done.[19]

This was all the more regrettable because it took attention away from all those fields where dedicated UNESCO staff and projects had been doing well—oceanographic research, the problems of desertification and cell biology, the preservation of endangered cultural monuments (for example, Machu Picchu in Peru), the identification and support of world heritage sites, and, above all, teacher training and literacy programs in the developing world and in war-torn societies. The latter have sometimes been controversial, as, for example, the teaching programs for Palestinian refugees in their camps. But it was noticeable that when, in September 2002, President George W. Bush surprised the world by telling the General Assembly that the United States would return to UNESCO, the hope was immediately expressed that the body's next task would be to help in the educational and cultural rebuilding of Afghanistan.[20] Under new leadership, depoliticized and streamlined, the organization has also been asked by various Arab governments to devise sensitive ways of overcoming mutual prejudices between the West and the Muslim world. That is surely a much tougher job than the preservation of Angkor Wat, but it is also a nice sign that after a stormy passage, UNESCO may at last be attempting to return to its original purposes of helping to avoid any "clash of civilizations." If so, it will have a heavy task ahead.

Such recent improvements hardly mean that the organization is now a shining success. It still suffers from an imbalance between personnel costs and programs. It still is too heavily Paris based. It still tries too much, in fields (girls' education, scientific training, technology transfers) that overlap with other organizations such as UNDP, UNICEF, and the World Bank, as well as with bilateral aid and NGO programs. And it is still regarded with deep suspicion by conservatives, who would prefer to abolish it altogether.

In a way, then, UNESCO's checkered career is symptomatic of the story of the UN's soft agendas as a whole. It, or rather the world, is nowhere near the goals proclaimed in the 1940s, and in some important areas—ethnic and religious tolerance or female poverty—very little progress seems to have been made at all. The many parts of the world organization frequently overlap and are top-heavy and inefficient. And the global agenda set out in the UN Charter, like that in UNESCO's own charter, may simply be too ambitious. It is tempting, in summary, to return to the language of the Brookings Institution report about there still being "much to be desired," whether in the social, environmental, or cultural spheres.

Yet there is another, more positive way of viewing these post-1945 journeyings. When the Charter was written, there were fewer than two billion humans on the planet. In the following half-century or so, and most probably unforeseen by those present at the creation, that number trebled, to six billion (2000). Those four billion additional mouths represent the greatest absolute increase of humankind, and in the shortest time, in all of history. Their need for food, clothing, habitats, health care, education, and jobs placed stupendous and unprecedented demands upon our society and our environment. Many of those demands are still unmet, at least among the poorest in the world; and others are only half-met. But it is difficult to imagine how much more riven and ruinous our world of six billion people would be today had there been no UN social, environmental, and cultural agendas—and no institutions to attempt, sometimes well and sometimes poorly, to put them into practice on the ground. It is a mixed record, but it is difficult to see how it could be otherwise.

CHAPTER 6

Advancing International Human Rights

At a time when slaughters and genocides continue in many parts of the world, it may seem foolish to argue that the UN's human rights agenda has advanced further than any of the other parallel tracks, such as the environment or peacekeeping. But the effectiveness of the international human rights regime has come a long way since Allied troops entered Nazi concentration camps in May 1945 and discovered the enormous atrocities that had been perpetrated there,* and the world resolved to reduce drastically man's inhumanity toward man. Since we have faltered so often and terribly in that ambition over the past sixty years, many will doubt this claim, so the onus is upon those who believe progress has been made to explain why.

The campaign for human rights and tolerance long preceded the holocausts of the Second World War and was deeply rooted in the Christian and Buddhist traditions. Nonetheless, in political terms it was a relatively modern idea that emerged near the end of the eighteenth century.[1] Thomas Paine wrote *Rights of Man*, the American Constitution talked of "certain unalienable rights," and the French revolutionaries declared themselves for *"les droits de l'homme et du citoyen."* In the nineteenth century, English evangelicals like William

---

*The first British officer into the Bergen-Belsen camp was, unintentionally, the redoubtable captain Brian Urquhart; see his description in *A Life in Peace and War,* pp. 81–84. It is easy to see why he and others who shared that experience were so committed to creating a better world.

Wilberforce campaigned successfully for the abolition of the slave trade and then of slavery itself, plus the end of anti-Catholic discrimination throughout Britain. The "laws of war," especially regarding the treatment of civilians during armed conflict, were slowly but surely developing, at least in regard to wars in the West. Prime Minister William Gladstone agitated against atrocities in the Balkans in the 1870s. In 1918, Woodrow Wilson (who had a portrait of Gladstone on his desk in the White House) pushed for national self-determination under his Fourteen Points, a clear reaction to the conquests of Belgium, Serbia, and other small European states and, more guardedly, to Western imperial rule. In 1941, Roosevelt and Churchill signed the Atlantic Charter, which declared that all peoples should live in freedom and without want, and FDR proclaimed his own expansive Four Freedoms.[2]

Yet the starting point for this story has to be 1945–48. The international human rights regime that the United Nations then set up was qualitatively different from anything that had gone before, even the advances made in the age of Enlightenment, because those earlier proclamations about rights had little or no place in international law—that is, governments had not agreed among themselves to abide by them. The laws of war, though important, were rules (through the Hague peace conferences of 1899 and 1907) specific to military actions, chiefly toward the treatment of civilians, and not a general claim about an individual's rights for all time. The UN Charter's articles changed that.

But exactly how much difference the Charter made in the lives of ordinary people across the globe is open to much dispute. Although the language in the Preamble on universal human rights is firm and clear, we have seen earlier that it was accompanied by Article 2, Part 7), stating, "Nothing in the present Charter shall authorize the United Nations to intervene in matters which are essentially within the domestic jurisdiction of any state or shall require the Members to submit such matters to settlement. . . ." How are world citizens and their governments to reconcile universal human rights with claims for state sovereignty?

The Universal Declaration of Human Rights (1948), a further international effort to advance and define human rights, complicated things further.[3] It certainly tilted the balance, at least on paper, away from states and toward individuals. It also is rooted in an abhorrence of the dreadful acts of the Second World War—the second paragraph of its preamble refers to the "disregard and contempt for human rights [that] have resulted in barbarous acts which have outraged the conscience of mankind. . . ." It enjoyed enormous global attention, partly because of the conspicuous role of Eleanor Roosevelt as the chair of the Commission on Human Rights, which produced the report, partly because the commission was swamped by appeals from all over the world for help against local human rights abuses, partly because the venerable W.E.B. Du Bois appealed to the United Nations to end discrimination against "citizens of Negro Descent in the United States"—an appeal that was taken up with intensity by the few Asian and African delegates and also hypocritically exploited by a Soviet government to embarrass America (at the same time, of course, that Stalin was terrorizing his own people and denouncing the Declaration as a threat to states' sovereignty).

Despite the controversial nature of its proceedings, the UN Commission on Human Rights pressed ahead, aided and abetted by an astounding number of intellectuals from across the globe with backgrounds in philosophy, law, literature, history, and the social sciences, including the ancient but still formidable H. G. Wells. Perhaps the most influential was French lawyer René Cassin, who brought to the commission decades of study of Catholic social thought about the need to temper brash capitalism with a due regard for the dignity of the individual and, being himself the son of a Jewish merchant, a deep loathing of the Holocaust.* But whichever group of drafters put it together, it was and is an astounding document, with an astounding range.[4]

The Declaration begins with eleven articles that are very much in the tradition of the U.S. Constitution and the French Declaration of

---

*It is not difficult to see the papal encyclical *Rerum Novarum* (1891), with its affirmation of "the rights of the poor and the helpless," peeping out of the entire second half of the Universal Declaration. Cassin would have known it by heart. The basic draft was done by Cassin over one long weekend. He was later awarded the Nobel Peace Prize.

the Rights of Man—that is, they proclaim the equality of all human beings and the right of everyone to life, liberty, and personal security. Then follow articles (numbers 12–17) that might be said to constitute rights in civil society—the right to marry, the right to own property, the right to free movement, and so on. The third segment or column (Articles 18–21) of what became known as "Cassin's portico" went back to ideas about the Athenian polis and dealt with democratic political rights, proclaiming the right to peaceful assembly, freedom of expression, and participation in government through "periodic and genuine elections."[5] The articles in the fourth cluster (numbers 22–27) are the most amazingly expansive—the right to social security, to leisure, to employment, to equal pay for equal work, to join a trade union, to health care and an adequate standard of living, to free elementary education. Article 25 may be the most breathtaking of all, since the right to a decent living standard was to include "food, clothing, housing and medical care and necessary social services, and the right to security in the event of unemployment, sickness, disability, widowhood, old age or other lack of livelihood. . . ."

Taking all the articles and proclaimed rights together, this was by far the largest bid that has ever been made, before or since, for the international prescription of human rights and dignities. It was instantly dubbed the "Magna Carta" of mankind and translated into almost all languages. It was brief enough to be printed on a single poster and was hung in schools and libraries across the globe. Its publication, and passage in the General Assembly, was greeted with jubilation, and its doughty chairman, Eleanor Roosevelt, was the heroine of the age. And it is, surely, one of the greatest political statements in world history.

However, it is sobering to read the archival accounts of the closed-door negotiations and trade-offs among the national delegates to the commission, the various reservations they expressed, and the criticisms by both the countries abstaining from the final vote and the vested interests who felt threatened by this new world order.[6] The many appeals for help from the colonized world were passed on to the ECOSOC, which ignored them. Eleanor Roosevelt, fearing a backlash at home, warned that Du Bois's appeal for Negro equality in the United States would ruin the work of the conference. Governments with colonial territories—including the host government to the commission, France itself—but also those with aboriginal and other minority tribes like Australia, wanted the language toned down. American conservatives were appalled at the social justice clauses and regarded Cassin as a crypto-Communist. Treasury officials everywhere shook their heads at the proclaimed rights to full employment, equal pay, and favorable remuneration.

Then there was the Cold War shadowboxing—hardly surprising, since just after the first meeting of the commission, the Truman Doctrine (March 1947) proclaimed that the world now faced a choice between totalitarianism and freedom. The USSR retaliated in this propaganda war, not only by attacking American domestic racism, but also by proposing that the abolition of the death penalty be put into the Declaration—an outrageous hypocrisy given what was going on in Stalin's camps, but which in any case was firmly resisted by Western proponents of judicial execution by firing squad, hanging, or the electric chair. In the end the Soviet bloc abstained, claiming the Declaration did not sufficiently support economic and social rights (!) or denounce Fascism. Saudi Arabia was unhappy with the religious freedom clause, and South Africa, at this time moving formally into apartheid, was opposed for many reasons, especially the "participation in government" clauses. The vast numbers of colonial peoples in Africa, Asia, the Caribbean, and other regions had no chance to vote on this solemn declaration of their inherent rights.

So what is one to make of this—a great step forward for humankind or a compromised and insincere document? There was a view among many governments at the time that since this text originated from the General Assembly, and not the Security Council, it was in no way binding upon states; that it was, literally, a "declaration" of principles of which one might take as much or as little as was desired. Indeed, the U.S. delegation had been firmly warned by the State Department to avoid any language in the Universal Declaration of Human Rights that would involve implementation or regulation, and no doubt most other governments felt the same way. In other words, it was one thing to proclaim that everyone has the right to "just and favourable remuneration," but quite another to compel government policies to be structured to that end. Again, while the preamble to the Declaration may have announced that "every individual and every organ of society" should strive to promote respect for its listed rights and freedoms, this was not the United Nations Charter, with its stricter requirements upon all members to comply.

Nevertheless, the Declaration was a step forward in humankind's story and should not be dismissed too readily. To begin with, a large number of groups and individuals—national and international bar associations, parliamentarians, human rights activists, trade unions, women's movements, and all those writers, scientists, and other intellectuals who had pressed for such a document—regarded it not as the end of a story, but as its beginning. Pressure groups representing races and religions deeply affected by the Depression and by the atrocities of the Second World War (Jewish groups especially, but joined also by radical social rights Catholics, Quakers, and political pacifists) felt that even more strongly. They saw it as a springboard or as a major step forward on a pilgrimage to universal human rights that had many more leagues to go.

Moreover, the media—not just the liberal press in the West, but oppositional journals in all countries of the world that abused these rights—had a topic that would not go away. There was now a set of guidelines by which they could measure a government's words against its actions, positive and negative. Finally, there were also governments (as usual, mostly among the more liberal or social welfare states in the North) that took the Declaration seriously and would set up offices to handle human rights cases. At the beginning, those governments were not many in number. Yet because the Document struck such a chord with international civil society, Professor Lauren notes, it "rapidly began to take on a life of its own." And, as Farer and Gaer observe, by the very openness and universality of the process and the fact that the text was passed without a single negative vote in the General Assembly, the Declaration seemed to require "binding norms of state behavior." It was indeed a fair start.[7]

How did this play out in the decades that followed? Again, the record is a mixed one, often outright disappointing. Institutionally, the weaknesses that are inherent in the UN system began to emerge almost immediately. The central instrument was the UN Commission on Human Rights, which reported to the ECOSOC and thus to the General Assembly. As such, it had no more legal and political status than the UN Statistical Commission or the Commission on Narcotic Drugs; it could report and advise, but not command. Part of its remit was taken away by the creation of the UN Commission on the Status of Women, part of it distracted by covenants regarding sex trafficking, international crime, and the minimum marriage age for girls. It almost goes without saying that the world organization produced many a resolution, and created various new bodies, in the human rights arena. For the first fifteen years or so, the story was one of declaration after declaration: the Convention Relating to the Status of Refugees (1951), the Convention on the Political Rights of Women (1952), the Standard Minimum Rules for the Treatment of Prisoners (1955), the International Convention on the Elimination of All Forms of Racial Discrimination (1965).

The biggest change, however, came from the decision to establish two separate covenants for states to sign, one regarding civil and political rights, the second relating to economic, social, and cultural rights—thus tearing apart Cassin's equally balanced portico.[8]

This was not done without much debate—indeed, the two covenants were not adopted until 1966. Unsurprisingly, the arguments advanced were close to those of 1946–48 about the nature of the Universal Declaration itself. Proponents of a single covenant held that it would be artificial and wrong to separate political from socioeconomic freedoms; that if the former existed without the latter, human existence would be hollow and the prescribed rights no more than nominal; and that the ability to speak and vote marched hand in hand with some basic economic dignity. Advocates of separate covenants contended that civil and political rights were the really "inalienable" ones, could be protected through the courts, concerned "negative liberty" (that is, protecting the citizen from unjust action by the state), and were immediately applicable. By contrast, economic, social, and cultural rights were more declaratory in nature, a vision of an ideal society, a set of objectives to be striven for but not instantly required. Thus, while the International Covenant on Economic, Social and Cultural Rights of 1966 was signed and ratified by virtually all governments and contained the usual catalog—the right to social security, to education, housing, food, and so on—everyone knew that these were aspirations, not statutory obligations, and that different countries would respond to these proclaimed "rights" in different ways. Sweden and Denmark might strive to provide their citizens with social and economic and health care security from cradle to grave; conservative American states certainly would not, though they would not object to the Universal Declaration of Human Rights covering political and legal freedoms. And three-quarters of the world's governments simply could not afford to do so, even if they had wished it. Perhaps the best that can be said is that these two general covenants consolidated the more specific declarations and made the human rights agenda even more public and measurable than before.

Since the UN's economic and social agendas are examined in the preceding chapters, our focus here will be upon the long, slow march to achieve civic and political freedoms—the right not to be subject to arbitrary arrest, torture, and death; not to be driven from one's dwelling place; not to be denied the right to speak openly or to vote; and not to be discriminated against because of one's race or religion or culture. These form the backbone of the international civil rights agenda, yesterday and today. And they provide yet another example of the distinction between good intentions and modest results.

The advances occurred on two separate but mutually reinforcing levels—that of follow-up monitoring and that of broadening public awareness and, with it, increasing public expectations. The follow-up story parallels the earlier tale about the economic and social agendas. These various covenants were innovative not only in setting universal standards, but also in establishing a system of data collection and reporting, so as to check on whether the new norms were being observed. The UN Congress on the Prevention of Crime and the Treatment of Prisoners was to convene every five years to assess progress (or lack thereof). All member states were to provide reports on the steps they had taken to comply with the convention against racial discrimination; moreover, the reports were to be scrutinized by an eighteen-member expert Committee on the Elimination of Racial Discrimination. In 1956, the ECOSOC resolved that all states be requested to send to the secretary-general, every three years, a report detailing what they had done to fulfill the Universal Declaration of Human Rights; and the UN's specialized agencies were asked to do the same. The ILO was tasked to report on instances of forced labor and slavery. For the first time ever, some parts of this machinery allowed *individuals* to file complaints.

Given the transgressions of these resolutions detailed in the pages that follow, it might seem that all this merely confirmed the opinion of the UN's conservative critics—that the world organization was high-minded but unrealistic, good at creating well-paid jobs for its bureaucrats in Geneva and New York City but poor at getting things done. Yet it can also be argued that the simple act of data collection and reportage in the follow-up process was the best way of keeping the world's attention on human rights issues and of embarrassing transgressor governments. Moreover, this monitoring process by official agencies was soon to be paralleled by the work of influential NGOs, the churches, and relief agencies, all of which had staff on the ground noticing abuses, and also from pressure groups in the West that campaigned against the mistreatment of Jews in the USSR and of Christians in China.

This larger awareness of human rights abuses coincided with the whole 1960s explosion of concern over an individual's "rights."[9] The greatest driver, surely, was the civil rights movement in America. The worldwide campaign for gender equality added to the pressures for change. The grim happenings of the Vietnam War stirred the pot. Pent-up frustrations at the unfair distributions of power and at rank discrimination could no longer be contained in an era of mass higher education, a new generation's challenges to authority, and the erosion of conservative social norms. As noted in the previous chapter, to liberals and radicals it was inconceivable that one campaigned for civil rights in the United States and did not stand against apartheid in

South Africa. To feminists in the North, gender equality was a universal "must." In both scope and vision, the cause became transnational.
This 1960s arousal of radical thoughts and movements occurred at
the same time as the rapid decolonization of dozens of Third World
countries, with their own agenda of complaints against the prevailing
system, whether it be "neocolonialism" or continued racial discrimination. By the time of the widespread street and campus protests of
the late 1960s, it really did seem that the world was being turned upside down and that the Universal Declaration of Human Rights might
come into its own.

Yet the fact was that the 1960s, 1970s, and 1980s witnessed some
of the most terrible abuses of human rights in the entire twentieth
century, apart from the Nazi Holocaust itself.[10] At the time, Western
liberals tended to focus upon abuses by right-wing authoritarian and
racist regimes. South Africa was a particularly frequent target because of its denial of equal rights to blacks and others, as were the lingering Portuguese colonies of Angola and Mozambique and the
settler regime in Rhodesia, since they all symbolized white colonial
oppression of other races. There was also sustained and rising criticism of the rule of the colonels in Greece, the continued authoritari-
anism of the aged Francisco Franco in Spain and of António Salazar
in Portugal, and of the slew of military regimes in Latin America
(Brazil, Argentina, Paraguay) that managed to "disappear" local journalists and activists. The heavy-handedness of the British military in
Ulster, or of the Indian military in Kashmir, also disturbed human
rights organizations.

But the largest atrocities really occurred elsewhere. Following the
tragedy of Mao Zedong's bizarre economic experiment of the "Great
Leap Forward" in the late 1950s, which led to perhaps as many as
thirty million deaths, his Red Guards terrorized anyone in China with
a bourgeois background and smashed ancient works and temples—
their own ancient works and temples. And what of the continual
Soviet and Warsaw Pact oppression of teachers, intellectuals, and
others who yearned and spoke out for civic freedoms, and of their
suppression of protests in Budapest in 1956 and in Prague in 1968?
This all made a mockery of the Universal Declaration. And it will

be noted that United Nations agencies—as opposed to, say, Amnesty International—were not prominent in highlighting and protesting these transgressions. How could they be, when their very existence rested upon consensus among the powers?

Cambodia in the late 1970s, probably, was the most terrible of all. When the Khmer Rouge took control of the country, millions of innocent Cambodian people, old and young, were driven out of the cities to die. In one schoolhouse, converted into interrogation center S-21, nearly twenty thousand people were tortured and murdered by Khmer Rouge fanatics; their skulls now form a testimony in the "genocide museum." Even Stalin or Hitler might have choked at the sight. More than one-eighth of the population was wiped out, which according to one scholar makes this genocide "the greatest per capita loss of life in a single nation in the twentieth century." Little wonder it was termed "the Killing Fields."[11]

But little could be done about the Cambodian slaughters. The General Assembly had no powers of intervention: It might approve conventions galore, the Commission on Human Rights might report to it via the ECOSOC, annual statistics on "progress" toward implementing the Universal Declaration or the convention against racism might be dutifully filed, but this was a dog without teeth. The only UN body that could intervene was the Security Council, but it was deep-frozen by the antagonisms of the Cold War and by the veto power of the Permanent Five. China acted as protector, if not mentor, of the Khmer Rouge, so there could be no peacekeeping operation in Cambodia. Beijing would also not tolerate inquiries or resolutions concerning its internal affairs or its suppression of liberties in Tibet, which it declared to be a domestic matter. Likewise, the Soviet Union would resist any Security Council debate upon its crushing of the "Prague Spring" in 1968 or its heavy-handed treatment of internal dissidents. The dark shadow of Article 2, Part 7, of the Charter hung over these affairs, rendering powerless the noble words of the Universal Declaration. Nor were the faults all on the Communist side. France gave consistent economic and military support to dictatorships in West Africa that had once been former colonies. And the United States, frightened by the possible inroads of world Communism in Latin America, Africa, and Asia, offered aid and protection to authoritarian regimes in those continents—provided they leaned toward Washington and not toward Moscow or Beijing. Many a liberal and radical in countries like Chile and El Salvador suffered prison, torture, and death from governments that enjoyed the White House's tacit blessing. Eleanor Roosevelt would have been appalled.

The fact was that unless the Security Council agreed on an intervention, the United Nations could do little or nothing to prevent human rights abuses. The Secretariat and its agencies could not offend the larger powers, so it strove earnestly to be as apolitical as possible. Its own fiftieth-anniversary report, "The United Nations and Human Rights 1945–1995" (introduced by Secretary-General Boutros Boutros-Ghali), gives the game away. Although it is an excellent collection of documents, and a fine account of how the two main covenants were arrived at, the volume simply collapses into as neutral a text as possible in its (potentially vital) Chapter IV, "Operating the System: From the International Covenants to the Vienna World Conference on Human Rights (1967–1993)." The language is bureaucratic and defensive. The Human Rights Committee, the reader is told, is "advisory and monitoring," it is a "conciliatory" body, it is simply an "enquiring and investigative" entity. Its chief activity is to receive reports. It may engage in "constructive dialogue" with governments concerning matters that relate to the covenants. There is no mention of individual countries—no El Salvador, no Tibet, no Cambodia—in this account of how the system operates.

Even the world organization's most intrusive instrument—the committee set up by the Convention Against Torture and Other Cruel, Inhuman or Degrading Treatment or Punishment, which is the only UN agreement that authorizes the holding of an inquiry into "the situation existing in a State party"—has turned out to be weak and ineffective. There is no recourse, no sanction, and no enforcement; the process "is confidential, and at all stages the cooperation of the State party whose practices are under examination is sought." Greek colonels, Paraguayan strongmen, and Khmer Rouge fanatics must have sneered; Leonid Brezhnev's USSR would have yawned. Perhaps the most historically ironic aspect of the fiftieth-anniversary report is its solemn account of the General Assembly's designation of the year 1968 to be the International Year for Human Rights—to mark the twentieth anniversary—and its convening of an International Conference on Human Rights in, of all places, Tehran, where the shah's secret police were otherwise doing all manner of things explicitly forbidden by the Universal Declaration.

Yet such atrocities could not be hidden forever. Television was making its impact—witness the media's coverage of the war in Vietnam that so embarrassed the Johnson administration, or "Bloody Sunday" in Belfast, or Tiananmen Square. Amnesty International could not be subdued, nor could investigative journalists who popped up in all parts of the world and reported local atrocities. The UN Commission on Human Rights was receiving hundreds of thousands of individual petitions, and while states might angrily dismiss them or give evasive replies, they were openly embarrassed. New human rights journals and organizations were springing up. Dissidents as varied as the novelist Aleksandr Solzhenitsyn, the scientist Andrei Sakharov, and the cellist Mstislav Rostropovich continually chided the fading Soviet regime regarding its suppression of free opinion. In the mid-1970s, almost all at once, Spain, Portugal, Greece, and Turkey broke free of authoritarian rule and lurched toward democracy. In the United States, President Jimmy Carter took the human rights agenda more seriously than all his predecessors and turned it into a sort of Gladstonian international campaign. But he was soon to be joined by a coterie of conservative Republicans like Elliott Abrams and Jeane Kirkpatrick, who saw that advancing "the American way" (that is, political but not socioeconomic rights) was a great device for embarrassing Marxist regimes, whether in the Warsaw Pact nations, the People's Republic of China, and Cuba, or in Mozambique and other decolonized, socialist states in the developing world. Human rights were no longer an under-the-table matter in international politics. Given the transformations of the global economy, the communications revolution, the new social dynamics, and decolonization, much of this was likely to happen in any case. It is a pity to record that United Nations agencies usually felt too constrained to lead the charge.

The whole process was given a major boost by the Helsinki Final Act of August 1975. This accord, which followed two years of East-West negotiations, was signed by representatives of thirty-three European countries (all except Albania), Canada, and the United States.[12] The process was formally named the Conference on Security and Cooperation in Europe (CSCE) and was a key feature in the Nixon-Brezhnev détente that Henry Kissinger was orchestrating so adroitly. World opinion thus paid more attention to the security dimensions of the Helsinki Act, especially the formal recognition of the existing political boundaries of Europe (including the two German republics) and the exchange of observers at NATO and Warsaw Pact military excercises. But in retrospect, its greatest feature might have been the human rights provisions of the treaty, since they allowed for monitoring and reporting on both sides of the Iron Curtain. It is likely that Brezhnev paid no more than lip service to those provisions—to him they were like the Yalta accords on "free" Polish elections. But by now the circumstances were different. First, there were to be review conferences, at Belgrade (1977–78) and then at Madrid (1980–83); the critical element of follow-up was at play once more. Second, and with the backing of the Ford Foundation, there was established Human Rights Watch, the most significant NGO in this field since Amnesty International was founded two decades earlier and one dedicated to monitoring the political and human rights clauses of the Helsinki Act. Within another year, Charter 77—set up by dissident Czechs such as Václav Havel, and with American support—was a stunning symbol that the suppression of the Prague Spring nine years earlier simply had not worked. A short while afterward, Polish shipyard workers in Gdansk set up their Solidarity movement to advance both economic and political rights. It was a clear challenge to an authoritarian regime, but how could it be suppressed after the Helsinki accords and with the immensely influential Catholic Church now led by a Polish pope? (Stalin's jeer, "How many battalions has the pope?" now came back to haunt the atheist Soviet regime.)

The 1980s were thus a curious decade for the human rights story. The authoritarian ice was cracking in so many regions of the globe—South America, Central Europe, parts of Africa, Korea, even China (at least with respect to economic freedoms)—yet remained rigidly frozen in others. Perhaps the main point was that these broadening norms were universal, that there would and could be no exceptions or distinctions even if certain interested parties wanted to preserve them. By the early 1980s, under instruction from the Congress, the U.S. State Department was publishing annual country reports on the condition of human rights in all nations of the world (except, of course, America itself). There were harsh and revealing surveys of abuses in Communist countries, but a drawing of the veil over, say, massacres of Indians by the Guatemalan army. But it was no good. Try as it might, the Reagan administration could not sustain a two-faced policy of asking the Soviet leadership to "pull down that wall" on the one hand and supporting brutal Central American governments on the other. By now, Human Rights Watch had set up an America Watch, and later an Asia Watch—no region was to go without scrutiny. Amnesty International received the Nobel Peace Prize (1977), an award that was gaining more attention every time it was given. The murder of Archbishop Oscar Romero while celebrating Mass had shocked the Catholic hierarchy in Latin America, which distanced itself from the right-wing regimes. Totalitarianism was going out of fashion, both East and West.

Three events in the years 1989–90 capture this bewildering, contradictory scene. In June 1989, an alarmed Chinese government ordered the forcible suppression of a student demonstration in Tiananmen Square, a sort of throwback action reminiscent of Budapest (1956) or Prague (1968) and an act forever captured on the world's television screens. Here was a Communist regime still strong and coherent enough to get away with the use of force, including tanks, against its own citizens. Perhaps as many as several thousand students were killed; others were rounded up and executed. Elsewhere, however, the tides were running in a different direction. The year 1989 also witnessed the coming down of the Berlin Wall and the collapse of the German Democratic Republic, to be followed in the next year by the unification of Germany and the dissolution of the Warsaw Pact, and still later by the dissolution of the USSR itself. The Cold War had

ended, and peacefully, except in Romania and the Caucasus. The Soviet experiment in forcing social change was over, a "short twentieth
century" indeed.[13] Five thousand miles away, another relic of the
1940s was crumbling. F. W. de Klerk had entered office in South
Africa in 1989 and within another year had started the systematic de-
molition of apartheid that would soon lead to black majority rule.
Prisoners and dissidents of the 1970s like Nelson Mandela and Václav Havel were now assuming national office. President George H. W.
Bush would later be derided by some for declaring that "a new world
order" had arrived, but it certainly seemed like that at the time, and
human rights activists across the globe rejoiced, even as they admitted there was still much to do.

It was time to make a new assessment, and in 1990 the General Assembly, under pressure from the Non-Aligned Movement, voted for a
UN global conference on human rights, to be held once the necessary
preparatory committees had done their work. As it happened, the
conference did not take place until June 1993, in Vienna, a sign in advance that reaching agreement was not going to be easy. Ostensibly,
the meeting had all the trappings of success and seemed a further display of how the human community was coming together in pursuit of
universal principles. "Approximately 10,000 people assembled in Vienna, including eight heads of state, nine heads of government, ministers of justice or foreign affairs from 171 countries, 3,000 delegates
from NGOs and some 2,000 journalists from all over the globe." The
UN World Conference on Human Rights was preceded by a three-
day NGO forum called All Human Rights for All. The formal conference issued the Vienna Declaration and Programme of Action
(VDPA), a lengthy document containing a set of principles and a plan
of action that was to be monitored regularly, and with a report upon
the progress to be made within five years. Most important, it recommended the creation of the Office of the UN High Commissioner for
Human Rights (OHCHR), a proposal the General Assembly adopted
a few months later.[14]
    Much of the language during nine days of debate and in the con-
ference's documents made the by now common assertion of the

post–Cold War era that everything was linked to everything else. Human rights were seen as an intrinsic part of development, and development as a means to secure human rights. Poverty, malnutrition, social exclusion, and lack of health care were declared to be violations of human dignity and thus as hurtful of real human rights as, say, unjust imprisonment; so, also, was severe environmental degradation. Coming as it did between the Rio conference a year earlier and the Cairo and Beijing conferences of the two following years, perhaps this was to be expected. What it suggested was that the pendulum had again swung in the debate between social and economic rights vis-à-vis more narrowly defined political and legal rights. At the time, supporters of the expansive view were certainly encouraged by this.

Yet it is hard to come away from the VDPA without a sense of déjà vu. Delegates agreed to proclaim "the right to development." They called for further steps to enhance the rights of women in the world. They called upon all nations to ratify the Convention on the Rights of the Child by 1995. They asserted the rights of indigenous and aboriginal peoples. They called for special attention to be given to migrant workers. They proposed "the right to request and be granted asylum." They called for an end to all forms of discrimination and of unusual and cruel punishments. Put together, this seemed to bring the world very close to the NGOs' demand for all rights for all of mankind.[15]

But, as was usual with solemn UN declarations, there was a lot more disagreement, anger, and reluctant compromise behind the scenes than appeared on paper. The disagreements were now much less between East and West and more between the West and the South. Governments in Southeast Asia and China feared that influential NGOs, politically correct foundations, and socially liberal nations in developing countries were going to push for tougher international standards on feminist agendas, challenges to state authority, and conditionality regarding development aid. There was an attack upon the universality of Western norms, and a major debate erupted about "Asian values"—a term favored particularly by Malaysia and Singapore. ASEAN foreign ministers actually met in Singapore to forge a combined statement that insisted that due regard be paid to "specific cultural, social, economic and political circumstances," which was a coded way of saying that they did not want to be judged according to the liberal gender and individualist lifestyle norms of Sweden and California. China, always sensitive to outside criticism of its human rights record, weighed in vigorously against "hegemonism and power politics" and became even more furious when the NGOs pressed (in vain) for the Dalai Lama to be allowed to address the conference. Needless to say, human rights advocates of all persuasions—and not just in the North, but women's rights speakers from Africa and advocacy lawyers from India—fought just as strongly to get their agendas advanced and resisted the arguments about cultural relativism.

But most of the latter groups were, by definition, nonstate actors, and the Vienna UN conference was, also by definition, a meeting of the representatives of sovereign nation-states. The NGOs had to learn this the hard way. They had come into Vienna with great expectations, riding on the prominence gained at Rio, believing in a new world order (their order), and passionate about spreading human rights. Angry governments would not allow this. The NGOs then found that because their preconference forum was held in UN-leased space, they could not carry out certain planned activities—they were told not to do so by the UN Centre for Human Rights itself, a bitter irony. Although the NGOs had provided many, many more ideas and draft resolutions than governments themselves prior to Vienna, their participation in the conference and in the drafting committee was much reduced. As the professional diplomats searched for compromise language for a final text, the head of Amnesty International denounced the proceedings as "a sham," and the executive director of Human Rights Watch remarked bitterly that he was glad that human rights conferences occurred only once every twenty-five years. Still, as a contemporary article observed, with gentle irony, one ground for optimism about the UN's human rights journey and its future was "the effort so many governments have made to restrain the organization's forward progress. . . . By their acts they have acknowledged the influence the idea of human rights has acquired over the minds of their subjects."

All this explains the particularly tortuous language of the Vienna document, as its drafters danced between universality and sovereignty. The best they could come up with was Paragraph 1 (5):

> The international community must treat human rights globally in a fair and equal manner, on the same footing and with the same emphasis. While the significance of national and regional particularities and various historical, cultural and religious backgrounds must be borne in mind, it is the duty of States, regardless of their political, economic and cultural systems, to protect and promote all human rights and fundamental freedoms.

On the face of it, it seemed as if the universalists had won, but then again there was the old problem that General Assembly (and thus UN conference) documents are only declaratory. Unless and until a member state swears to observe and uphold a particular principle, and agrees to targets, these are simply statements of goodwill; a country like Yemen, with no intention of changing its domestic arrangements regarding the rights of women, could sign off on the text, as did a grumpy China. As Clarence Dias (a human rights expert and consultant to the Vienna conference) observed, proclamations like those on women's rights "may well prove pyrrhic unless they can ensure that the UN moves from mere affirmation to the creation of effective mechanisms for monitoring and realizing women's human rights."[16]

It was a fair comment. There were six conventions on human rights either contained within or subsequent to the Vienna protocol, but only a select number of worthy-minded governments signed and ratified all of them. Owing to conservative political pressure at home, the U.S. government continued to decline to sign the Convention on the Rights of the Child, just as it refused to ratify the International Convention on the Elimination of All Forms of Discrimination Against Women; and it had never signed the International Convenant on Economic, Social and Cultural Rights. These UN world conferences were becoming uncomfortable places for American policy makers, well aware of their own constituents' traditional suspicion of anything more than local governance. But this cultural difference, manifested as we have seen in other areas, regrettably made the United States seem increasingly out of step with the rest of the developed world and thus become the focus of criticism from developing nations, the NGO movement, and the liberal media. At Rio, the United States had been lambasted not only as the number one producer of trace gases, but also for having the nerve to ask the South to reduce "dirty" industrialization. Later it was criticized for its very high rate of prison incarceration and its continued application of the death penalty. All this had the unfortunate results both of confirming the dislike American conservatives felt toward the United Nations and of giving developing nations the opportunity to express resentment at being preached to concerning human rights—while also permitting them not to undertake the reform measures pledged to in the covenants. Here was an interesting question: Which was more at fault, a country that signed the Vienna protocol but declared it would not follow through with some of the covenants or a country that ratified the covenants with little or no intention of acting upon them?

Where, if anywhere, could one count progress emanating from the United Nations itself in the human rights field? The first was in leadership at the top. The new UN secretary-general, Boutros Boutros-Ghali, had made it clear that he believed the agendas regarding human rights and sustainable development should command as much attention as the problems of peacekeeping and peace enforcement; and his documents *An Agenda for Peace* and *An Agenda for Development* were soon to be complemented by *An Agenda for Democratization* (1996). Consequently, the UN agencies directly under his supervision (UNDP was the leading example here) did their best to incorporate the Vienna resolutions into their programs. UNICEF had been given a large boost, as had the various women's programs and agencies, partly because of a reaffirmation of their importance, but also because the conference called upon the secretary-general to find ways of increasing their resources. The World Bank had the human rights dimension firmly on its checklist by now. By the mid-1990s, the main lending bodies had made it clear that corrupt and abusive regimes could not expect sympathy if they came looking for

loans. Governments might pay lip service to the Vienna accords or re-
ject them openly; international organizations could not.

Second, Vienna greatly reinforced reporting and data collection on
human rights abuses as a central part of the follow-up process—
rather like the Helsinki procedures, though with a global span.[17] In
setting a five-year deadline until member states came together again
(at the ECOSOC and the General Assembly in 1998) to review how
far each had moved toward the principles of the Universal Declaration and Vienna protocols, the conference created time pressure. The
Vienna conference had not only urged every government to ratify all
international human rights instruments, to accede to the Geneva conventions, to move toward the establishment of an International Criminal Court, and to educate and train its officials in this field by that
later date, but it had also asked UN bodies—most notably, the Centre for Human Rights in Geneva and the Commission on Human
Rights—to devise indicators to measure the realization of these
rights. Every UN agency, it was proposed, should have an office concerned with the global human rights agenda. Working groups should
be set up, and data exchanged, while the rather messy structure of
overlapping machinery should be streamlined. The habit of appointing special "rapporteurs" or "representatives" to visit a country and
investigate claims of human rights abuses (religious discrimination,
"disappearances," mistreatment of ethnic minorities)—already established with respect to Myanmar, El Salvador, Afghanistan, and South
Africa and in many ways providing the stimulus for the Vienna
resolutions—was to be intensified. Finally, the secretary-general was
to provide the General Assembly with regular reports as to how much
(or little) had been accomplished.

Third, the creation of the Office of the UN High Commissioner for
Human Rights meant that there was at last one high-level "point person" for the human rights agenda, someone whose office was tasked
to bring all the pieces together, someone who was given the responsibility to produce a full report five years hence on what had been done
since the VDPA. Clearly, so much would depend upon the personality and integrity of the high commissioner, but in its second incum-

bent, Mary Robinson, former president of Ireland, the burdens of office were exceedingly well borne. The Geneva office was shaken up, the OHCHR presence in New York strengthened (to further the agency coordination process), and field operations expanded. Monitoring the international response to the conventions, assembling evidence of human rights abuses, and preparing for the Vienna+5 meetings made the OHCHR a hubbub of activity. Robinson acted as both gadfly and inspiration, raising staff morale, delighting the NGO community, and sending a clear message.

Alas, not even this new agency (and those with which it worked) could deal with all the world's evils and atrocities. The OHCHR had been tasked with "removing the current obstacles and in meeting the challenges to the full realization of all human rights and in preventing the continuation of human rights violations throughout the world." But the years around and following the VDPA were to see some of the largest and nastiest cases of genocide and abuse in the second half of the twentieth century. The Yugoslav Federation had imploded in 1991 with the declaration of independence by Slovenia and Croatia, triggering Serb military action and an open civil war. The three-way bloodletting was awful, with the unfortunate Muslims suffering the most. As ethnic tolerance collapsed, millions fled their ancestral homes. The atrocities multiplied, village by village. And all this was happening only a few hundred miles southeast of Vienna and in a continent that believed it had freed itself from war and the holocausts that many could still remember.

This assumption about perpetual peace was one that few held about Africa. It is true that many rather amazing democratic transitions—and with them the enhancement of civil rights—had taken place across the continent within a short space of time. According to one tally, "In January 1989 only five of the forty-seven states in sub-Saharan Africa could be described (using generous criteria) as having a multi-party system: Botswana, the Gambia, Mauritius, Senegal, and Zimbabwe. By the end of 1994, the figure was thirty-eight." This was at least as big a shift toward democracy as those occurring in Eastern Europe, the former USSR, and Central America.[18] Unfortunately, while some African countries were able to vote their former corrupt governments out of power, others suffered under continued dictatorship and the denial of human rights—not only intolerable in themselves, but offering more ammunition to conservatives in the North who claimed that providing assistance to Africa would be like throwing money down a rathole.

Dictatorial abuses by deranged leaders and one-party governments paled in comparison with the disasters afflicting many other parts of Africa. In the Horn, Eritrea became engaged in a vicious cross-border conflict with Djibouti, and then later with Ethiopia, producing deaths, displacements, and all the other horrors that the VDPA had so recently condemned. In Sudan, a northern Muslim regime was waging a brutal campaign of genocide against the Christians and animist tribes in the south. Little outside attention was paid to those atrocities, because the Western media was not focused upon them, in contrast with the attention they gave to the civil wars raging in Somalia in the early 1990s. There, American television was heavily present, night after night showing graphic scenes of hundreds of thousands of starving, displaced women and children and provoking the Bush and Clinton administrations to commit troops to Africa under a UN peace enforcement operation. The failure of that mission, as described in Chapter Three, dealt a severe blow to the very notion of humanitarian peacekeeping and led to U.S. opposition in the Security Council to authorizing a peacekeeping force for Rwanda and Burundi, where a much more massive disaster was looming. Here the slaughters matched those of Cambodia in size and enormity.

Of course, it was a horrible coincidence that the dreadful abuses and mass murders of Kosovo, Srebrenica, Somalia, and Rwanda occurred in the afterglow of Vienna. The discourses there had been about state sovereignty versus universal or individual rights. But most of the dreadful human rights abuses of the early to middle 1990s were being done by the anarchic forces of fractured states like Serbia and Rwanda, or were taking place in a civil war with mutual atrocities as in Bosnia, or were perpetrated by warlords and tribes that lacked any government, as in Somalia. Terrorist attacks were on the rise from Nairobi to South Yemen and beyond. In other words, the abuses were being committed by groups that were never at Vienna, never even knew where it was, and would probably never attend a UN-sponsored conference. How, then, was the international human rights regime, created by and with its focus upon governments, to work? If the UN secretary-general or the OHCHR sent a special representative to Burundi, with whom should he negotiate?

Of course, this raised some very big questions about the nature of the state itself and its supposed capacity to protect its citizens. By the mid-1990s, the world community was grappling with the phenomenon of "collapsed states," something the UN's founding fathers could not have conceived of. Certain commentators argued that these failed societies needed to go into international receivership or that the Trusteeship Council (which had never been formally abolished) should be reactivated—ideas that enraged many an African and Asian foreign ministry. Still, it could hardly be denied that the power of nation-states was under challenge. NGOs and other groups that felt pushed aside at Vienna continued to agitate for international governance and were particularly vocal as the United Nations reached its fiftieth anniversary in 1995. Warlords, ethnic leaders, illegal drug cartels, and terrorist movements had no interest in the state, except to keep it weak. The rapidly swelling globalization of finance and trade suggested that many giant multinational corporations had more real influence than most governments of the world. Nations as seemingly solid and unified as Thailand and Malaysia could be brought low by runs on their currency. Experts argued that "a relocation of authority," away from states to higher or lower bodies, was under way.[19] One did not need to get involved in all the details of that political-science debate to recognize that if the power and influence of governments really was weakening, it would be more difficult than ever to advance a states-centered, treaty-driven international human rights regime.

Boosted by the VDPA and the establishment of the Office of the UN High Commissioner for Human Rights, yet battered by events in Bosnia and Central Africa, the United Nations agencies in this field limped into the twenty-first century. The "two steps forward, one step back" analogy again comes to mind and naturally fueled the debate between internationalists and isolationists, the UN's advocates and its critics. Those dubious of the world organization's capacities, or suspicious of its powers, pointed to the failures and disasters, in the Balkans, Central and West Africa, and elsewhere. And there were many in the world's most powerful country who increasingly claimed that the pretensions of the United Nations were a threat to American liberties or that peace enforcement worked only when the United States got reluctantly engaged. By contrast, the defenders and supporters of the UN system preferred to point to the successes, the slow advances, the jobs well done, from Central America to Namibia to the new human rights regime itself.

Both, of course, were correct. At the advent of the twenty-first century, conditions were again worsening in the West Bank and Gaza Strip, where increasingly militant Palestinian groups (such as Hamas and Hezbollah) clashed against an increasingly aggressive Israeli government; the bulldozing of settlements or the act of a suicide bomber on a bus full of civilians was a long, long way from the Universal Declaration, not to mention the Oslo accords of 1993, which were supposed to bring peace to the Holy Land. Most (though not all) Arab nations denied full political and social rights to women. Iraq's dictator, Saddam Hussein, ordered unspeakable atrocities against the Marsh Arabs, the Kurds, and the Shia majority. The fanatical Taliban movement turned Afghanistan into a human rights purgatory. The regime in North Korea was, if conceivable, even worse, its population wasting away in a deluge of propaganda and a dearth of decent food and health care. China continued to suppress its dissidents. Russia kept a heavy hand on Chechnya, whose citizens responded with atrocious bomb attacks in Moscow. Worst of all was the human rights situation in Africa, with appalling one-party dictatorships in West and East Africa, continued slaughters in the Congo that spilled over to neighboring states, and genocides in Sudan and Rwanda. Just to read the State Department's or Amnesty International's annual country reports on the atrocities of any previous year is to induce outrage that such things can happen in today's world.[20]

But limping does not mean falling, or dying. The ending of the apartheid regime in South Africa was inspirational, especially in the decision of the new Mandela-led government not to crush the white minority (as happened in East Africa), but to have old wounds settled through a "truth and reconciliation commission." The smoothness of the first genuine election process in South Africa—supervised by the UN and with millions of people lining up for days to exercise their right to vote—had an impact that spilled like a tidal wave across much of the rest of the subcontinent. Cuban troops went home from Angola. Mercenaries dispersed. Namibia became independent and also enjoyed its own UN-supervised elections. The wars in Central America, which had produced so many offenses against human rights, were slowed and then ended, with Oscar Arias duly receiving the Nobel Prize for his efforts to extend Costa Rica's model democracy to its troubled neighbors. (In 1978, only Costa Rica had an elected civilian government; by 1995, all six countries of the region had one.)[21] The rule of the generals in Argentina and Brazil was over. Above all, perhaps, the peoples of Eastern Europe and the Baltic rushed to embrace an open society, the free market, and full human rights—Hungary, Poland, the Czech Republic, and Ukraine were now full of intellectuals, journalists, and philosophers who were allowed to talk about anything, and also full of native entrepreneurs who wished to buy and sell anything. The same was true, although to a considerably lesser extent, in Russia. Each year, the editors of the New York–based Freedom House recorded the advance of democracy and civil liberties, though they were also careful to notice backsliding and the many outstanding cases of human rights abuses.

Probably, much of this was going to happen in any case, regardless of the UN. The collapse of the Soviet system and the Warsaw Pact, China's transition to a market economy, and the steady globalization of production and market flows all combined to make more and more countries, whether willingly or reluctantly, adopt Western norms—not just stock markets, but the rule of law, transparency, increased rights for women and ethnic minorities, and relaxed censorship of the media. The argument might be made, therefore, that the United Nations had little claim to this global transformation toward democracy, yet that, too, would be overly simple. It is not unreasonable to argue that certain of the peacekeeping and nation-building efforts of the world organization had, cumulatively, the effect of impressing political leaders and publics in other societies that it was good (or prudent) to accept the broad movement toward democracy and the establishment of a human rights order.

The transition from authoritarian rule to multiparty democracy in South Africa and Namibia, as noted earlier, had taken place under United Nations electoral monitoring—in fact, this was a function that showed the world organization at its best. Who else had the legitimacy to guard ballot boxes, count votes, and declare election results in countries seething with suspicions and discontents? Human rights were usually advanced in lockstep with peacekeeping, and as noted in Chapter Three, this often required considerable resources from the international community or from individual nations that stepped up to the challenge. More than twenty thousand blue helmets had supervised the process of establishing democratic elections in Cambodia, while sixty thousand NATO troops (one-quarter American) kept the peace in Bosnia. Australia assumed responsibility, delegated by the Security Council, to lead a multinational force that restored order and brought elections to East Timor; Britain took the lead in Sierra Leone; Nigeria and the United States led the UN coalition in Liberia. This whole pattern made an obvious point: that human rights could not advance simply as the result of declarations made at UN global conferences or, for that matter, of NGO protest marches. They had to be accompanied by the willingness of key nations (that is, their governments) to supply resources to get noxious and evil actors off the world scene. And since judging who was an evil actor was culturally and ideologically charged, one could never expect uniformity among the Security Council members who made the final decision. There would always be anomalies and inconsistency of principle, some of them deeply disturbing.

But why not consider the UN's successes? Can one imagine the Indonesian government relaxing its grip upon East Timor and permitting (of all things) an Australian-led peacekeeping force into that territory to supervise the holding of elections and the coming of free expression had it not been for enormous international pressure? Would a settlement in the decimated state of Cambodia have been possible without the UN? Could one conceive of a political settlement in Namibia or Mozambique without the world organization? These were things to chalk up to its credit.

What was more, the human rights agenda was not staying still. By the beginning of the twenty-first century, Secretary-General Kofi Annan was advancing the notion of "the right to protect"—that is, the idea that individuals who were being abused by their own governments had the right to be protected by the world community, a direct reference back to Eleanor Roosevelt and the Universal Declaration. The OHCHR was now regularly producing its reports, carefully stated but somber. Human Rights Watch accounts were more abrasive. The Quakers and the Catholic Church were both weighing into this publicization of human rights abuses. And Amnesty International was relentless in its recordings. As the twenty-first century began, it really was very hard for any state to transgress the corpus of international human rights law without the global civic community knowing about it—and raising a fuss. Even the world's most powerful government, reeling at the international outrage over its treatment of captured foes in Guantánamo, Abu Ghraib, and Bagram military prisons, came to learn this lesson.

Thus, despite all the setbacks and ghastly actions, there has been a bigger advance in the idea and practice of national and international human rights in the past sixty years than in any comparable period in all of history. The gap between the rights enjoyed by a citizen of Sweden and those granted a citizen of Sudan at present is still far too wide. But the point is that we all know about that, and that there is a collective world effort to close the gap. It is not unfitting to end this chapter with Professor Lauren's conclusion a decade ago:

> In the fifty years that have transpired since the adoption of the Universal Declaration of Human Rights the world has witnessed a veritable revolution in transforming visions of international human rights into reality. Never before have there been so many achievements in extending rights to former colonial peoples, setting standards through declarations and binding covenants, protecting rights through mechanisms of treaty implementation and

non-treaty procedures, promoting rights through education and the media, and enhancing rights through such means as advisory services and technical assistance in the field where people actually suffer.[22]

But Lauren is wise enough to note also that this is an unfinished revolution in human affairs, that abuses continue, sources of resistance remain, and many problems persist. Who could disagree? Forces of evil, prejudice, and deep-rooted hatred still abound. But since 1948, few of them can hide in the darkness or act with impunity. That is not a bad beginning.

CHAPTER 7

"We the Peoples": Democracy, Governments, and Nongovernmental Actors

The issue of global representativeness and democracy is the most diffuse of the strands of the UN's history between 1945 and the present day. It is also the most problematic for the world that is to come, because it encompasses so many tensions, puzzles, and contradictions. Given all the quarrels among member states (especially on the Security Council) in recent decades, it seems hard to believe that those proud, sovereign, and suspicious Great Powers assembling at San Francisco allowed their interstate contract to be prefaced by a poignant reference to "We the Peoples." A cynic's view would be that the governments meeting there simply wanted a lofty preamble before the nuts and bolts of the new world order were hammered out in the succeeding chapters. After all, the very same opening statement concludes with, "Accordingly, our respective Governments . . . have agreed to the present Charter . . . and do hereby establish . . . the United Nations." Thus, while the early paragraphs of the Charter's text are an amazingly bold and idealistic proclamation of the human enterprise, within another few pages there is a constant affirmation that states and governments are the only important actors.

The post-1945 record suggests that even if the Charter's Preamble were little more than persiflage, we should recognize that the issues those few sentences raised—of governance, democracy, representation, and voices of the people—have had a continuing power and presence in the UN's evolution and possess great relevance in many circles for today and the future.[1] Of course, the reader should also admit the many contradictions that flow from a statement about "the Peoples" in a document that is an intergovernmental postwar settlement.[2] It raised, but without settling, the issue of states' rights versus universality, a matter not resolved either by the Universal Declaration three years later. It posed a set of lofty goals against the reality and harshness of the world—this, indeed, is the story of the United Nations in every arena. It ignored the issue of big states versus small states, not in any explicit way, but rather in what was not said: Should "the People" of Namibia (about 1.8 million today) really have the same voice at the UN as the billion inhabitants of India, as is implied in the articles about equal and sovereign membership? For that matter, should the British and French peoples have far greater power at the world body than India, with almost tenfold their combined populations?

On another front, the Preamble made way for nonstate actors to present their views, for why should not NGOs, the media, minorities, and resistance groups claiming to speak for "the Peoples" have a voice as well as their otherwise exclusive governments? Above all, at least to those feeling that the nation-state itself was the problem, not the solution, it raised the tempting prospect of some form of world democracy, over and above—or, at least, separate from—the phenomenon of governments coming to speak their minds at the General Assembly each autumn.

This chapter, then, is the story of the United Nations with the Great Powers left out—and in many of the areas treated in the following pages, it is not just the larger members that are left out, but governments themselves. It is about claims and ideas and movements that sought to clamber onto the world stage and are still clambering. It is about structures, but also about concepts and aspirations. It is about assumptions regarding democracy, legitimacy, and civil society. It is about change from below and not from on top. It is therefore a very messy chapter, but not an unimportant one.

Because it includes such a confused and volatile cast, the tale is best divided into three discrete but complementary stories: first, the role of the General Assembly itself, as the "democratic" organ of the United Nations; second, the much slighter history of those movements that, dissatisfied with the General Assembly, have sought to transcend the international system and achieve a genuinely representative world government; and third, the tale of the remarkable growth in prominence of groups that now claim to constitute "international civil society" (NGOs, churches, foundations, and the media)—that is, bodies whose actions and very existence challenge statist assumptions of the international order and may, in their varied ways, relate more closely than governments to the broad mass of peoples of the world.

Of those three parts, that played by the UN's General Assembly has clearly been the longest lasting, the most visible, and the most openly fought over, simply because it has been a discourse among governments themselves. It is quite possible to argue that the Assembly, whose size has risen from the original 50 members in 1945 to 191 as we entered the twenty-first century, is the closest we are ever going to get to a parliament of man; and that this is an entirely representative body since ambassadors who are partaking in General Assembly debates and decisions have been appointed on behalf of their own sovereign nations (regardless, alas, of whether their governments were elected democratically). Here is an argument on which U.S. congressmen and Indian parliamentarians are likely to agree, for whatever their other differences, both assert that the United Nations is a collection of governments and does not have to pay attention to the (usually unelected) bodies yapping outside or bother with arguments for a world government. If anything, this protective tendency increased when more and more recently decolonized countries joined the UN, since they have been at least as jealous as the older powers of their claims to sovereignty. In sum, this view goes, states themselves had signed on to membership of the world body, and states pay the bills. Nobody else counts—or should count.

But this blunt view still leaves myriad problems and massive dissatisfactions in various quarters. The first is that the General Assembly's principle of "one Member, one vote," though sounding like "one MP, one vote" and even "one person, one vote," is badly weakened by other sections in the Charter, especially the sheer realities of international power. The largest contradiction with the democratic principle is, obviously, the special privileges accorded the five permanent and veto-bearing members of the Security Council, especially when one also remembers the great authority and roles that are assigned exclusively to the Council as a whole. This is why medium-size states like Australia, Brazil, and Mexico railed against the Charter's Security Council provisions in 1945 and why countries like India and Brazil continue to this day to protest against its lopsidedness (although would no doubt happily accept permanent Council membership themselves, if offered it).

After all, how could the General Assembly really be some global equivalent to a parliament or a congress when the entire issue of international security was removed from the representative body? When its declarations on security matters—like the many pronunciations about a Middle East settlement—are toothless in international law and authority compared with Security Council resolutions, which are binding? Or when it has little power of the purse (the reason why the English Parliament originally gained its bargaining power against the king), but in contrast can be brought into crisis and debilitation by major contributors refusing to pay their dues? When it meets in solemn ritual for a few months each year (unlike the Security Council, which can meet at a few hours' notice), receives reports from its many committees and agencies, passes declarations, affirms a budget that might or might not be realistic, and then dissolves for much of the rest of the time? When its hoped-for economic powers have been eroded by the independence of the Bretton Woods institutions? And when any amendment to the UN Charter or preferences for a new secretary-general have to run the gauntlet of being vetoed by one of the P5?

It is surely for this reason that whenever a new report, book, or article appears discussing "UN reform," or when politicians call for changes in the way the world organization is run, the role of the General Assembly gets but little mention, save for some reference to its place in the UN family and a call to improve its efficiency.[3] Writings upon the Security Council probably outnumber those on the General Assembly by about a hundred to one. There have also been many more writings about, and attention paid to, the role of NGOs, multinational corporations, or the global media. It is difficult to believe that this absence of mention of the General Assembly is because people at large are so content with its record that they see no reason to change things: It is probably because they do not care about it, or do not think that it is important enough to try to improve it, or do not even know what it does. No permanent representative to the UN would admit it openly, but privately most concede the General Assembly's lack of real powers. And the frequently expressed urgings, like that in Brazilian president Lula da Silva's fine speech of September 2003 for the assembly "to take on its responsibilities for maintaining international peace and security," appear to have no lasting impact.[4]

This is not to say that the General Assembly is redundant. It does vote its own budget. It does supervise, chiefly through the ECOSOC but also through its own six main committees, the work of many ad hoc bodies and important policy-relevant programs like the UNDP, as well as interact with the world's technical and specialized agencies. Its structures suffer from well-publicized bureaucratic overlaps— a plethora of food agencies, committees on women, and human rights bodies, as already noted—but it is difficult to know of a government, congress, or parliament that does not have the same "shared turf" problem, and at least the Assembly, under pressure from many states, has striven to improve itself and merge some agencies.

Much more significant is the General Assembly's role as a barometer of world opinion, with its autumnal sessions in New York being like the global equivalent of a town hall meeting and with almost all national leaders journeying there to address the Assembly. Now, it must be said again that its claim to representativeness is weakened by every single government (for instance, China, Sudan, and others) that itself has not been voted into office by open, democratic elections. It lays itself open to further criticism when, because of its strict rotation principles, an inappropriate member state becomes president pro tem of an important General Assembly body.* It is also true that the Assembly can, by majority vote, pass extremely silly resolutions, for example the "Zionism equals racism" vote of November 1975, which become even sillier because they have no binding force in international law and politics.

Still, the Assembly's role as a "global barometer" cannot be easily dismissed. It repeatedly debated and sought to press resolutions against apartheid in South Africa and the white supremacist regime in Rhodesia (though it was very quiet about Mao Zedong's domestic horrors). Eventually, its African–Asian–Latin American majority embarrassed the richer countries (the United States and the United Kingdom in particular) into joining the international pressure on the government in Pretoria to end its racist regime. It—or at least a number of regional members—played a key role in the Central American peace process. It has often requested the UN Secretary-General's Office to issue statements on critical global matters; and it was the force behind the holding of the important international conferences on the environment, population, the habitat, women, and human rights of the 1990s that were detailed in previous chapters. The relatively high impact of those conferences and of the often impressive changes that follow them again suggest that the General Assembly works best when it focuses on the soft agendas.

It achieves much less when it entangles itself in security matters, where it often finds itself torn between its own ambitions on the one hand and the constraints of the UN Charter on the other. One recent example will suffice. In July 2004, the International Court of Justice (ICJ) offered an "advisory opinion" on the decision of the Israeli government (under Prime Minister Ariel Sharon) to build a massive wall between Palestinian and Israeli settlements on the West Bank. The Court's opinion had been requested by a majority in the General Assembly (in its tenth emergency special session on the Israeli-

*The most notorious case in recent years was Libya's six-month presidency of the ECOSOC's Commission on Human Rights—grist to the mill for UN critics like *The Wall Street Journal*, which forgot to mention that the United States had not objected to the rotation and regional weighting principles for such bodies in the past because it did not deem the matter important.

Palestinian issue), which constitutionally it is free to do. The 14–1 opinion of the Court (the American judge dissenting) was predictably critical of the Sharon government's bulldozing policies. But what a tangled web it was: The two parties had not agreed to this jurisdiction, a prerequisite for ICJ action; the opinion to the General Assembly paid no attention to Israel's right of self-defense; it neglected the fact that all earlier Security Council resolutions called for a negotiated agreement on the boundaries, thus leaving moot the issue of where a "wall" might be drawn; and it inserted General Assembly activism into an international peace and security matter of which the Security Council was very much "seized." The General Assembly, and the ICJ, for that matter, had crossed a constitutional turf line, although most media reports spoke favorably of the Court's opinion and described the Palestinians as being on the "moral high ground." Nevertheless, the judgment made Israel more of an international outcast and embarrassed an American government increasingly drawn into the Palestinian issue. It did not stop what the Israelis were doing. And realists will tell us that this resolution will not matter in any case because only the Security Council has authority in such matters and a U.S. veto will demolish all other pretensions.

It is difficult to specify where all this leaves the Assembly, both in its constitutional role and in its inherent claim to represent "We the Peoples" through governmental forms. Clearly, it is not a cipher. It is especially significant to developing nations, to medium-size richer countries such as Sweden and Canada, and to smaller states that have little chance of getting onto the Security Council. It is the place where they can raise their voice, and some of those smaller states (Singapore, for example, or New Zealand) use this opportunity to express non-P5 viewpoints very well and forcefully indeed. And even if the General Assembly's resolutions lack the powers accorded the Security Council, it is no small matter if a majority of its members call for sanctions against a rogue state or condemn, say, the 1990 Iraqi invasion of Kuwait. Even its recent request for an ICJ opinion on the Israeli wall, legally tortuous as that judgment may be, is not insignificant. Although it may often pretend to powers it does not possess, the General Assembly remains the only sounding board at the governmental level for what much of the world thinks and feels. Without it, there would be no United Nations.

However impressive or limited one judges the General Assembly's achievements, it is clear that it falls well short of the role that many at its foundation hoped it would play. Some thinkers have thus returned to those early notions of "We the Peoples" that seemed to suggest that in the future there might be a sort of third chamber of representatives alongside the General Assembly and Security Council— a global parliament of some form or other whose members are voted directly into office by the peoples of the world. This is an idea that floats in and out of the public debate, like a ship in the mist. Many of the proposals are extremely vague, suggesting a Tennysonian vision but not really laying out what it means in reality. An early example here would be Wendell Willkie's book *One World* (noted earlier), the work of someone who traveled around the globe in 1942 and 1943, and returned to the United States to campaign on an "equality of opportunity for every race and nation" ticket. Generating a great deal of debate at the time, it gave a boost to the World Federalist movement (founded in 1947), which to this day calls for the creation of democratic global structures accountable to the citizens of the world.

But what exactly would those structures be? The Commission on Global Governance had a crack at this knotty problem in its 1995 report, "Our Global Neighborhood," yet while it ably outlined the worldwide transformations that were making both the Westphalian states system and the post-1945 international bodies less and less effective, it did not really push for systemic or constitutional change in the form of a third chamber with real legislative powers. In fact, it was at pains to stress the difference between "global governance" and " global government" (perhaps because of the unrelenting hostility to the UN of the Republican majorities in the Congress at that time).[5] Thus, it left the reader with rather familiar proposals: Increase the number of permanent and nonpermanent members on the Security Council, revitalize the General Assembly, resuscitate the Trusteeship Council as a steward of the global commons, replace the

ECOSOC with a more authoritative Economic Security Council, establish a permanent UN volunteer force, and so on. The report also
suggested that there be a "forum of civil society" consisting of NGOs
and other citizens' groups able to petition the General Assembly. Although many of these ideas had and continue to have validity, the
commission was clearly not making a fresh attempt at a parliament of
man, but rather offering ideas that they felt would improve existing
structures and allow them to work better.

Other authors, however, have pushed further ahead and argued,
literally, for such a parliamentary chamber. In an important article in
Foreign Affairs (2001), Professors Richard Falk and Andrew Strauss
suggest that the pressures of globalization now make it imperative for
international civil society, especially activist NGOs and concerned
business leaders, to create a global parliament to reduce the evident
democratic deficit in today's structures. "Even an initially weak assembly," they maintain, "could offer some democratic oversight of
international organizations such as the IMF, the WTO, and the World
Bank." The British radical journalist George Monbiot has argued on
numerous occasions that the existing system is so corrupt, so tilted in
favor of a few states (the P5), vast corporations, and, in general,
white men, that it should be superseded by a world parliament of six
hundred members, each representing ten million constituents. And he
is not alone. Some people—indeed, a lot of them—take the idea seriously.[6]

The practical and political problems with this sort of utopian
thought are numerous. A world assembly of self-important NGOs
and others is likely to be strongly opposed by parliamentarians and
congressmen who fought hard to win their seat in their national legislatures and believe that they constitute true democracy. It is worth
noting that the European Parliament, which is elected democratically,
can do little because of its limited authority. In any case, even if one
could organize ten-million-member constituencies (including minuscule Caribbean and Pacific island-states?) and send them off to debate
and vote at the designated global headquarters of a third forum, what
powers—of the purse, of constitution making, of voting the executive
in and out of office—could they possibly claim without nation-states

having somehow surrendered their sovereignty, without the implicit and explicit assumption behind the UN Charter itself—an agreement among countries—being set aside? The further implications of this scheme are even more mind-boggling. At ten million an MWP (member of the world parliament), and with an assembly of 600 voting members, China would have 140, India 120 and growing, Britain and France about 5 or 6 each, Russia about 14 but shrinking—and the world's superpower around 27 members! It's a lovely, idealistic proposal, but it's destined for the dustbin of history.

Thus, while the debate continues about formal institutional changes to further the agenda of greater representation and democratic control, many more crusaders on behalf of "the Peoples" have looked beyond traditional structures of global governance toward newer actors. As the twentieth century ended, "global civil society" was a phrase being increasingly heard. A diverse collection of NGOs, churches, foundations, and the media was becoming increasingly prominent, vocally challenging the exclusive rights of governments to speak for their people. To their supporters, these organizations represented an authentic flowering of a citizen-led politics that could speak directly for the voiceless and powerless. However, to their critics they were unelected meddlers, special interest groups that had allowed their self-proclaimed virtue to go to their heads. The following sections will examine some of these civil society groups as they strive, in their view, to refashion the globe. What were their successes and failures, and how far have they advanced in their campaigns for greater transparency, democracy, and stewardship of the planet?

The most vocal of these groups are without doubt the nongovernmental organizations. Relatively small in number at first, they have expanded rapidly in recent years and by their very informality and amorphousness, they are hard to count—some sources claim there are up to thirty thousand NGOs in the world today. Such bodies have a distinguished provenance—was not the antislavery movement in nineteenth-century Britain an NGO? Various public organizations (the American Bar Association, women's groups, World Federalists) were present at the San Francisco deliberations in 1945, some being allowed to submit their viewpoints to the delegates. Thus, the idea of forming associations with a declared purpose to affect public policy goes back a long way and is linked with the rise of democracy and civil society. Moreover, the UN Charter embraced this relationship in Article 71, which declared that the ECOSOC "may make suitable arrangements for consultation with non-governmental organizations which are concerned with matters within its competence." That was vague enough, but recognition nonetheless.

What is different in today's world is the sheer number and range of NGOs. The blossoming of the movement was very much connected with the global public protests and self-mobilization that occurred in the 1960s.[7] To many people, especially the young, the structures of power, whether in the selfishly capitalist West or in the stiflingly Communist East, seemed more and more out of date. Injustices were rife, both within countries and between North and South. The civil rights movement in the United States was a major catalyst, in the depth of the change that it demanded, the publicity it received, and the political changes it achieved. The women's rights movement in Europe and America energized and organized other parts of democratic society and spilled rapidly across frontiers. The suppression of the Prague Spring in 1968, far from checking agitation in Warsaw Pact countries, spurred underground organizations within such lands and "human rights watch" bodies outside. Environmentalists began their campaign about the fate of the earth. Other bodies formed to campaign for a new international economic order.

The story of this social and intellectual transformation is a rich but messy one, and very difficult to categorize, simply because these many organizations had very different purposes and pursued radically different lines of action. Some activists who campaigned for political change and human rights reforms (Nelson Mandela, Václav Havel, Lech Walesa) would, years later, end up running their national governments; as such, they were in a different category from those agitating against seal culling or foxhunting. But what they all had in common was a conviction that change was necessary and that national and/or local politicians and officials had to be persuaded, or even compelled, to agree to the proposed changes.

Thus, some NGOs, like Greenpeace, have preferred direct action to make their point; others, such as the World Wildlife Fund, wish to work through establishments or through the United Nations system itself. Some are extremely practical, such as Médecins sans Frontières (MSF). Some were, and are, very strictly focused, such as the Committee to Protect Journalists, whereas others have a very broad agenda. Many of them are associated with churches—like Quaker or Catholic associations for international peace and development—and try to keep a distance from political agitation. Still others are passionate about the fate of a single country or people—the Kurds, Israel, Taiwan, Tibet, the Amazonian tribes. Generally, and because they are operating outside government systems and are often suspicious of governments, they are left of center; they want change, improvement, human and environmental betterment. But they are certainly not all marching to a leftist tune. The American Catholic bishops press for social and economic justice in Latin America but oppose the practices of abortion and contraception favored by American feminist organizations there. Human rights groups protest against bulldozing in the Gaza Strip, which supporters of current Israel policies defend. The American "Christian Right" has shown formidable powers of self-mobilization. Whatever the ideology, each campaign and attempt to influence affairs is usually generated from below, so it is not surprising that traditional politicians are made uneasy by the NGO phenomenon, even if treating certain groups with considerable respect. These organizations are, by definition, not controllable by, and very often embarrassing to, governments.

Among the NGOs, a considerable number work closely with the world organization. From the very first session of the General Assembly (London, 1946), there began a process of accrediting a growing number of NGOs to the United Nations. These organizations, by gaining consultative status to the ECOSOC, would use their "international personality" both to influence governments and to spread the gospel of world order, peace, and cultural understanding. To be sure, their input is suitably screened by an ECOSOC standing committee, which considers requests for consultative status (many are turned down) and receives requests from NGOs for items to be placed on the ECOSOC's agenda—at least if the NGO in question is accredited to the ECOSOC's Category I status. Direct access to the General Assembly, let alone the Security Council, does not occur, and the cynic may wonder whether the ECOSOC's role, at least in this regard, is simply to act as a UN buffer to civil society's concerns and agitations.[8]

Yet even if relatively few of these organizations can submit documents (to a maximum of two thousand words), and even if it is just the ECOSOC with which they have a consultative relationship, small steps have been taken toward public democratic participation. Furthermore, the UN's Department of Public Information has also opened its doors to the NGO movement and has a lengthy list of accredited organizations; other NGOs are accredited to UN offices in Geneva, Vienna, and Nairobi, without the consultative status that derives from approval by the ECOSOC. Around 3,900 NGOs are registered with either the ECOSOC or the DPI alone. Finally, there are the thousands of NGOs that receive permission to attend UN global conferences, where they can lobby government delegations, offer information/support to smaller countries, stage parallel events (the NGO forums), and in general make their presence felt.

Yet for all the work of the NGOs outside and inside the United Nations, it seems clear that their greatest impact is elsewhere, upon public opinion and the media. Because the UN Charter accords special and protected privileges to governments, they in their turn (especially when meeting in General Assembly and Security Council sessions) can be aloof to outside voices. It thus makes sense for most NGOs to concentrate on their own mission and generate their own publicity, trusting that by their very actions they will influence broader opinions and help change the world for the better. By the same logic, it also makes sense for our analysis to focus on select examples of different types of NGOs and the policies they pursue.

The first example is Amnesty International, in the field of human rights. It has been mentioned before. This is an extremely activist

NGO that focuses on ending grave abuses to the rights to physical and mental integrity, to freedom of conscience and expression, and to freedom from discrimination; it seeks to compel governments and others wielding authority to respect the Universal Declaration of Human Rights. Emerging as a small acorn (it started in 1961 when British lawyer Peter Benenson called for a campaign against the Portuguese government for imprisoning two students who raised a toast to freedom), it is now a mighty oak. With more than one million members in 160 countries, it receives information from all manner of sources about human rights abuses and then campaigns for reform. It is difficult to think of a government that has not been embarrassed by Amnesty's reports one way or another—the USSR and the People's Republic of China for cracking down on dissidents, Britain for abuses in Ulster, the United States for police brutality, Arab states for cruel punishments and the denial of basic human rights to women, Sierra Leone for arbitrary killings, Israel for its excessive force in the Gaza Strip, Indonesia for political "disappearances." In 1977, Amnesty International was awarded the Nobel Peace Prize.[9]

To its critics, Amnesty International is too interfering, too judgmental, too quick to take the case of the victim and not of the authorities, who may have genuine security reasons for, say, imposing martial law. Its local enthusiasms and self-promotion may outweigh prudence. Very often, Amnesty's confrontational stance is contrasted with that of the International Committee of the Red Cross (ICRC). The latter is, indeed, a very different sort of humanitarian organization. Although also founded by private initiative—the shock of several Swiss citizens at the neglect of wounded soldiers at the 1859 Battle of Solferino—the ICRC (and its Muslim equivalent, the Red Crescent) is much more of an intergovernmental organization even if it does receive funds from its various national committees and state grants.

The ICRC prides itself on its absolute neutrality and impartiality—in the Second World War, it paid visits (with food parcels) to British prisoner-of-war camps holding captured Germans, and to German camps holding captured Britons. Originally conceived of as an organization working in wartime, it later moved to the broader remit of assisting victims of internal violence and helping to coordinate relief activities. It holds to a policy of strict confidentiality about its prison visits, except in extreme circumstances of abuse. It strives to reunite families and protect POWs on all sides. This implies that it often has to negotiate with loathsome regimes—ones that Amnesty International or, for that matter, American conservatives would condemn outright. The ICRC works on the assumption that even nasty governments would agree to cooperate with a discreet and neutral organization. Ultimately, it is the prisoner's well-being that takes precedence, whatever the nationality of that prisoner or his jailers.

Both Amnesty and the ICRC interact importantly with the purposes of the UN, therefore, and more deeply with the work of the Office of the UN High Commissioner for Human Rights, but they do so in radically different ways. One is the gadfly, rushing in where angels fear to tread, ready to be confrontational if the need arises, appealing to world opinion to support its causes and replenish its coffers, keen to publicize (its 2005 publications catalog in the United States is forty-three pages long), and refusing to accept moneys from governments lest it become in any way beholden to them. The International Committee of the Red Cross pushes in the same noble direction of establishing protection for the basic human rights of those wounded, displaced, abused, and imprisoned through conflict. Yet it seeks to achieve those purposes more diplomatically and discreetly, invokes governmental accords (especially the Geneva protocols), receives block grants from UN member states, and attempts complete neutrality.

Both the activist lobby and the quiet operators have their own strong supporters. In today's complex world, where no human conflict and suffering is quite the same, it seems unnecessary to have to prefer one to the other. Perhaps the ICRC's interventions are better in one situation and Amnesty's campaigns have more effect in another. It may also be the case that both campaigns—in parallel with those of many other human rights organizations, churches, and media—are needed to persuade an abusive regime to admit the need to change its ways. Either approach might help to convince the world community to be moved by a particular tragedy. No doubt the Foreign Ministries of the world prefer the ICRC's more tactful manner; but the media and parliamentarians, plus the rest of the NGO community, are likely to lay their sympathies alongside those of Amnesty International. There is room for both—alas.

Médecins sans Frontières operates on a different plane, or in a different way, though again pushing in the same direction. Founded in 1971 by a group of French doctors to provide emergency medical assistance in wartime and crisis areas, they strive like the ICRC to be neutral in any conflict, yet they also are willing, like Amnesty International, to speak out against atrocities being committed. This they did in recent times, for example, in Darfur, where the Sudanese government had shut out foreign news correspondents. Being one of the very first NGOs on the ground (along with, say, local missionaries or the Catholic Agency for Overseas Development [CAFOD] and OXFAM), they can draw international attention to a burgeoning crisis. As such, they act as an "early alert system" for the United Nations itself, even if they insist on being seen as a nongovernmental player. They are usually welcomed by all sides in a dispute or a famine, because their intentions are so transparent: to bring medical services, food supplies, sanitation—in a word, relief—to the tortured parts of our earth. The MSF is certainly more willing to wear a public face than is the ICRC. In 1999, the MSF's head openly requested President Boris Yeltsin to stop the bombings of civilians in Chechnya. In the same year, it received the Nobel Peace Prize and used the moneys to raise public awareness of the need to fight neglected diseases such as tuberculosis and malaria.

The charter of the MSF proudly states that its volunteers "are aware of the risk and dangers of the mission they undertake, and have no right to compensation for themselves or their beneficiaries other than what Médecins sans Frontières is able to afford them."[10] These 2,500 volunteers (doctors, nurses, technical support) join with roughly 15,000 local staff worldwide to provide medical aid—in 2004, that was in eighty countries. It was a bitter blow, therefore, not just to the work on the ground, but to the MSF's careful operating principles, when five of their team were killed in Afghanistan on

June 2, 2004, accused, absurdly, of being agents of American imperialism. Within a couple of months, the MSF had withdrawn its 80 international volunteers and terminated the jobs of the 1,400 local staff in that country.[11] The organization had been in Afghanistan for twenty-four years, in earlier times becoming famous by bringing medicines by packhorse to stricken communities. Such killings—and they are not just of MSF personnel—raise a larger question that will be addressed later in this chapter: Can any operation that has its original inspiration (and its existing headquarters) in Paris or London or New York City or Geneva avoid the suspicion that it is a foreign influence in a troubled land, to be denounced and attacked as just another face of Western intrusion? By extension—and the most dismaying thought of all—can humanitarian aid and human rights agencies and NGOs continue to be respected by all sides to a conflict, given this spate of recent attacks?[12]

Another massive and growing field of NGO activity has focused on environmental issues, in parallel with (and often in advance of) the expansion of UN agencies in this field. Here is a movement that must nowadays comprise thousands of NGOs. At one end of the spectrum, there is the ultra-activist organization Greenpeace, which first attracted media attention in the early 1970s after some spectacular protest actions, each with the clear intent of embarrassing governments and commercial firms into stopping practices that its leaders judged harmful to nature and the environment.[13] This, of course, raised questions that attend all such organizations: How can a group of self-appointed persons claim to be speaking for the people as a whole, for the environment, for the forests and the whales? And how can they be tolerated if they deliberately break the laws during their protest actions? Here Greenpeace's answer was firm. Like the U.S. civil rights movement a generation earlier, they felt they had to ignore certain regulations (regarding trespass or against assembly) in order to achieve their larger purposes. This was civil disobedience, now carried onto the high seas—literally.

Greenpeace activists were therefore not hesitant to put themselves in danger if it drew attention to their cause and compelled authorities to change policies of which they disapproved. Physically interrupting the slaughter of gray seals in Canada and Alaska was an early example of this, as were actions at sea against large-scale drift-net fishing. Sailing into the French nuclear-testing grounds in the Pacific and protesting against reckless logging practices (especially in tropical rain forests) were other ways of catching public attention. International oil companies, large forestry concerns, and the Norwegian and Japanese whaling industries have been special and repeated targets for Greenpeace. Moreover, strong physical countermeasures by the authorities have often backfired, the most spectacular case of this occurring when the organization's ship *Rainbow Warrior* was sunk by the French secret service in 1985 to stop it from sailing into a nuclear-testing zone in the South Pacific. Although the French government defended itself, the resulting furor, plus Greenpeace's gathering of millions of petitions worldwide, did a great deal to drive the major powers, including France, into much less testing. No doubt it was the altered political climate between East and West that chiefly explains the coming of the Comprehensive Nuclear Test Ban Treaty (1996), but it is not unreasonable to argue that a gadfly organization had played a considerable role in shifting public opinion in the first place.

This is not, then, merely symbolic protest. Greenpeace, like many other NGOs, nowadays employs lawyers and lobbyists to advance its case, recruits scientists to test products and survey damaged environments, and conducts sophisticated public relations campaigns, working through its widespread network of local groups and volunteers and a sophisticated use of the Internet. In recent years, it has campaigned with particular vigor against genetically engineered crops, forcing company after company to pull out of that field. It recognized very early on the importance of getting what it wanted enshrined in international law and of working through international bodies and treaties. Intense lobbying of many governments resulted in UN sanctions on Liberia for illegal logging. Other campaigning caused the International Maritime Organization to increase restrictions on oil tankers and other dangerous cargo vessels in the Baltic

Sea. As it celebrated its thirtieth birthday in September 2001, it announced, as if we hadn't realized, "Greenpeace thrives on committed activism. . . ."

The World Resources Institute (WRI), founded in Washington, D.C., in 1982, is much less confrontationist. And where Greenpeace now has a network of self-mobilized, virtually independent groups in more than thirty countries, the WRI has concentrated its personnel in one office—although its one hundred or more scientists, engineers, consultants, mapmakers, and other specialists fan out across the globe in pursuit of a multitude of projects aimed at improving environmental sustainability. It, too, acts to mobilize public awareness through its many press releases and publications, the best known of which is its impressive "World Resources" annual report. But its greatest role is to create partnerships with bodies in the developing world, usually securing the major funding from government agencies and foundations in the North.

Two examples may suffice.[14] In June 2004, the WRI and the Confederation of Indian Industry announced a collaboration on projects to support environmentally sustainable enterprises in India—a not inconsiderable event, given that India is (after China) mainland Asia's largest economy and a country whose impressive economic growth could well affect the struggle to control global warming. The Godrej Green Business Centre, which will do most of the groundwork, is supported by the state of Andhra Pradesh, the Godrej Foundation, and the U.S. Agency for International Development (USAID). In the same month, the WRI announced a collaboration with the Asian Development Bank to study "environmentally sustainable urban transport" in Asia—which anyone who has coughed in the fumes of Bangkok or Shanghai will agree is a much-needed goal. The holding organization on the ground is funded by the Swedish International Development Agency. The WRI's organ for advising on all this (its Center for Transport and the Environment, which goes under the weird acronym EMBARQ) is supported by the Shell Foundation. This is a long way from Greenpeace's campaign against Norwegian whaling. Yet both organizations, and thousands of others, push in the same direction.

Even more extraordinary is the range of NGOs dedicated to the advancement of women's and girls' rights—that is, to the claims to dignity and citizenship of more than half the human race. Their chief focus is, understandably, on the denial of basic rights to women in so many parts of the developing world. Here again, though, the observer gets the sense of overlap among a large number of self-appointed bodies. But overlap is not necessarily redundancy if the general result of these bodies' disparate actions is to improve international civic society. Still, it is difficult to keep pace with the founding of new NGOs in this field, springing up like mushrooms—almost always in response to reports of new plight and outrage. For example, in 1983 a group of U.S. female activists traveled to Nicaragua to observe the effects upon women and children of the Contra war and returned so incensed at what they had seen and heard that they founded MADRE—as their website describes it, "an international women's human rights organization demanding human rights for women and families." It has a particular interest in Latin America, where it links up with indigenous women's movements, and politically it is acerbic about how American governments, big business, and trade accords like NAFTA have hurt the social fabric of that region. Then there is Equality Now, founded in 1992 to promote women's rights around the globe through the appeal to international and national law—nine years later, it established the Lawyers' Alliance for Women (LAW) to carry that mission from country to country, testifying in courts, tribunals, and other public bodies. A quite different group is the Global Fund for Women, which since 1987 has raised enough money from outside donors to allocate approximately $32 million to more than 2,300 women's groups around the world: It supports about four hundred new projects a year with grants that may seem small in Northern eyes but are gratefully received on the ground.

Still, the critic is entitled to ask, What does all this activism and expenditure of energies really achieve? Clearly the results are mixed. Many of these organizations are too scattered in their aims, too angry and unpolitic, too likely to dissipate their strength on any and all related causes. MADRE, for example, openly states: "Our programs reflect a human-rights-based and people-centered approach to achieving the UN Millennium Development Goals, which aim to: eradicate extreme poverty and hunger; achieve universal primary education; promote gender equality and empower women; reduce child mortality; improve maternal health; combat HIV/AIDS, malaria and other diseases; ensure environmental sustainability; and develop a global partnership for development."[15] This has been a tall order to fill, even for the entire United Nations organization itself.

Other NGOs, focusing upon one clear mission, do make a difference in practical and everyday terms. Consider the irrepressible Professor Wangari Maathai, founder of the Green Belt Movement (GBM), the first woman ever in East and Central Africa to earn a doctorate, and the recipient of the 2004 Nobel Peace Prize. When she first started the GBM in 1977 by planting trees to replace those cut down by irresponsible logging, the Kenyan government was merely baffled. When six hundred tree nurseries, all run by women, were established within a decade, President Daniel arap Moi's corrupt government became worried. When the GBM opposed the construction of a sixty-two-story building in Nairobi to be the headquarters of the ruling political party, the government became violent. Dr. Maathai was physically assaulted on at least three occasions. The result of this clumsy intimidation was that the world's human rights and women's organizations weighed into the fight, the global media suddenly had a new item of interest, Northern foundations offered moneys for her tree-planting project (to date, she and her movement have planted more than twenty million trees), the awards and prizes to her and the GBM from across the world have multiplied, and the Kenyan government has had to back off. In 2002, she was elected to parliament, then to a ministerial position. Years earlier, her husband left her and was granted a divorce on the grounds that she was "too educated, too strong, too successful, too stubborn, and too hard to control. . . ." Exactly. And she made things move.[16]

Yet what does all this mean in terms of the global structures of power? Probably not very much. The government of Kenya might have shifted its stance but is certainly not yet committed to a women's rights agenda. The vast majority of governments are male dominated, as are their bureaucracies. Women's rights are denied across the Muslim world and most of Africa. And real power in the world of international organizations remains firmly in the hands of the Security Council, the IMF, and the World Bank. Yet if an early-style global activist of the late 1940s were to return to survey the position of NGOs in the world community today, he or she would be astonished at their prominence.

Could the same be said of other nongovernmental bodies, like the churches, the media, and the philanthropic foundations, in the development of international civic society? There is no doubt that institutionalized religions such as Islam, Christianity, Buddhism, and others have a profound impact upon the lives and thought of billions of people, but does that fact itself translate into a significant interaction with, and influence upon, international organizations? In most respects, the answer is surely negative. Families and individuals worship in pursuit of a yearning to come closer to the Almighty, not to alter the ECOSOC. Still, what the churches say and do often has massive ripple effects upon world politics both because of the size of their memberships and because they, too, turn to the UN and its member states to get international change.

This is not to imply that the churches' public roles are all political. The Quaker Relief Services work quietly and effectively to relieve suffering in many parts of the world and rarely make the headlines. From assisting victims of the Irish potato famine in the mid-nineteenth century to their relief efforts among the German people after both world wars (for which they received the Nobel Peace Prize in 1947), the American Friends Service Committee moved on to a global role and now operates in twenty-two countries: It has supported flood victims in Mozambique, famine victims in the Horn of Africa, and victims of violence in Chechnya. A similar pattern of international service is carried out by many Scandinavian church and missionary societies. Then there is the largest player of all, the Catholic Relief Services (founded 1943) and certain national-based organizations like CAFOD in the United Kingdom, which nowadays operate in ninety-four countries, providing emergency relief, nursing for HIV/AIDS victims, health, education, microfinancing, and peace building. Although they often work alongside UN relief agencies and

NGOs, in some more distant parts of the world these religiously based aid bodies *are* the international community.[17]

Churches sometimes have the power to make governments move that NGOs could only dream of possessing. A great example of this was the political mobilization by the American Jewish community at the news and images of emaciated Muslims held in camps in Bosnia in August 1992. When the American Jewish Committee, the American Jewish Congress, and the Anti-Defamation League published a full-page advertisement in *The New York Times* entitled "Stop the Death Camps" and organized a march on the White House, U.S. policy makers suddenly snapped into action. Twelve years later, when the U.S. Council of Catholic Bishops asked Secretary of State Colin Powell to intensify efforts to stop the Sudanese governments from the genocides in Darfur, the State Department's attention soared—and increased again when the main southern Protestant churches also expressed a belief that if necessary, the U.S. government and the Security Council should seriously consider intervention.

The interplay of church politics and international politics is sometimes much more controversial—and problematic. A generation ago, the storm center of church-state relations was in Central and South America, where the influence of the Catholic Church was unmatched. Traditionally, the church's leaders (just like those in Spain and Portugal) had tilted in a conservative direction, often supporting dictatorial regimes. But the coming of new "liberationist" ideas, the emergence of some radical bishops during the civil wars that racked Central America, and the growth of a fresh generation of priests, especially Jesuits, preaching socioeconomic as well as constitutional reforms changed the entire landscape. The church became associated with the radical wing of politics and sometimes paid a heavy price. When it set up an investigation of human rights abuses in Guatemala over the previous decades of conflict and concluded that 79 percent of the fifty-five thousand cases were perpetrated by the "security" forces, the head of the final report, Bishop Juan Gerardi, was bludgeoned to death two days later (April 26, 1998)—a chilling replay of the 1980 El Salvador assassination of Archbishop Oscar Romero, who was shot by right-wing officers while saying Mass. Romero's murder was investigated twelve years later by a UN Truth Commission, which ultimately identified the perpetrators. Gerardi's case (or rather the case made by some of his supporters) was brought to European attention under the sponsorship of Amnesty International. On this occasion, agencies, churches, and NGOs were marching together.

On other matters, these various actors disagree. Although the liberal Protestant churches of Northern Europe normally associate with progressive global causes, this is not true of the conservative U.S. churches concerning the role of international agencies over abortion and family planning, and certainly not true of the Vatican. The Holy See's unique position—it has official nonmember observer status in the General Assembly (which it elected to take in 1945 rather than the obligations of full membership, as did Switzerland)—gives it the chance to influence UN policies way beyond that of any NGO or any other religion. One of those many privileges is the right to a vote at UN global conferences and to shape the resolutions of such meetings. This is usually an uncontentious matter, or at least accepted as historic fact. But the Vatican's determined interventions to mold the text of the Programme of Action during the 1994 global conference at Cairo on world population (it claimed the draft language encouraged abortion on demand, teenage sexuality, and homosexuality) stunned many delegates and caused feminist organizations to call for the Vatican to be downgraded to the status of an NGO. Since the Holy See has full diplomatic relations with more than one hundred states, and since its special position is nowadays supported, ironically but understandably, by conservative Protestants, Jews, and Muslims, this call was futile. What this furor, and the compromise language in the final text of the Programme of Action, perhaps most suggests is that the usually liberal NGO movement, despite its growth in voice and influence, has its limits.[18]

There is no doubt at all, however, that many NGOs have benefited greatly from the expansion of the philanthropic foundations, mainly American and mainly liberal, in the advancement of global democracy. Established by law early in the twentieth century and designed for both philanthropic and tax purposes—Carnegie and Rockefeller were the first, with the Ford Foundation being created only in 1936—foundations are able to leverage their financial power in a variety of ways. It is extraordinarily difficult to obtain accurate statistics here, and many figures conflict, even within the annual report of the same foundation (they are all required by U.S. law to produce an annual report and to spend 5 percent of their assets each year). As of 2002, the nearly sixty-five thousand private American foundations had assets of $435 billion and were dispensing $30 billion a year—a sum equal to the entire GDP of Zimbabwe or El Salvador. The overwhelming share of this money goes to domestic U.S. constituencies such as schools, inner-city needs, and medical research. Even so, much is spent on what is usually termed "international affairs" programs, and it is these that probably gain the most attention, since the political Right sees many foundations as being too progressive and subversive, radicals on the Left view them as elitist and undemocratic, and many developing world countries regard them as being too intrusive even if they offer a welcome supply of funds.[19]

There seem to be two main ways in which philanthropic foundations affect international civil society and can be related to the stated purposes of the UN Charter and the Universal Declaration. The first is in the fields of cultural exchanges, educational scholarships, research and training programs, and the dissemination of information about international matters—a rather UNESCO-like agenda, since the declared intention is to promote knowledge and understanding among and between peoples. Funding East-West scientific conferences during the Cold War would be one example among many, the argument being that it could help to promote policies of coexistence rather than confrontation. A great deal of foundation money was poured into Western Europe during the 1950s and 1960s, subsidizing journals, making gifts to educational institutions, and encouraging an appreciation of American culture so as to reduce European anti-Americanism and any drift toward the USSR. Funding libraries in the developing world was another typical investment. Since the USAID and CIA were doing much the same, it is not surprising that many foreign individuals and their governments suspected that the foundations were just another arm of American strategy—despite the fact that they were by this stage pushing agendas altogether more progressive and liberal than their tough, conservative founders could have imagined.

The second cluster of projects offers practical support to human rights groups and funds environmental and agricultural improvements, especially tropical medicine research and experimentation. By definition, therefore, this flow of moneys goes from the First World to the Third World. The Rockefeller Foundation was probably the trailblazer here. As early as 1916 it began making grants in India, and in 1932 it funded the All-India School of Hygiene and Public Health. Rockefeller was also the leader in grants to assist community projects in Latin America and the Caribbean, while Ford, when it entered the field in a serious way in the 1950s, decided to devote much of its funds for international affairs to the Indian subcontinent. Both those foundations played a significant role in supporting the so-called Green Revolution in Asia, allowing countries to boost their agricultural productivity.

What does this mean in monetary terms? The annual reports of two huge players, the Ford Foundation and the Gates Foundation, give us an idea. Ford's total assets at the end of 2003 were $9.97 billion, which allowed it to make grants of $489 million—much less than the annual moneys available to USAID or the World Bank, of course, but important because of its far greater flexibility and freedom from political (that is, government) interference. In certain regards, the foundation has the attributes of a medium-size state. It has offices in Mexico City, Rio de Janeiro, Santiago, Lagos, Johannesburg, Nairobi, Cairo, Tel Aviv, Moscow, Beijing, Hanoi, Jakarta, and New Delhi—the last named being its largest overseas office. Between 1951 and 1995, Ford allocated hundreds of millions of dollars to some 2,500 grant projects across India. Just to watch the visitors flowing into its offices on Lodi Road in New Delhi is to gain the impression that one is observing an embassy or large consulate in action.

The Gates Foundation is a latecomer to this world, but within a decade it has become the largest donor ever, due to the family earnings in Microsoft. In 2003, its assets stood at almost $27 billion, and it was spending more than $1 billion in grants each year. Its largest program concerns what it calls "global health," where $576 million was given out in 2003 alone, chiefly in combating deadly diseases like HIV and malaria. It has become a particularly important player in the fight to combat AIDS in Africa, with moneys going to everything from medical research to health care provision for those affected by HIV/AIDS. It therefore does not have Ford's range (or overseas offices) but places large money on large projects. Ford's policies are more general, and it happily contemplates smaller-scale grants, for example, to village-based initiatives on environmental cleanup, water supplies, and microcredit for women's ventures. But it has also played a distinct role in advancing human rights in the developing word, often to the fury and embarrassment of authoritarian regimes. When the Argentine military regime violently intervened at the University of Buenos Aires in 1966, the foundation helped Argentine scientists resettle in other Latin American countries. And when the apartheid government in South Africa discriminated against African scholars in higher education, Ford set up the South African Research Program (SARP, at Yale) to assist their research and education. Currently it supports the Colombian Commission of Jurists and a Jesuit think tank in Bogotá called CINEP, in each case to fight and report on human rights abuses. Many of these grants by the foundations are not well spent because of mismanagement or wrong techniques, but the cumulative effect of the past half-century of giving has undoubtedly been to advance international awareness and cooperation.

There are, of course, similar philanthropic foundations in other countries—the Krupp Foundation in Germany, the Sasakawa Foundation in Japan, the Leverhulme Foundation in Britain. But most of them concentrate on domestic projects or on cultural and educational exchanges. And the domination of American bodies in this whole arena is enormous—some years ago, it was estimated that of thirty-two foundations across the globe with assets exceeding $100 million, twenty-nine were American.

At first glance, one might think the same Western dominance exists with respect to media coverage of international and UN-related agendas. Two cases would reinforce this impression: the role of the

American cable television network CNN and the rather different role of the BBC World Service. No one would argue that either organization was at the forefront in a global "We the Peoples" campaign, but their dissemination of news and information to so many countries across the globe strengthens the notion that, for all the differences among states, more and more citizens (especially the younger generation) are exposed to what is happening elsewhere. Furthermore, CNN has assumed a rather special role—the so-called CNN effect—in causing governments to engage in, or disengage from, international crises, especially in the developing world. The argument here is best put by Professor Viggo Jakobsen: "The causal mechanism of the CNN effect is usually conceived in the following way: media coverage (printed and televised) of suffering and atrocities—journalists and opinion leaders demand that Western governments 'do something'—the (public) pressure becomes unbearable—Western governments do something."[20] The key examples here were the triple crises of the mid-1990s, Kosovo, Somalia, and Rwanda-Burundi. In the words of John Shattuck, U.S. assistant secretary of state for democracy, human rights, and labor at the time, "The media got us into Somalia and then got us out." UN secretary-general Boutros Boutros-Ghali said wonderingly, "Television has changed the way the world reacts to crises"—a judgment that the global reaction to the Indian Ocean tsunami of December 2004 has borne out.

This is surely true, yet not the whole story. Atrocities and humanitarian disasters that were covered by CNN (and other networks that scrambled to keep up) certainly got more attention than the many that were not much covered—like Abkhazia, Angola, Sudan, Liberia, Nagorno-Karabakh, Kashmir, and half a dozen others. The situation in Sudan was even more horrendous in the early 1990s than in Somalia, but CNN was in Somalia, not Sudan, so Somalia was where the UN and the United States intervened. It is also true that television coverage is episodic, depending on whether the human rights abuses are acute or the region is accessible to an expensive news team or the story itself is "sexy" enough; few of the networks devoted much footage to, say, rebuilding efforts once the Rwandan atrocities were over.

But all the attention given to the CNN effect as the chief or sole "driver" of international governmental action ignores so many of the other actors on the stage, including those discussed previously—the NGOs, the human rights organizations, the many UN agencies in the field reporting directly to the secretary-general, the diplomatic and consular officials reporting atrocities to their own governments, the churches. Clearly, the French and Canadian governments did not need CNN to cause them to urge intervention in Rwanda. Prime Minister Blair did not need the media to make him decide to send two thousand Royal Marine commandos into Sierra Leone. It is probable that the U.S. Catholic bishops were a more important influence in arousing Secretary of State Powell's concern about Sudan than was any news media. American black congressmen with a deep interest in the fate of Africa keep up a pressure all their own regarding events on that continent. In sum, the Western media certainly adds to the momentum for debate and action regarding peacekeeping and humanitarian issues, but it does not walk alone.

A very different influence in the arena of global opinion and perceptions are the radio broadcasts of the BBC World Service (not to be confused with the domestic BBC services that broadcast within the United Kingdom itself). This remarkable organization decided from very early on in its long career—it was founded in 1922—to adhere to two principles that have stood it in good stead: first, to broadcast across the globe, not just in the English language but in a host of foreign languages (Swahili, Hindi, Hausa, Turkic, and others) spoken by native speakers who had immigrated to the United Kingdom; and second, to offer factual, often understated reports of world news in as impartial a manner as possible—in direct and deliberate contrast, half a century ago, with Dr. Joseph Goebbels's Propagandaministerium.

The result was credibility, an immeasurable asset. During the Cold War, tens of millions of Soviet and Eastern European citizens listened in to get the truth in their Orwellian world. Today, approximately sixty-nine million people in Africa and forty-eight million in Asia hear its nightly broadcasts. Although one may want to take with a grain of salt the BBC's own polling data, they claim that 64 percent of Nigerians and 55 percent of Indians believe that the World Service "provides unbiased and objective news and information"—this in contrast with the Voice of America and the main U.S. networks, which to many foreign audiences are regarded as being too patriotic and self-centered (in that they talk about events in America, not the world). As noted *New York Times* columnist Paul Krugman sarcastically observed in May 2003, during the Iraq war even many Americans were turning to the BBC for their news because networks like Fox News "wrapped themselves in the American flag and substituted patriotism for impartiality."[21]

The largest listenerships to the BBC are in countries of the commonwealth, which is unsurprising. In Ghana, it is the biggest station in the country. But what is one to make of the fact that there is a weekly audience in Iraq (!) of 1.8 million people? Or that of those who listen to radio news in Kabul, 60 percent to 80 percent listen to the World Service? Or that when Iranian lawyer Shirin Ebadi was awarded the Nobel Peace Prize, she said in an interview: "We hear from the BBC (Persian Service) news and views which we can't get from our own media. The BBC is often first in reporting the important news in our country. Indeed I have often heard it first from the BBC if a colleague has been arrested"? Given also that the World Service's staff monitor more than three thousand TV, radio, Internet, and agency sources in up to one hundred languages, there simply is no equivalent.

Still, in neither the case of CNN nor that of the BBC World Service should one overestimate their global impacts. There are simply too many other domestic contenders. In India, which has such a vigorous local press, radio, and television, only 1.7 percent of the adult population listens to the World Service. In China, where there are about 3,300 local TV stations, foreign networks are not allowed to beam news (as opposed to entertainment, presumably) into the country. Most of the major cities of Latin America have a lively domestic media; where it is suppressed, one can listen to broadcasts from neighboring states. And the truth is that even the 146 million of the BBC World Service's listenership in the non-Western world are overwhelmingly of a literary and professional class who play political roles but represent only 1.5 percent of humanity. One should add to this the extraordinary influence of the al-Jazeera network across the Arab world. Regarded by many in the region as the most authoritative source of news, it enjoys the sublime fate of being criticized by both American conservatives and Muslim fundamentalists. And it now broadcasts in English, an intriguing turn of the tables. Finally, a more in-depth investigation of the place of news and cultural communications in the evolution of international affairs would need to consider the pervasive and transnational nature of the Internet. Since it has grown so fast in the past decade, and its popularity is exploding in the giant states of India and China, it is extremely difficult to get a good measure of its many impacts; but it seems fair to remark that because this is a medium that can be used and abused by anyone with electricity and a computer, it may become less and less a Western-dominated instrument.

Surveying this profusion of nonstate actors, agitators, and agencies, the observer must be struck by two thoughts, one positive, one negative, regarding the possibility of establishing a truly global civil society. The positive aspect lies in the emergence of synergy or, better, synergies that run across the entire spectrum. Foundations and NGOs and the media and the churches are working with, or at least interacting with, one another on an ever increasing scale and also often interacting with the governments of the UN member states as well as with specific UN and specialized agencies. The AIDS pandemic in Africa, for example, attracts the attention of the world's press and (occasionally) television. Discussions about this problem are broadcast by the BBC World Service in English, Swahili, and Hausa. There are heartrending accounts in *The Guardian* and *Le Monde*. NGOs of all persuasions seek to assist. Foundations such as Gates and Rockefeller lend their resources. Catholic Relief Services and those of other denominations tend the sick and dying. The World Bank enters as a powerful player. UN bodies and specialized agencies ranging from the World Health Organization to UNICEF and UNDP are participants. Richer governments allocate additional aid.[22]

The same is usually true of major human rights abuses or of a widespread famine disaster: UN agencies, the world's media, national and international human rights organizations, the churches, and the foundations find themselves drawn into, or rather bring themselves into, the ring. These are no longer matters for governments alone to handle (if they ever did), and most governments are usually grateful for that. Many of these bodies also attend and play a significant role in UN global conferences, because their agendas (health, population, human rights, the habitat) also converge. Of course, there will be duplication and some confusion—among various sorts of women's organizations or food supply agencies and distribution programs that are acting independently, for example—but that is in the nature of the system. To the historian of these developments, though, there remains one critical methodological problem: Where exactly can one say that the United Nations itself was responsible for progress when the actions of its many agencies are marching in lockstep with the myriad nongovernmental players? Perhaps that is a question that cannot be fully answered and may after all be a secondary matter compared with the main story—a tale of variety and inventiveness and sheer range of the actors involved, all pushing toward common goals: the assistance and improvement of fellow human beings. But governments and parliaments that fund the UN's programs are entitled to ask the question.

The negative thought is this: Since so much of this activism is obviously generated and funded by richer, Northern foundations, media, churches, and NGOs, will it not inevitably be viewed by governments and peoples in the developing world as lopsided, patronizing, intrusive, and a mere sop to the fact that we have entered the twenty-first century with one-fifth of the world's population still possessing four-fifths of its wealth? And is that general suspicion reinforced by the particular prominence of the United States in today's international system, so that the activities of CNN, the Voice of America, the giant foundations, and the U.S. churches seem to be the tacit or even active allies of great multinational corporations, the Bretton Woods institutions, and the Pentagon's assertive global strategy? Such a notion would deeply upset the Quaker Relief Services and the liberal foundations, but that is not to say that these suspicions do not exist, perhaps especially these days in more troubled parts of the Muslim world. It is manifested in its most extreme form by the killing of Western journalists, attacks upon the Médecins sans Frontières, and bombings of UN offices. But the feeling that the richer countries patronize and then guiltily seek to emolliate the rest of the world is more broadly held.

However, many of these actors are working for the developing world and increasingly working with developing world partners. The Ford Foundation's long-standing support of village-level projects concerning the environment and women's empowerment in India, or the massive investments by the Gates Foundation to combat AIDS/HIV in Africa, are not condescensions but genuine attempts to help. Relief and nursing and educational services provided by the churches are motivated not by a power calculation, but by a deep sense of commitment to our common humanity. And while much of the Northern (chiefly U.S.) media is ignorant and patronizing about the rest of the world, a far larger number of liberal newspapers and journals go out of their way to empathize with and push the case for the less developed peoples of the globe. Finally, most of the UN agencies and specialized agencies have the matter of global poverty, disaster, relief, and development at the center of their mission. But, as the case of Wangari Maathai or the microbank loans in India demonstrates, this is not a matter of de haut en bas. There is a genuine North-South cooperation in thousands of places, and local actors count more and more. Perhaps that means little to the power brokers in Moscow, Beijing, and Washington. But it is there.

Is there something that can fairly be called "international civil society"? Yes. Is it growing and evolving? Yes. But there remains a problem. Our material, social, and scientific world is changing before our very eyes, and it will have changed much further when our children and grandchildren reach their maturity—yet the main instruments to deal with these transformations are still the nation-state structures so familiar to us, though palpably inadequate for the tasks ahead. This is why there are repeated calls for enhancing the powers of the General Assembly on the one hand and why there has been such self-mobilization of international civil society via the NGOs and other nonstate actors on the other. This is why there are the campaigns, however vague, for a world parliament or some analogous body. This is one reason there is such broad unease and dissatisfaction with the prevailing state of world affairs. All this, as Karl Marx remarked in another context, is the cry of the soul in a soulless world. And these pressures for a greater international arena, and more integrated action, will increase. Meanwhile, the member states will resist, especially the very large states, until perhaps sheer necessity forces a reconsideration upon even them.

PART 3

The Present and the Future

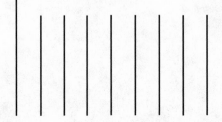

CHAPTER 8

The Promise and the Peril of the Twenty-first Century

There is an old analogy about perspective and history that suggests we are all members of a vast caravan that winds its way through the desert, with a range of mountains to one side. Those peaks appear to have a certain shape when advancing from the south. Yet they look different when the observers draw level to the mountains, and different again when casting a backward glance upon them. Perhaps we should approach our understanding of the UN in rather the same way. The founding fathers of the world organization, and the interested groups and media of the time, obviously viewed the meaning and purposes of the United Nations differently from the way we do—how could they not, especially in those epic years of 1943–46? In today's world, all of us (whether friendly, hostile, or indifferent to the organization) naturally view the UN in another light, one affected by sixty years of history. By 2050, publics, interest groups, and governments will doubtless regard this grand experiment of world governance in a very different way, as a result of the UN's various successes and failures in the decades to come. It would be unnatural not to do so.

This makes it extraordinarily difficult to suggest where advances might be made and where the chief obstacles to progress lie: The story is so complex and contradictory that it confuses the mind. But that is precisely the point. The message from the six parallel tales in Part Two is that the UN's record is a mixed one. Who could be surprised at that, since it is a human-based and fallible organization so dependent upon the whims of powerful national governments and the foibles of individual UN senior administrators? So if there has been a mixed success rate for the first sixty years of the body's life, we might reasonably assume that, along with progress, we will witness failure and disappointment in the decades to come. A complete collapse of the United Nations is not going to happen—so many nations and peoples have invested in it to prevent that happening. On the other hand, a massive constitutional restructuring of the world body as advocated in many radical reform schemes is also not possible right now, even if its merits are undeniable.

When the UN changes, if it changes at all, the transformations will therefore have to be partial and gradual. That is not to say they will be unimportant. They will matter a great deal. So a "softly, softly" approach to reforming the United Nations is critical, to get around the usual roadblocks by the Great Powers, national legislatures, and others who prefer things to stay the same. Change is not impossible, but the burden is on the reform-minded critics of the present system, whether they are indignant groups in the developing world or liberal internationalists in the developed world, to propose changes that might work. Any such proposals have to pass two tests: First, do they actually offer a prospect of measurable and practical improvement in our human condition; and second, do they have a good chance of being agreed to by the governments that control the world body?

The argument for reforming the United Nations organization to make it more effective, representative, and accountable is of greater urgency today than it was, say, twenty-five years ago because of various developments.

The first concerns power politics, as vital now as it was at the UN's foundation. The 1945 peace settlement was, as noted earlier, the first postwar order that gave veto privileges to a pentarchy of nations indefinitely, in a way that the earlier post–Great War settlements had not. But the ever changing nature of the international political system—in a word, the rise and fall of Great Powers—cannot be frozen or halted by a mere contract. The world moves on. Sweden and Spain were major players in 1648, minor actors by 1814, and barely involved at all by 1918 and 1945. So the international system in our unfolding twenty-first century faces a major systemic problem that national leaders have not even begun to contemplate, let alone tackle. The balances of global economic and military weight are altering, and swiftly. Perhaps the recent slew of predictions regarding those shifts are too assured, but unless there is some major catastrophe in Asia during the next decades, the general points are clear:

- By the time the United Nations celebrates its centennial in 2045, China could well constitute the largest economic and productive force in the world, bigger even than the United States;
- India may possess the third largest economy in the world, larger than Japan's and that of any individual European state (though not the European Union as a whole, which itself may have a gross national product [GNP] markedly larger than America's);
- Brazil, Indonesia, and possibly a revived Russia could be advancing fast, overtaking the traditional European states in economic heft.[1]

These are heady predictions, and it is unlikely that all these scenarios will unfold as today's forecasters suggest. But the basic point remains: The world's economic and, ultimately, power balances are changing faster than at any time since the 1890s, and if the United Nations remains encrusted in its 1945 constitution, it will appear—and really be—increasingly anachronistic. Governments and congresses that resist sensible proposals for modernizing the world body should recognize that they are condemning it to irrelevance. They might also in all decency cease from attacking the UN as an ineffective instrument when it is precisely they who have sought to make it so.

The second development that calls urgently for a revamping of the United Nations relates to the various global pressures upon humankind's capacity to maintain itself. These pressures are known to most literate people on this planet and contended only by eccentrics recruited to write pseudoscientific "denial" articles for conservative magazines. Pretty well all the environmental/atmospheric data now suggest that we face serious pressures on our ecologies and that global warming in particular is a certifiable fact. With glaciers disappearing throughout the Swiss Alps and the icefields of Antarctica vanishing into the sea, how could they not be? Bound up with this is the industrialization of Asia, very much driven by the need of their national regimes to provide better living standards to the peoples of China, India, Indonesia, and Pakistan—how exactly do you create prosperity for three billion people without destroying much of the globe? Even collectively we may not be able to solve this critical problem, but what is sure is that no single nation can do it alone. The challenge is an international one, to be tackled by international means.

The same is true with the relatively new phenomenon of international terrorism. One does not have to accept that this is the greatest danger to humankind (AIDS will claim many more victims) to admit that no society on the planet is free from random and beastly attack. Yet dealing with terrorism cannot be done by one country alone, however powerful. It will need consistent international action, through combined police work, shared intelligence, the destruction of terrorist cells, and heavy pressure against regimes that harbor terrorists. Complete success here seems unlikely—there will always be some wild breakaway terrorist organization bearing grudges and making unacceptable demands—but reducing their activities to the level where most people in the world can go about their normal business without fear or unreasonable inconvenience should be an aim accepted by all member states of the UN. To do that, they must cooperate.

Finally, and perhaps most important, the world community faces the challenge of how to deal with failed states; stanch their internal genocides, famines, and other calamities; and steadily restore such nations to their rightful sovereignty. As events in Bosnia, West Africa, Somalia, Afghanistan, and many other parts of the globe have shown, this is no easy task; it is one that in most cases will be a labor of many years and will see many setbacks. But dealing with failed states is unavoidable, since it is precisely here that one witnesses unacceptable levels of violence, abuse of women and children's rights, environmental degradation, and, very often, a nesting ground for terrorists.

All these are challenges to the 1945 constitution of the world body. The power-political implications of the rise of, say, India and Brazil to greater economic and strategic influence inevitably challenge the stranglehold that the five permanent veto-owning members have had in the Security Council over the past sixty years. It was an axiom of the UN's founding fathers that Great Powers had somehow to receive special (if negative) rights in order to prevent them from leaving or blocking the international system, as happened in the 1920s and 1930s. It would be hard to deny that argument to India if its GDP sails past that of Britain and France over the next decade or so. But the transnational changes described previously challenge the 1945 state-centered constitution even more, simply because they lie well outside the assumptions and expectations of the politicians who assembled at Bretton Woods, Dumbarton Oaks, Yalta, and San Francisco. There was no place in those days for such matters as international terrorism, global warming, or failed states; now they begin to occupy center stage. This leaves the international community with the fundamental question that many of its member states have been avoiding for decades: How are we to reconcile the "old" United Nations with the "new" and transformed global scene, thus making it more effective for today and tomorrow's great problems?

Before we grapple with that question, let us try to understand better what people mean when they use that all-important term *United Nations reform*. If one studies the varying "reform" proposals carefully, it becomes clear that the word is being used in three different ways or applied at three different levels, which accounts for much confusion.

The first, which one might call the "clean out the stables" approach, is essentially this: Shake up the system, cut back on overlapping agencies, and sack all those high-paid international bureaucrats living along the shores of Lake Geneva, thus reducing the cost to (especially American) taxpayers. In fact, a great deal of this has been done over the past decade, driven by the demands of critical

American congressmen and the responses of reform-minded senior UN officials. This approach is, obviously, negative. It involves reducing the United Nations in size and certainly not giving it any further powers. While pointing to undeniable inefficiencies in the present system, this school of thought is basically suspicious of international governance and the threat it might pose to unilateral national actions.

Second, and at the other end of the spectrum, there are calls for reform that would involve major changes in the UN's constitution—that is, an alteration in the Charter itself, which as noted earlier requires a two-thirds majority vote in the General Assembly and a concurrence (or at least a nonveto) by the Permanent Five.[2] These are the reforms that ardent internationalists, plus some aspiring governments, press for and are usually very bold indeed. Thus, the Ford Foundation–Yale University report of 1995 recommended an expansion of the Security Council (including five more permanent members), a reduction in the application of the veto (solely to urgent issues of war and peace), and the abolition of the ECOSOC (to be replaced by a more powerful Economic Council and a sister Social Council). Other reports, like that of the recent High-level Panel on Threats, Challenges and Change, recommend abolishing the Trusteeship Council.[3] Some call for a reduction in the independence of the Bretton Woods institutions, requiring them to report to the General Assembly. All of these imply significant shifts in power and privileges, and each and every one has already generated and will continue to produce strong debates. The question is, how likely are any of these to succeed?

The third approach occupies a middle position. It certainly does not want to diminish the United Nations; in contrast, it seeks to enhance its capacities and effectiveness, thus boosting its position in the eyes of governments and publics. Yet, recognizing the political and constitutional hurdles in the way of major Charter reform, it seeks for a package of incremental and practical changes—with the more distant hope that if these improvements prove successful, it might later be possible to secure significant constitutional alterations. This school of thought contains members who advocate some amendments to the Charter but maintain that their proposals are reasonable and that no government should feel threatened by them. Such views (also held by this author) disappoint the root-and-branch reformers for their lack of combativeness, and alarm the clean-out-the-stables groups, which are fearful that they might make the United Nations look better. As every study on UN reform has discovered, there is no easy way forward, only thickets and hurdles. Negotiating them is no easy task.

This point about the different possible "depths" of UN reform as well as their respective practicality can readily be seen in the debate over altering the membership and powers of the Security Council, the issue most mentioned when demands are made for change. Here one can identify three clusters of arguments (leaving aside the impractical notion that no member states should have special rights). The first is to leave things as they are. The 1945 arrangements are certainly not perfect and would not have been made if today's 191 members were setting up a new organization. But it is simply too difficult to pass large-scale Charter amendments these days. All the proposals to alter (that is, increase) the Security Council's membership would make it more cumbersome and thus less likely to work well. And the matter is so contentious and problem-strewn that the only thing such a debate would do is worsen many diplomatic relationships. Just don't touch the hornets' nest. One suspects that a fair number of politicians and officials in each of the P5 countries privately incline to this conservative way of thinking, even if their public statements often suggest that they are more open to considering additions to the select club.

The objection to this argument for stasis is explained a few pages earlier: It is that the shifting array of world forces will make the present array of exclusive privileges more and more anachronistic and less and less respected. The P5 might preserve their oligopoly for the next ten years, perhaps even twenty; but what would be the point? If the substructure of global power is altering, the superstructure cannot remain unaffected. It is for this reason that many of the governments that seek a place at high table (variously referred to among

UN diplomats as "aspirant," "contender," or "pretender" permanent veto nations), and many of the recent and distinguished international commissions and panels on Security Council reform, have pushed for important amendments to the Charter. Generally, they look to an expansion of the size of the Council from its present fifteen to around twenty-three to twenty-five members, but that overall increase would usually include additional permanent veto members as well as more nonpermanent, rotating members. The names of the candidate countries most often short-listed for elevation are Japan and Germany (as the second and third largest contributors to the UN budget), together with some rising pivotal states in the developing world, India, Brazil, and South Africa. Occasionally this scheme is accompanied by the idea that there be only one European Union permanent seat, occupied on a rotating principle. As a result, it is argued, such an amended Security Council would allow the world body to recover the legitimacy and respect it has steadily been losing.

This is where the fur begins to fly. Would China welcome giving the veto to India and, more particularly, to Japan? One doubts it. Would France and the United Kingdom agree to surrender their single national seat? Unlikely. Could a rotation of European Union states, large and small, bring any consistency of policy to the Security Council's deliberations, if it was Denmark for six months and then Greece, with the larger European powers not occupying a Security Council seat for the next three years or so? Would Russia agree to a Japanese veto? Hmn. When Germany is mentioned as a front-runner, the Italian government strongly opposes the idea. Pakistan, joined perhaps by other nations in the Muslim world, would be exceptionally uneasy at the scheme to elevate India. Japan's neighbors (quite apart from China) are not enthused by Tokyo's arguments. In Latin America, the assumption that Brazil is the "natural" representative of the region is stoutly denied by Mexico and Argentina; and in Africa, the idea that the Union of South Africa is the obvious choice is contended by Nigeria and by Egypt (whose government makes the additional point that no Arab nation possesses a permanent seat). Then there are the objections of the smaller member states, which don't want any additions to the privileged club: Five veto powers are bad enough.

Such regional political jealousies are accompanied, or clothed, by other reservations that have some force. It is often difficult for the Security Council to agree on war and peace resolutions, even with only five countries capable of blocking common action. Having ten countries constitutionally able to put a spoke into the wheel would, logically, make the chances of Security Council authorization regarding some contentious future crisis twice as hard. The greater the number of governments with a veto, the lower the number of peacekeeping and (especially) peace enforcement cases upon which all can agree. Is that what the reformers want?

This combination of political rivalries and practical worries has caused some scholars to seek to a middle way in regard to Security Council reform. Being compromise proposals, they look messy and arcane to the outside observer, and even expert insiders have to parse the language carefully. For example, the recent High-level Panel of 2004–5 offered a complex package of alternatives, one of which suggested: Do not disturb the P5's privileges, or nothing will get done at all; increase the total number of Security Council members from fifteen to twenty-four; divide the nineteen rotating members according to regions (Africa would get six in total, Europe a smaller number because it already possesses three veto seats, and so on); and, finally, create some six new permanent (but nonveto) seats or establish eight new four-year memberships, regionally based, as well as regular two-year memberships. This clearly is an attempt to square the circle or several circles: Avoid angering the P5, respond to the demands that the Council should be bigger overall, and give some regional powers a special place, thus creating a three-tiered Security Council membership. Desperate to get at least some changes, a majority of the General Assembly may, in the future, vote in favor of something like this; and the P5, their privileges preserved, may not oppose. But it is a clumsy device, like aircraft designs around 1910.

There are simpler and rather more cunning ways to advance the prospect of making the Security Council more representative and

breaking the logjam by recognizing that certain of the non-P5 countries are indeed "special" and most likely candidates for promotion
to a higher status. The first would be an amendment to the UN Charter that would merely raise the number of rotating members from its
present ten to around eighteen or nineteen, thus recognizing the
world body's growth in numbers over the past forty years. There
would be no conditions about four-year and two-year memberships.
Simply increase the number of rotating states, so that more of them
could have exposure to being on the Council. Second, just amend the
(Article 23, Part 2) restraint that nonpermanent members have to re-
tire after two years. The old principle has its merits (giving everyone
a turn), but frankly, if a nation such as Singapore or Germany has
done great service over the preceding two years on the Security Council and is supported for prolongation by its friends and neighbors,
why make that impossible? Then—a real act of faith—let us see how
the combination of these two nonthreatening amendments would
work over the next years. If, say, South Africa was reelected for a second or a third time, the notion that it might become a permanent
member, and then one with a veto, would seem less and less strange
to the P5 and others.

The specifics of these middle ground suggestions are not as important as what they have in common: attempts to crack the ice. Simply
getting a couple of amendments to the UN Charter with respect to
Security Council membership would be a step in the right direction, a
precedent in themselves. Not swift or decisive enough, perhaps, in
light of our changing world. But any serious and thoughtful effort to
turn this vast ship away from foundering on the rocks ahead should
be supported.

The privilege of permanency on the Security Council is the first
distinction of the P5. The second is the power of the veto, which,
though intimately linked, is a separate matter. After all, one could in
theory have some large nations always on the Security Council but no
one having a veto. But that is, indeed, pure theory. Then there is the
suggestion that in any future expansion of the Security Council, certain substantial nations (the usual list, Germany, India, and so on)
could have permanency but without the veto, while the P5 retained

their 1945 rights. This would most definitely create a three-class system, one that has been vigorously opposed by the leading "pretender" nations (although some of them are so desirous of permanency that they may soften their stance) and by most countries that would, in effect, be in the lowest tier. A third idea, both desperate and ingenious, is that a Security Council resolution could be blocked only by the veto of two permanent members, something that, again in theory, makes a lot of sense if the P5 should ever expand to be P10. Yet it seems highly unlikely that neuralgic governments in Washington and Beijing would make this concession, or those in Moscow and Paris, for that matter.

Thus, proposals to make modest changes in the size of the Security Council seem to have more prospect of gaining broad agreement—or provoking less opposition—than the various schemes to amend the sacred, encrusted veto. Perhaps the best that might be done under the present charged circumstances would be for the General Assembly to ask the P5 to agree to the principle of using the veto only as a measure of last resort, in decisions about war and peace that directly affect national security interests—which is, of course, what the UN's founders envisaged. Were this to be agreed upon, the vetoing, for example, of a certain candidate who was supported by the vast bulk of nations to be the next secretary-general would not transpire. Even this might be too much for certain hypersensitive members of the P5. One is left only with the hope that the five nations enjoying these remarkable privileges will always recognize how sparingly they should be used and how heavy a blow they deal—to the world body and to themselves—when the veto right is abused. Truly, the establishment of a hard-to-alter constitution for the Security Council in 1945 has come at a very high price.

Because of these difficulties of Charter amendment, some reformist groups have been looking at other ways to make the UN's security apparatus more effective. All of them are incremental, though not without controversy, since they pertain directly to the issues of peacekeeping and warmaking that were discussed in Chapter Three and continue to excite passions today. And because opinions on peacekeeping/enforcement divide so bleakly into those who think the world body has been trying to do too much and those who protest that it has done too little, suggestions about future improvements assume the same risks as a convoy steering through a minefield. Virtually all of these writings (even the negative ones) focus on ways to improve the international community's capacity to deal with human disasters, civil conflict, and the severe weakening or collapse of member states. And their discussions concern those 1945 worries about one nation attacking another less than they do today's internal wars and transborder mayhem about the newer threats to state sovereignty.

One example of this pragmatic reformist agenda is the push to improve intelligence on impending threats. It is a lesson derived from the multitude of exploding crises during the 1990s—namely, that the international organization needs a much better system of gathering and dissecting data regarding unfolding disasters. There are, of course, many local sources of information about troubled places, spreading famine, and rising ethnic conflict, sources such as NGOs, human rights organizations, the churches abroad, and reporters from Reuters, AP, and other news agencies, all of whom are networked electronically. So the real question is, across which desk can all this information be assembled and analyzed, in order to brief the secretary-general when he alerts the Security Council to a worsening crisis within a member state or a broader region? And the only feasible answer is that this UN central intelligence office has to be located in, or beside, the Department of Peacekeeping Operations itself. Suspicious neocons may whine at the idea of the world body having its own CIA, and neuralgic oppressor states will surely protest that the collective gathering of data about atrocities in their territories is an invasion of national sovereignty. But all such yelps should be dismissed as self-serving and obstructionist. The need is too great, and the work that has been already done in this field should obtain greater empowerment and, where necessary, resources in the future.

Although that idea addresses the challenges antecedent to a state's breakdown, there is an even greater urgency for better coordination of the UN's responses to crisis. To head off a deteriorating situation in its early stages is the ideal, but the world body is usually constrained by political factors (some members suspicious about too early interventions) and by the fact that it is already grappling with so many problems elsewhere. Thus, whatever is done to strengthen the UN's "proactive" strategies, the international community definitely needs many improvements in its "reactive" capacities to civil wars and social breakdowns. Practically speaking, all of the components are already identified: UN blue helmets (or other delegated military forces) to provide physical security; specialized bodies to help (re)train local police, judges, administrators; World Bank and UNDP capacities, alongside those of the UN Regional Banks, to identify priorities for economic and social recovery; experienced election monitors; a track record of working with international NGOs; and much else besides. What is so often lacking is political will and a lead body to coordinate the multiple efforts. Without falling into the trap that there is a UN state-rebuilding template to be moved from one situation to the next, it is clear that the world organization and its agencies have been building up formidable knowledge of best practices, which now needs to be harnessed to assist future rescue endeavors. Once again, it is hard to see how this can be done without some central coordination and the active participation of the Secretary-General's Office or a designated offshoot.

A further lesson from the peacekeeping operations of the past fifteen or so years is that it is almost always a mistake to assume that the restoration of collapsed states takes only a relatively brief amount of time; that all that is necessary is to send in a military force to defeat the "bad guys," then commence civilian reconstruction and democratic elections and smoothly withdraw from the scene, marking up another success score. The cases of backsliding are considerable (Haiti, East Timor, Cambodia, West Africa), with newer examples possible (Afghanistan, Iraq). Many recently established regimes are often weak, partisan, and possessed of little regard for the claims of the opposition, or for any critics and opponents at all. Tribal and religious differences resurface. The amount of aid and technical assistance is never enough. And when the foreign legions go home, so too do many NGOs (usually to a new crisis) and much of the world's media. What is clearly needed here is a better "after-care" or "after-sales" service, something that a partially rebuilt country may find difficult to obtain when open civil war and genocide is occurring in other regions, unless, of course, it suffers its own further relapse. When that happens, it may attract less help from richer states burdened by donor fatigue and prone to ask: "But I thought we had fixed the problem in [for instance] Haiti?"

A midlevel reform as just suggested makes sense to most people. Governments and agencies will certainly quarrel about processes and priorities, but no one would dispute that having a better early-warning system is a good thing. Much more controversial, though, are the various ideas about how to give the United Nations more physical (that is, military) resources so as to act faster and more decisively when a catastrophe or genocide is unfolding swiftly. The practical argument for this is incontestable. The failure in recent times of the world community in general and the Security Council in particular to get an international force into a troubled area in time to stop the bloodshed (Rwanda being the worst example) rightly caused much hand-wringing and provoked a flood of new ideas.

As we have seen, the real problem has been that while the Security Council seemed increasingly willing to mandate lots of peacekeeping and peace enforcement actions, it left it to the secretary-general to go, cap in hand, to member states and ask them to contribute troops. Governments in turn might need to consult their parliaments, take advice from their own militaries (many of which are ill equipped for distant operations), and thus respond slowly—if at all. Were there to be UN standing forces, equipped and trained to the same standards and positioned in some select bases around the globe, their battalions and brigades could be dispatched to the trouble spot just as soon as the Security Council had authorized action.[4] Whether the troops in question were individual volunteers or battalions recruited nationally and then given blue helmets could be experimented with. The main thing would be their availability. Cost is a secondary consideration; most probably, this scheme would save money.

Roughly, one could divide member states into those incapable of contributing (often being failing states themselves or too poor or small), those unwilling to assist (China), and those willing in theory to contribute but by that stage suffering a form of military donor fatigue. Perhaps the most commendable efforts have been experiments by the Canadians, who studied this problem carefully and then established an advanced force (in Fredericton, New Brunswick) ready to move as soon as the government agreed to the secretary-general's request for troop contribution. This is an intelligent measure but is only a drop in the bucket. Still, were it to be imitated in the future by other nations, many of which possess considerably larger armies than Canada, it may be that a combined total of up to one hundred thousand UN-designated troops (plus specially trained police) would be available.[5] That would certainly be a step forward.

Another stumbling block to the establishment of a UN army is the paranoia of some American politicians. Ignoring the fact that the United States would always have a veto on any proposed Chapter VI and VII actions, but determined that the world body should be kept weak lest it threaten national sovereignty, such politicians warn that any steps taken to establish a form of UN army would be regarded as a hostile act. Given the power of Congress, that is a serious threat. So this proposal lies on a back shelf, at least for a while. It will be worth looking at it again sometime in the future.

Whatever the category and constitutionality of the forces deployed in the various operations the UN is conducting and will continue to initiate, there clearly is some need for a professional military body to oversee things. Preparatory work before troop contingents are sent, establishing an intelligence system to understand local conditions, creating effective chains of command, ensuring that the flow of logistical supplies never breaks down, and defining the military's role when it is actually in the area are tasks that only professionals with many years of staff training can perform. This is vital for success at the local level, but the need for more general (and comparative) oversight, and thus some central office to watch all this and report to the secretary-general and the Security Council, has caused a revival of the notion of using the UN's Military Staff Committee. It may be recalled that the committee still exists, although in a moribund state owing to disagreements during the early Cold War. Yet anyone who peruses

Article 47 of the Charter—"There shall be established a Military Staff Committee to advise and assist the Security Council on all questions relating to the Security Council's military requirements"— might be forgiven for assuming that this problem is easily solved: The requisite body is there, merely sleeping. Why not resuscitate it?

Here is an idea that meets a triple roadblock. The first is that the traditional leading contributors to UN peacekeeping missions (the Scandinavians, Dutch, Latin American states, old British Commonwealth countries) are uneasy at the disposition of their readily available forces being in the hands of a military staff dominated by Great Powers, for that would enhance the latter's special privileges even more than at present. Second, this feeling that the Permanent Five could influence events in favor of their own national interests rather than in fulfillment of the peacekeeping mission's stated purposes and indeed of the Charter itself is even more strongly held among G-77 countries. The very sentence (Article 47, Part 2) that representation on the Military Staff Committee by non-P5 military personnel requires a test of their capacity to carry out "efficient discharge" of required duties for a particular operation can only remind India, Brazil, and other members of their second-class status, even if their track records in peacekeeping are better than certain other militaries in the developing—or developed—world.

The third objection comes from some of the armed services of the developed nations, as always with the United States military to the fore. American enthusiasm for joint staff arrangements, which might mean U.S. troops being under a foreign commander and U.S. war aims being compromised by the demands of allies, has never been strong; it reached a (medium) high point under Roosevelt and Marshall in World War II, but since then has slid continually downhill. The two wars against Iraq simply confirmed the Pentagon's prejudice: It could act more swiftly and decisively when not hampered by layers of multinational consultation and decision making. Peacekeeping operations were bad enough; reporting to a UN command would be anathema. From a strictly military standpoint, such concern about effectiveness is probably valid, and one supposes that the defense ministries of the other P5 nations hold similar (though less strongly expressed) reservations.

It is clear that a large-scale military action like the recent Iraq war could not be managed from an office in New York. But that conclusion does not help the Security Council and Secretariat work out how the world organization may better exercise responsibility over a plethora of smaller and less contentious peacekeeping operations or supervise the preparatory and force coordination measures. If the revival of the Military Staff Committee is politically impossible, and if the number one power blocks any attempts to create a UN standing force, how can present and future emergencies at this level be handled from the center? How do the larger and more capable member states (one excuses very small and impoverished states here) live up to their solemn Charter pledge (Article 1) "to take effective collective measures for the prevention and removal of threats to the peace, and for the suppression of acts of aggression"?

The obvious, rather desperate reply is that the Big Five, and those countries capable of giving to rather than taking from the world community, should live up to the great responsibilities to which they legally committed themselves upon entering the world body. But until that happens, one simply has to turn elsewhere and be as creative as possible, acknowledging that the measures taken will be far from ideal. It may be that, as we suggested in Chapter Three, perhaps a standardized response to international crises is not in itself the best way to proceed. As we have seen, the instinct in the early 1990s to produce a peacekeeping template (as in An Agenda for Peace) that would serve for all cases was too tight; East Timor simply was, and is, different from Macedonia. So, while the experiences of the past decade and a half have been bruising, what they offer, collectively, is a caution against uniformity. They suggest instead a multitool approach, using different instruments, combinations, and institutions for different crises—a strategy, one suspects, that the ever pragmatic P5 have already adopted privately.

Consider, for example, the array of the forms of peacekeeping that now exist in today's fractured world:

- There are the traditional UN "blue helmet" operations, most of them very long-standing, usually occupying an intervening strip of land following a cease-fire between the two parties, with the peacekeepers required to be completely impartial and the former belligerents agreeing not to cross the provisional cease-fire line. If the UN negotiators cannot broker a final and political settlement, then the blue helmets continue to stay in place, as has been the case in, for example, Kashmir (UNMOGIP), Cyprus (UNFICYP), and Lebanon (UNIFIL). The troop contingents usually come from distant and noninvolved member states, and such operations are normally run under the supervision of the Department of Peace-keeping Operations and thus the Security Council itself. This is the sort of peacekeeping that many medium-size and neutral states prefer, believing it to be most approximate to the intentions of the Charter. The Great Powers contribute little here, which means that the UN units committed have little "punch"; but that is not re-garded as a major problem, since they are not expected to fight.
- There are the regional peacekeeping efforts, involving a combina-tion of neighboring states that have received Security Council sanction (under the perfectly plain Articles 52–54) to attempt to restore peace and order to a troubled or failed nation in their part of the world. The work of the ECOWAS group of states in West Africa to improve the situation along the borders of Liberia, Guinea, and Sierra Leone is a case in point.
- There has increasingly occurred the "farming out" of peacekeep-ing and, especially, peace enforcement missions to regional defense organizations, which may also—if one pushes it—be interpreted as being within the Charter's provisions but is much more con-troversial because it involves heavy action by some of the P5 and essentially is removed from any purview of the Depart-ment of Peacekeeping Operations. The most prominent would be the NATO peace enforcement missions in the Balkans and Afghanistan, involving powerful and well-resourced military units, including, of course, vital contributions from a Pentagon that prefers almost anything to direct UN supervision.

- There are the operations in which an individual member state, usually with the Security Council's blessing, has undertaken to quench slaughter, interethnic mayhem, and political collapse. But the "lead nation" here usually enwraps the enforcement mission with the trappings of an international enterprise by obtaining small-scale troop and police contributions from other countries, especially those in the area. The Australian lead role in quelling East Timor's convulsions and Britain's in Sierra Leone are examples of the kinds of operations that are likely to be repeated in future.

In some places like Afghanistan, it is indeed possible that various of these formats may operate alongside one another—clumsy on paper, no doubt, but not outrageous if they prove to work on the ground. This seems to be the general drift: Do not insist upon a uniform recipe for peacekeeping and peace enforcement, but let each case be considered in its own context. At present, this is probably more effective than any other route, given the insistence of such grumpy P5 powers as the United States and China that the world organization not assume too much authority and control in this ultrasensitive area. All crises should be referred to the Security Council, as the Charter requires, but the circumstances alone—on the ground and in the delicate balances within the Council itself—would dictate the response. Authorization of a regional response, or a lead country's role, or farming out to an organization such as NATO, or simply deciding to take no action would each become acceptable options.

To those who strive for a more enhanced and uniform role in peacekeeping for the United Nations, such an ad hoc policy smacks of failure. If each case is to be treated sui generis, and the responses to them are also negotiated individually, then it may be more difficult to prepare standardized resources and to train mixed-nation contingents (if a member state has committed troops to a mixed force but doesn't agree to a particular operation, how does that affect the force that is ready to go?). It probably implies more work for the overstrained Office of the Secretary-General and for the Security Council itself. It clearly brings more risk of inconsistency and of double standards. It may be that one catastrophe is treated differently from others and that the fate of the Kurds is deemed more important than that of the inhabitants of Chad. The Department of Peacekeeping Operations can handle the lesser cases while members of the P5 run the more politically charged operations, as in Afghanistan and Iraq. Such a flexible response strategy, despite its advantages, affirms the privileges of the veto powers to decide how much action they wish the world organization to take. This is not a happy result, but faced with an alternative that nothing gets done in distressed regions, various sorts of UN peacekeeping operations, however compromised and circumscribed, are better than none at all.

Finally, whatever the definition and scope of a peacekeeping and peace enforcement action authorized by the Security Council may be, it is clear that much more attention has to be given to the dynamics of the "transition" or "recovery" phase. (It has been mentioned earlier, but the point needs reinforcing again and again.) This stage is absolutely vital for the reputation of the world body, as well as the long-term restoration of the country under treatment. It is one thing to drive away limb-chopping thugs in Sierra Leone or to topple dictators like Saddam Hussein, but quite another to devise a due process for a nation's long-term recovery. While recognizing that each crisis will contain different elements and obstacles, we ought to admit that there are common procedures, although most are in need of clarification. When, for example, should a UN peacekeeping operation no longer be a Security Council item but one that is transferred to another body? Which agency should normally take the lead role in long-term reconstruction? One candidate here is the World Bank, simply because of its relatively larger resources (and leverage) and its experience in drawing up "country plans." But perhaps there needs to be a special coordinating office in each of the failed states, since the tasks outrun the expertise of even the biggest agencies. After all, who would supervise the transition from a UN military framework for internal security to a regular police administration in, say, the Congo? Who would be responsible for working with local leaders and groups to plan and execute elections, the rule of law, and the creation of civil society? When does the task end?

There is, of course, one nifty answer to those questions: Why not return to the Charter itself and give new life to one of its principal organs, the Trusteeship Council? We may recall that its declared purpose is "to promote the political, economic, social, and educational advancement" of the lands in question and assist "their progressive development towards self-government" in accordance with their peoples' wishes (Article 76). Broadly interpreted, that could extend to current and future UN efforts to help failed states recover their independence and sovereignty; and, after all, the Trusteeship Council and its specific national administrations were and are to report to the Security Council on "strategic" matters and to the General Assembly on all other matters. This surely covers any worries about accountability.[6]

The reason this notion will not work is that mere mention of this Council infuriates countries that were not sovereign in 1945 and remain sensitive to any hint of covert Western colonialism and patronizing. Reviving the Trusteeship Council is thus politically impossible. In fact, if in the future a group of Charter additions and deletions were being pushed through, it would be appropriate to abolish this anachronistic section (Chapters XII–XIII, Articles 75–91); it would also reduce the Charter's length by a sizable amount.[7] Yet those who seek abolition have themselves an obligation to explain how we might find better mechanisms to help broken communities recover their governance and move toward stability, prosperity, and democracy. The developing world has certainly much to criticize about our unbalanced, unfair global system. But it does not help to invoke the dictum of no interference in domestic matters when millions of human beings may be encountering mass poverty, ethnic slaughters, or other violations of human rights even after a UN peace enforcement mission has driven a villainous regime from the field. Something more positive is needed, especially given the weakness of the Economic and Social Council.

It is evident that, as the peacekeeping and peace enforcement operations in any particular country wind to their close, the responsibility of assisting distressed communities will normally move from the UN's "hard power" instruments to the panoply of civilian actors dedicated to rebuilding and to longer-term assistance. This suggests two steps, at least, that ought to be taken. The first is that the Security Council, after consulting interested (that is, regional) members of the General Assembly, should give the secretary-general the power to appoint a country coordinator (with an adequate office) and instruct all parts of the UN organization to cooperate with that office for the larger purpose of restoring the sovereignty and advancing the quality of life of a collapsed state. This implies not only an integration of the efforts of immediate UN bodies, but also the harnessing of the expertise and resources of the independent agencies and Bretton Woods institutions as well as an imaginative enrollment of significant NGOs. Attempts at this sort of coordinated rebuilding are being attempted, of course, but it is clear that the firm (if distant) mandate of the Security Council gives the greatest authority and legitimacy to any program of national restoration.

A second, somewhat more novel idea would be to involve the General Assembly in a larger consultation about the rebuilding of collapsed societies. As many observers note, the division between the work of the Security Council and the interests and potential contributions of the General Assembly has often been artificial and damaging. Already, ideas exist about joint Security Council–General Assembly cooperation, through a working group, on matters of arms control regarding weapon systems large and small.[8] But the case for establishing some new forum (not necessarily by Charter amendment) for allowing elements of the General Assembly to provide input into the process of rebuilding is even stronger, because it is precisely during this transition phase that the military security dimensions of the task give way more and more to civilian activities, and here non-P5 members, not capable of heavy fighting, might reasonably take on rebuilding and training efforts. One recent report (that of the High-level Panel) has anticipated this reasoning by arguing for a new and powerful Peacebuilding Commission, whose remit would run from anticipating (and heading off) state collapse to coordinating the rebuilding efforts if the nation should break down. However structured, this type of activity would not only give more legitimacy to the UN, it would also show that the General Assembly is not being excluded by the Security Council in matters and regions in which many member states take the deepest interest.

These suggestions for improving our peacekeeping and peace enforcement strategies constitute a formidable list. But no single proposal is decisive; journalists searching for a "hot" theme in this analysis will go away disappointed. And the same might be said for all and any of the ideas that may help to address the equally tangled issue of advancing socioeconomic justice for the world at large. As we saw earlier, the Charter itself asked members to pledge themselves to "employ international machinery for the promotion and economic advancement of all peoples" and to solve "international economic, social, health and related problems"—no small task at the best of times. Yet, however ambitious, this is the area of prime concern to the majority of nations in the General Assembly, which have frequently expressed irritation that the world body focuses too much on security and not enough on development.

The debate about advancing the UN's economic and social agendas takes a different form from the Security Council/veto discussions precisely because it does not possess a "P5 versus the rest" dimension (even if the voting arrangements within the Bretton Woods institutions decidedly enhance the privileged). Yet this does not mean that the debate is less charged. After all, it is in the economic, social, technological, and environmental arenas that the world has changed fastest of all. Our planet really is different—demographically, environmentally, socially, geopolitically—from the world our grandfathers created in 1945. How could it not be when, in one person's memory, the earth's population has tripled from around two billion people (1950) to six billion (2000) and expanded tenfold in its total product, from $4 trillion to $40 trillion, in the same period?

The world economy, and global society, has thus been transformed and changed at a faster pace in recent decades than in all history. The big question as concerns our inquiry is, what might the United Nations organization do in the socioeconomic fields that no one else can do? To the founding fathers in 1944–45, it seemed obvious that the international machinery they were creating was necessary because so much of the world was in end-of-war distress and needed acute help. If the United Nations itself, and the Bretton Woods organizations, could not provide that help, little would happen. Such large-scale institution building had to be done, both to meet current needs and as a demonstration that the neglect and isolationism of the interwar years would never be repeated. It is so difficult nowadays to recapture that budding optimism and the high spirit of those who, sixty years ago, thought that a new world order was approaching, or had arrived.

The same challenge is here today, in a different form. There are, though, two major constraints on the international community coming together to push for ambitious social and economic policies. The first is the miserable and neglected condition of the ECOSOC, not all its own fault but miserable nonetheless, together with the controversial status of the IMF and World Bank, whose legitimacy is contested from many sides. The second and even more fundamental problem actually arises from a positive trend: the fact that so many former Third World countries like Singapore, Chile, and Hong Kong have developed themselves without much aid from the global financial institutions.[9] With giant nations like China and India (40 percent of the world's population) following the same trajectory, and under their own steam, it is no wonder that many economists nowadays question whether international instruments—other than market-enforcing bodies like the WTO—have a role. Thirty years ago, the G-77 was a recognizable and self-defined group. Today, with Singapore enjoying an average per capita income more than forty times that of Mozambique, the solidity has gone. So, too, perhaps, may have gone the appeal of collective economic action.

This suggests that whatever measures the world body undertakes for the greater economic and social good of its citizens should be done on a selective basis, in those fields where member states can have little impact acting alone but can move things by working collectively. The first area is in regard to financial, currency, and trade instabilities among the major economic zones, to avoid a meltdown of the international economic order; in that respect, we have advanced little since the 1930s and 1940s, with Keynes's wrestlings on those matters (which still represent some of the most acute observations upon this tricky field). The second concerns the rescue and rehabilitation of the world's poorest sixty states, which, as the UNDP and World Bank recognized years ago, are in such a desperate plight that they simply are not going to recover by themselves. In particular—though pointing to a single ailment may seem rash—the forecast explosion in poorer countries of the number of men, women, and children with HIV/AIDS demands massive international effort. The third field lies in the need for measures to reduce the impact of human action upon our tender world ecologies. In all these dimensions of our lives, we must indeed all hang together or, most assuredly, we will hang separately.

But it is far easier to state the problems than to propose the solutions, and in all cases the reason for the difficulty is political. Take the case of global fiscal and currency instabilities. It is nice for neoclassical economists to echo Adam Smith and proclaim that what is needed for prosperity is good governance, fiscal probity, and an encouragement of fruitful industry. Alas, politicians and publics often do not act that way. Governments run fiscal imbalances, mortgaging themselves to the markets. They keep their currencies artificially high or artificially low, as if either will help them in the long run. They protect insecure and inefficient sectors of the economy (agriculture, heavy industry, old bureaucracies) and thus throttle world growth. When they allocate foreign aid, a vast proportion is not an open gift at all but tied firmly to domestic agricultural subsidies and military transfers. There are few good Samaritans in this story.

More specifically, a United States that runs colossal fiscal and trade deficits, relying upon Asian banks to purchase its Treasury bonds, is a force for trouble. A China that deliberately keeps its currency low is no help at all. European states that solemnly sign Maastricht principles regarding fiscal discipline but then abandon them weaken the system and themselves. An India that, though bursting to join the globalized economy, protects its favored service industries is another drag. And corrupt regimes everywhere—nicely highlighted these days by the reports of NGOs like Transparency International and Amnesty International—make sure that Keynesian high principles for fair economic cooperation and good governance do not come to pass. Gradually, perhaps, each will see the folly of its actions. But until then, genuine international coordination is cramped.

Yet washing one's hands of the UN's work in these fields represents both intellectual defeatism and political escapism. However messy, the repair job has to be attempted and pursued. Diplomats, public servants, and scholars with decades of experience in this realm have pointed to changes that, undertaken seriously, could bring improvements—and not just to the organization's image, but to its effectiveness. It is important, though, that suggested reforms be presented not as a lengthy shopping list, but as a shorter list of ideas that have a practical chance of being followed.

First of all, the specialized agencies that focus on economic and social matters, particularly the World Bank group and the IMF, but also the others (WTO, ILO), have got to take a serious further look at how they "shall be brought into relationship with the United Nations," as Article 57 of the Charter coyly says. The dubious 1947 legal opinion that the Bretton Woods institutions carry out only economic and not political measures makes less and less sense in a world where financial and sociopolitical instabilities grind against each other. This means, of course, that the governments of those large and powerful economies that think they have virtually permanent entitlement to being on the Executive Boards of the IMF and World Bank also have to grapple seriously with the prospect for change.[10] Perhaps they need to be reminded that the very constitution of those bodies implies that their membership will be altered soon if the forecasts of the shifting global economic balances turn out to be correct. To give but one example, what would be the implications for future policies of the World Bank's board of executive directors (five out of the twenty-four are appointed by the countries having the largest number of shares) if China, India, and Brazil were indeed to have bigger GNPs than Japan and individual European states? Membership at the high table of the Security Council remains deep-frozen, but that may not be so for the financial institutions in the years to come. The agendas of the new leading economic powers by the year 2025 will certainly differ from those of the present. Better to think about it now.

It is also incumbent upon the directors (and thus their governors and central banks) to come through with sensible proposals to reduce the "Holy Roman Empire" structures of the global financial and trade institutions. Will G-7 or G-8 meetings and their solemn declarations in the future make much sense with the emergence of a broader-based G-24 (or some other total figure); and how will the twenty-four directors of the IMF and World Bank relate in real policy terms to G-24 intergovernmental agreements? How, above all, will these various parts of global economic management forge a more understanding relationship with giant free market companies, banks, and investors who are transforming our early-twenty-first-century society? Naïve laissez-faire advocates argue that the capitalist world is marching in a different direction from that of the semi-socialist international creations of 1945, but no intelligent CEO of a multinational corporation—BP, Toyota, Pepsico—believes that it's possible to thrive without global stability and security, and they are the first to admit where the private market's role is inadequate and desperately needs the contribution of international agencies. What they don't know— does anyone know?—is how to achieve a symbiosis between the business world and international governance, and to that end much thought and work is essential. Yet the situation that faced the planners and businessmen of 1944–45 was even more challenging. This is not the time to be daunted or evasive.

The central weakness here is the feebleness of the ECOSOC, for what is the point of a coordinating body that cannot coordinate? This is recognized by every serious study of the world organization. Traditionalists urge that the matter can be promptly rectified if all member states agree to honor the wording of the Charter (Chapters IX–X) and infuse the Economic and Social Council with the powers and roles set out in that document. More radical schemes propose the creation of a powerful Economic Security Council—with the stature, indeed, of the Security Council itself; or suggest that the ECOSOC's many tasks be handed over to two smaller and nimbler bodies, a UN Economic Council and a closely linked Social Council. Both, clearly, imply the high hurdle of Charter amendment. And the problem with all such ideas, and indeed of every neat suggestion issued by "high-level" and "distinguished" commissions, is that without positive support from the larger powers, nothing significant will get done.

Yet the present weakness of a "principal organ" of the UN like the ECOSOC is such that the General Assembly ought honestly to confront the blunt alternative: Kill it or cure it. The latter will be the only acceptable solution for those governments that see the ECOSOC as an antithesis to the Security Council—a place where the weaker and poorer countries have their voice, a body where regional membership rotation stands in contrast with P5 privileges, a world institution whose many agencies and committees do useful work on behalf of the less powerful. Furthermore, it is not as if all parts of the ECOSOC have failed. One would not wish to abolish its Commission on Narcotics Drugs or its Commission on the Status of Women. True, one's eyes glaze over at the mention of the Committee of Experts on the Transport of Dangerous Goods and on the Globally Harmonized System of Classification and Labelling of Chemicals, but in an age of possible biochemical terrorism, its role may be rising, not shrinking.

The ECOSOC problem, then, lies not in its parts but in the whole. A body of fifty-four (three-year rotating) members who meet "in substantive session" for only four weeks each July is not a serious enterprise. Whatever the howls of protest from the international levelers, surely it makes more sense for a smaller body of, say, twenty-four member states (one-third from the developed world, one-third from the larger developing states, one-third from small countries) to meet more regularly, with the power to bring all international entities into consultation and cooperative planning? The World Health Organization, for example, simply cannot be expected to carry the burden of global AIDS/HIV, nor can the UN Environment Programme work alone in its critical field. Yet without a coordinating body of some considerable authority, agency efforts will be splintered. When one thinks again of the challenges of rebuilding a single collapsed state and the lack of an overall coordinating agency, the point becomes compelling. Both at the local level and in New York/Geneva, there is a crying case for more simplified but also more authoritative structures if the UN's remit here is to be carried out.[11]

But such reforms of the ECOSOC (and, by implication, of the General Assembly itself) require a chance of general acceptance. Proposals from the Left—to fully "democratize" the United Nations—have no prospect of acceptance by the established powers. Criticisms from the Right, that the ECOSOC is corrupt, ineffective, and mired in its own past, are of little help. Yet those conservative observers make valid points that all who wish to enhance the UN ought to take seriously. There is a need for more transparency and commitment from every member state that is elected to the ECOSOC and its committees and to other bodies that are part of the General Assembly's "family." There is a need for challenging a strict regional-rotational system of national representation if an incoming candidate nation is remiss in its own governance. What a wonderful boost the ECOSOC would have given itself had it declared in 2004 that the government of Sudan was not qualified to become a member of the UN's Commission on Human Rights! As the recent High-level Panel on the UN's future tartly observes, the reinforcement of human rights "cannot be performed by States that lack a demonstrated commitment to their promotion and protection."[12]

The reader can by now guess the way this argument is going. In an ideal world, it would be good for significant structural changes to be made to the UN's economic and social architecture and policies—as good, no less, as an ideal transformation in the membership of the Security Council and in the practices of peacekeeping. But failing seismic amendments to the Charter, there is still a lot that can be done to improve today's rather sorry state of affairs: the further reduction of overlapping agencies; a greater insistence upon the quality of incoming UN officials; less rigid emphasis on rotation; and greater consistency regarding standards when applying ECOSOC and more general UN policies. The same recommendations also apply to the Secretary-General's Office itself; like Caesar's wife, it has to be above suspicion, a house of rectitude, efficiency, and fairness. Much has been done in this respect, but the larger point is that, because of unfriendly and disdainful feelings toward the world organization in some quarters, the Secretariat needs to have a record that is spotless and unchallengeable.

Thus far, this chapter has suggested various "middle of the road" recommendations for improving the representativeness of the Security Council, the effectiveness of UN peacekeeping and peace enforcement, and the capacities and authority of the ECOSOC. Each recommendation would have to be negotiated by governments, perhaps as a package rather than singly; and they would help to move the caravan on. In the areas that remain—in other words, in the areas covered earlier in the chapters on human rights, cultural understanding, environmental protection, and the advancement of international civil society—it is much less certain that institutional alterations would make much difference. The issue here is not so much that of fossilized structures as that of a failure by member states, individually and sometimes collectively, to live up to the serious language of the treaties to which they signed their names. The matter is one of genuine compliance with the UN's purposes, about which the governments of Sudan, Belarus, Zimbabwe, Cuba, and so many others, at this time of writing, appear to know little.

Advancing the cause of international human rights is a case in point. Chapter Six finished on a mixed and troubled note, but that was not because of any glaring defects in the overall architecture of our existing human rights regime. On the contrary, the world community has further advanced its machinery in this dimension of its mission than in probably any other field, and the international consciousness about genocides and other abuses of rights is higher today than at any time. No, the disappointments come with the knowledge—amply provided by UN agencies, the churches, Amnesty International, Human Rights Watch, and others—that so many governments, large and small, are still acting in defiance of the Universal Declaration, the Geneva conventions, and all subsequent protocols. Few countries have completely clean hands, a number of them are major culprits, and where political order has collapsed, the atrocities multiply. Without this basic human need of the right to be protected, either from one's own government or from foreign assailants, world society will continue to stand ashamed. The major consolation—indeed, a fact to rejoice about—is the power of international opinion these days to expose human rights abuses and cause even recalcitrant and vicious regimes to consider the consequences of their evil. This international pressure against abuses has to be kept up, and where necessary, interventions to stop genocide must be sanctioned by the Security Council. But the real improvements will come in the hearts and consciences of humankind, not in additional machinery.

The same is true, surely, in regard to heading off global warming and the erosion of our environments. Of course, there are many supplementary and technical measures to be agreed upon, and better ways to organize humankind's struggle for sustainable development and to invest in recovery programs, but the key measure is whether major states are willing to enforce tough policies of reduction and conservation. The term *major states* says it all. It is no use asking small island nations to take steps to stop global warming. The burden is on the United States, the European Union, China, India, Japan, Russia, Brazil, and a few more large and/or prosperous states, precisely because it is their economic activities that contribute most to the deterioration of our planet. Here, unfortunately, the United States is put in the spotlight. If the world's largest economy and emitter of trace gases drags its feet over international restrictions (Kyoto, Montreal, or whatever), it gives a perfect excuse, whether fairly or unfairly, to laggard governments elsewhere. Today, in the environmental realm, all roads lead to Washington. Will it take action?

Advancing our cultural understanding of "others" (and thus of different ways of viewing the world) is another important item on the global agenda, although it would be wise not to place such weight upon UNESCO and related bodies, as was done by the founding fathers in 1945 or their ambitious successors during the 1970s. Sixty years of experience has shown us where UNESCO stumbles badly (ideologically charged, overly politically correct programs) and where it works well (international sports, education and environmental issues, identification of world heritage sites, and so on). There is no need here for altering constitutions, just for better practices in policy, plus the highest standards of appointments to redeem a tarnished past. Essentially, UNESCO's charge of "promoting collaboration among the nations through education, science and culture" is far more likely to be carried out by the drivers of globalization—the Internet, student exchanges, tourism, scientific collaborations, media networks, and global capitalism. Here are fields in which the UN's contributions will, sensibly, always be limited.

The same has to be said about the advancement of international civil society, discussed in Chapter Seven. This is a critical element, both present and future, because without it the United Nations would be a weak, stunted body, a meeting place for governments and nothing more. Yet while the UN remains an intergovernmental organization, it is also clear that its policies are best achieved when it operates alongside other bodies for the common good: volunteer organizations, NGOs, the churches, international business, local activists, and the world's media. It is these entities that are creating international civil society, and whether or not the world organization existed at all, it is obvious that other actors (ranging from Fulbright scholars to the Catholic Church to IBM to *The Economist*) would still be marching to a rather similar tune—that which promoted the links among the rich multitude of the world's peoples. For many citizens, both in the liberal North and in the aspirant South, the United Nations represents the best hope for our collective future. But that future is also being shaped by players and forces a long way away from New York and Geneva.

What, finally, can one say about the General Assembly? This is, after all, the closest manifestation we have of the parliament of man, yet its limpness is evident to all. Forbidden (essentially) to discuss and decide upon security issues, emasculated in its socioeconomic remit by the distance of the Bretton Woods institutions and the intergovernmental organizations, limited by the amount of time it is in session, cramped by its plethora of committees, paperwork, and formal bureaucratic practices, and weighed down by the need to be representative of its 191 members (with the recognition by most of them of the loss of efficiency), this is neither an effective nor a happy principal organ of the UN. No serious person suggests that it might be a candidate for abolition, as is often said about the Trusteeship Council or the ECOSOC, but that merely returns us to the big question: How can the General Assembly be made more effective and more respected?

Perhaps it can't. The nineteenth-century English writer Walter Bagehot made the distinction between the "dignified" branches of government (the queen, the House of Lords) and the "effective" branches (the cabinet, the House of Commons, the civil service). One would not want to push this analogy too far, but when one reads the two weeks of declarations of high principle by the world's leaders at the opening of the General Assembly each autumn, then contrasts that with the daily activity of the Security Council or the World Bank, those same adjectives spring to mind. Perhaps the General Assembly is a sort of global House of Lords—a collection of peers, rich and poor, large and small, all entitled by their heritage as sovereign states to a single vote, all willing to pronounce upon matters political, economic, and social, but not really able to exert much power.

This may be too cruel. The Commission on Global Governance (1995) makes a good case for the General Assembly's relevance.[13] After all, it has to approve the UN's annual budget, so in that regard it does act somewhat like the original House of Commons. It is the only real forum for world opinion—or, better, the opinions of the world governments that we have. Its resolutions may lack full follow-up because it is a deliberative body with no power to make decisions binding on member states; but those pronouncements are often a good barometer of international opinion and in many quarters regarded as having more legitimacy than the Security Council itself. Its demands on the Secretariat for reports upon a pressing issue, such as its request for what would become the secretary-general's An Agenda for Development (1994), can have institutional consequences, perhaps triggering new practices, reforms, and agencies that fill certain needs. It is the only principal organ with the capability to convene international conferences to address major social, economic, and environmental issues requiring global attention. The Assembly is, therefore, a body with many creative powers.

So the real question is, how can it be made more responsive and more effective and appear less like a talking shop to puzzled or hostile observers? There are, in fact, a surprising number of proposals in the air regarding the improvement of the General Assembly. Most of these begin by emphasizing its special role as the forum for world discussion and heartily defend the fortnightly September sessions of heads of states and foreign ministers in New York as being of value, indeed vital, to international understanding. But they rapidly admit that the Assembly's agendas are unwieldy, ineffective, and repetitive— too many governments are pushing for policies that fit ill with our twenty-first-century realities, even if they had been attractive back in 1970. The agendas should also be shorter and the committees smaller and more focused. Some of the six main committees might be candidates for merging or outright abolition. The first half-century of the world organization's existence saw a steady expansion of its roles, offices, and bureaucracies; the second half-century might hopefully witness a better recognition of where the Assembly and its subparts work well and where they do not, plus an identification of where they could respond better to the newer needs of humankind.

Some of the other proposals for raising the efficiency and stature of the General Assembly were mentioned earlier in this chapter. A shakeout of the ECOSOC is clearly necessary, and that can be done only by member states within the Assembly agreeing to make that sister body leaner, less somnambulant, and a lot more focused—or (most unlikely these days) by creating another organ. As the ECOSOC rises in estimation, so rises the General Assembly itself. The second, equally important set of ideas concerns an enhancement of the Assembly's relationship with the Security Council. Since there already exists the General Assembly's Special Committee on Peacekeeping Operations, why not build upon that to create better interactive machinery at a "principal organs" (Security Council–General Assembly) level? This consultation might also occur by enhancing the liaison powers of the president of the General Assembly, a rotating office to be sure, but it makes a lot of sense for the person holding that office to be able to sit in on both regular and emergency sessions of the Security Council. Any stronger links that can be forged between the Assembly's president and the UN Secretary-General's Office could also help to grease the wheels of a very complex bit of machinery.

Last but not least, the General Assembly should take another look at the question of how the UN is financed. It is a commonplace that most national governments, city administrations, school systems, pension schemes, universities, hospitals, and other social entities are strapped for cash these days; but the United Nations may be unique in the sheer pace of burdens being placed upon it, combined with its constitutional difficulty of raising fresh income. This gap between ends and means has long become embarrassing, but the possible solutions are also bitterly contested. A decade or more ago, the idea of a small tax on international currency transactions was very popular— the reasoning being that since the global trading community relied more than others upon world stability, it would not mind this minuscule but special contribution to the UN's coffers. The notion plummeted quickly, shot down by the same American conservatives who had machine-gunned the proposal about a UN army. One doubts if international bankers themselves had the time to ponder this scheme before it was dead: They might perhaps have approved of it. It may still be worth a fresh look, for the idea was a fairly modest one and included some stringent controls over the scheme by member states and their parliaments. And in any case, the Assembly is going to have to reexamine the annual assessment criteria and the relative national contributions in light of the shifting global economic balances. This is a suitable moment for a thorough look at the UN's funding.

This chapter has sought to answer that basic cry "What is to be done?" The response is that the world organization is, by its very nature, so complex and massive that a single recipe for improvement would be absurd. Reforms will, or should, come piecemeal. Doing nothing at all is impossible, given humankind's needs for better cooperation and governance; and trying to batter through Charter amendments that totally transform existing power relationships would have no chance of succeeding. So we need a middle way, one that produces some changes now, with the possibility of more to come.

This ought to be incontrovertible. Given the sheer number of principal organs, agencies, commissions, technical organizations, and the like, and given the complexity of UN agendas regarding peacekeeping or human rights or development, no one can believe that reforming one part of this grand machine will solve all needs and problems. And, in fact, suggesting changes in one area is almost bound to bring forth calls that transformations are even more important in certain other areas. As we have seen, whereas some governments worry most about environmental decay, others agitate chiefly about the unfair North-South economic balances. If, therefore, the world community of nations can agree on UN reforms at all, they will have to come as part of a package. This may not be the "grand bargain" that some writers have called for, but it will be a deal that includes many parts. Every commission and report stresses that point, and it makes a lot of sense.

The other part of this argument is also true. To have no changes at all spells the increasing sterility of the United Nations, save for its technical agencies, yet proposals for Charter amendments that threaten those who control the levers of power cannot happen under present circumstances. The only way forward is through intelligent, piecemeal reforms such as expanding the size of the Security Council; improving operational effectiveness in all aspects of peacekeeping and peace enforcement; abandoning the Trusteeship Council and the Military Staff Committee (but finding better ways to do their originally designed jobs); shaking up or abolishing the ECOSOC; improving the performance of the human rights, environmental, and cultural agencies; establishing closer coordination with the Bretton Woods and other specialized agencies; and giving the workings and structure of the General Assembly a thorough overhaul. That is not a bad list. In fact, if the greater part of these reform proposals were adopted by the governments that control the UN—indeed, if only half of them were put into effect—this clumsy but worthy organization would be moving in the right direction. Slowly but surely, it would be getting better, strengthening that three-legged stool of peace, development, and democracy envisaged sixty years ago by the founding fathers. There is urgent need to start those changes now.

One final word needs to be said, however, about this struggle to improve the United Nations' record in these many important fields. If the events of the previous decades are any guide to the future, then—

even if reforms are made along the lines just proposed—we must brace ourselves for many surprises and setbacks, for dreadful failures of governance, for awful abuses of human rights, and for regimes that will not respect the purposes of the Charter and insist upon going their own way. This is an awkward fact, and a natural one. It should not deter us from responding as best we can, using our talents to improve this always mixed record of trying "to save generations from the scourge of war," "to reaffirm faith in fundamental human rights," and to promote "social progress and better standards of life in larger freedom." The original Preamble to the Charter of the United Nations had it right.[14] The question is, can we do it?

Afterword

TENNYSON AGAIN, AND A PARLIAMENT OF MAN

This study began by quoting those famous lines of Tennyson's poem "Locksley Hall" about a future "Parliament of man, the Federation of the world . . . lapt in universal law." How optimistic those early Victorians could be! It is bittersweet today to read that poem and others like it. Did Tennyson not understand that the advent of new technologies and awful world wars (including aerial bombardments), should they occur, might drive peoples not to a universal peace, but to the opposite result: mistrust, arms races, and genocides? Or that his Enlightenment ideas ignored the fact that many human beings have a stubborn, instinctive dislike of a universal order and prefer their own national control of policies, even if, time and again, they have led to war, bloodshed, and mayhem? Did he ever consider that he was a comfortable resident of a nation that was steadily acquiring about one-quarter of the surface of the globe, the inhabitants of which saw only a Hobbesian world of foreign conquest and strife rather than a Kantian vision of perpetual peace? Finally, did it not occur to him that humankind might simply be resistant to liberal and utilitarian dogmas, even if, to his own early-Victorian generation, the signs of progress were promising?

Clearly he did not, at that time. He was young and optimistic, and the world (he thought) was emerging from constrained, unenlightened times to broad, sunlit uplands. It is an irony to learn, therefore, that in 1886, a half-century after composing those soaring, optimistic stanzas, he recanted in a bitter poem entitled "Locksley Hall Sixty Years After."[1] Again, it is wild, passionate, flailing around, but this time pessimistic. By then in his late seventies, Tennyson had soured and become deeply mistrustful of the trends of modern life. The later poem is written to his grandson (though tactfully dedicated to his wife), but it is not a missive that any young person would care to receive. In Tennyson's opinion, almost all had gone wrong. Europe had been riven by the midcentury wars in the Crimea, Italy, and Germany and by wretched colonialism. The booming global economy had tumbled into the Great Depression of 1873–96. Evidence of the continued impoverishment of the lower classes was weakening Benthamite dreams of prosperity for all who worked hard. The laboring classes were organizing themselves and demanding a new sociopolitical order. The Irish were in revolt. Religious belief was eroding fast. Jingoism was on the rise. Rationality was fleeing out the window. The thin crust of civilization was crumbling. Thus, Tennyson's poem was bitter, almost manic:

> *Chaos, Cosmos! Cosmos, Chaos! who can tell how all will end? . . .*
> *When was age so cramm'd with menace? madness? written,*
>   *spoken lies?*

So the heady dreams of the Parliament of man were over. The Federation of the world was an impossibility. Progress was a chimera, a utopian dream. One could forget about any future United Nations.

The rebuttal came from a remarkable source. It was none other than William Ewart Gladstone, the greatest statesman of nineteenth-century Britain (and Woodrow Wilson's hero), four times prime minister, and temporarily in retirement. Gladstone was mentioned early in Chapter One as one of the great liberal thinkers and actors of his age. He and Tennyson were two of the best-known politically engaged intellectuals of the nineteenth century in the Western world (they were both born in 1809, the same year as Abraham Lincoln, Edgar Allan Poe, Charles Darwin, and Felix Mendelssohn, which makes for a remarkable vintage). Tennyson and Gladstone had entered and graduated in the same year from Eton College, the most elite private school in England, then proceeded to Oxford. Presumably they had started disagreeing there, though they were very fond of each other. They sailed around the Scottish isles together and frequently corresponded. It was the prime minister's pleasure to recommend the poet laureate to a peerage, and the queen agreed.

Yet Gladstone would have none of Tennyson's latter-day gloom and doom. In an astonishing article in the January 1887 issue of the respected journal *The Nineteenth Century,* the former and future prime minister took on the nation's most famous living poet, toe to toe, though with a wonderfully generous language toward his great year-mate. Looking back over the half-century of Queen Victoria's reign, and thus of "Locksley Hall" itself, Gladstone argued for a different interpretation. It was true, he conceded, that the more ambitious hopes of the early Liberals had not been realized. But there had been substantial progress on many fronts. Gladstone thus rejects the poet's "dark prospect" and attempts what he calls "some account of the deeds and the movement of this last half-century." The list is numbing, boring, and impressive at the same time. The percentage of children in schools had shot up, Gladstone noted, and the rights of women had been enlarged, the fair wage was much higher, the disgusting criminal code (game laws, inheritance laws) had been cast aside, restrictive trade measures like the Navigation Acts had gone, the press gang in the navy and flogging in the army had been abolished, and commerce had increased fivefold, while crime had greatly diminished.

Gladstone is smart enough not to stop there, with a shopping list of Victorian improvements. He acknowledges where things were still not right (the fraying social fabric for the underclass, the increasing reliance upon public expenditures), but he remains convinced that the balance sheet is positive. He is deliberately modest and understated as he comes to the end of his tract, reminding his readers that with all progress there is error and setback. Always, he suggests, we should expect failure and rebuff even as the world advances. Then, in the final page of his review, Gladstone pulls out a trump by quoting a couple of his classmate's lines:

> *Forward then but still remember how the course of Time*
>   *will swerve,*
> *Crook and turn about itself in many a backward streaming curve.*

For every two steps forward, the statesman suggested, there would usually be one step back. Overall, though, the movement went forward. The river did flow to the sea.[2]

Might not the same argument be made following the sixtieth anniversary of the founding of the United Nations? It is all too easy these days to point to the many failings of the world organization, the horrible gaps between the language of the UN Charter and the Universal Declaration on the one hand and, on the other, the brutal realities of our present world, the failure to protect the weakest and most vulnerable in our societies, and the disgusting and widening chasms between rich and poor across the globe. Many of those failings have been discussed in the previous chapters. Other mistakes are trumpeted in our daily media, especially by those who dislike the world organization and wish to curb its roles. Its errors, whether they be in ambitious peacekeeping or poor financial management or bureaucratic overlap, are easy targets for groups that have become fearful of the evolution of global society along liberal, cosmopolitan lines. Then there are the criticisms from the Far Left, which views the United Nations as part of the apparatus that the privileged of the earth use to keep the masses down. Given those multiple phobias, how can a relatively flimsy international body possibly meet all the demands being placed upon it? Clearly, it can't.

The cynic might observe that if the UN is being attacked both by writers of the conservative Heritage Foundation and by the Socialist Workers Party, and resisted by nasty autocratic regimes, then it must be doing some good. But the better answer is more a Gladstonian one and is of two parts. The first concerns what has been achieved by the United Nations and other international organizations since 1945. The second suggests what might be achieved in the future, if the common will is at hand. There is no reason to despair of the future of world organization. The real issue is whether member states will recognize that they gain more than they lose by empowering the United Nations to carry out tasks that individually they have no prospect of fulfilling.

An account of what has been achieved was offered at the end of each of the six substantive chapters that form the core of this book, and all too often the summaries read, at least to the author, rather like a school report: "Much achieved, but could do better." One only has to look at (for example) the story of UN peacekeeping operations in the 1990s—some real successes, some awful disasters—to agree that the record is a mixed one. Generally, it may be said the greatest progress has been made in advancing the agendas of international human rights, improving the position of women and children, increasing cooperation on the environment, and bolstering civil society, though in all areas there have been setbacks and the progress has not been as swift as advocates had hoped. The least change has occurred in regard to the UN Security Council, chiefly because of the deep-frozen nature of its voting structures; the Council is certainly at work in these troubled days, but the results remain heavily dependent on whether the Big Five have the will for collective action—which is no different, really, from 1950. Finally, assessment of the world organization's contribution to global economic progress and the eradication of widespread poverty has always been the hardest to make, because in those cases, unlike measuring the eradication of certain diseases by UN agencies, the story is complicated by other forces—especially by those amazing bursts of regional productivity and growth that probably are explained chiefly by internal factors. It is much easier to link the UN to the elimination of polio worldwide than to the economic growth of Singapore, which is why the world body's advocates focus on the first achievement and the critics point to the second.

However, without repeating simple listings of "here the UN did good," the overall record is clear: Without the actions and existence of the world organization, humankind would be a lot worse off than it is today, warts and all. It would be much more fragmented, and countries would be much less understanding of others and much less capable of taking collective action in the face of grave crises. Though critics will protest at the thought, there clearly has emerged something that Woodrow Wilson liked to term "world opinion," which presses for collective responses to international problems and believes in the use of international instruments, whether to ensure peace in Bosnia or to coordinate assistance to countries affected by natural disasters, like the Indian Ocean tsunami of December 2004. Did the international body not exist, we would have to be constructing it or parts of it.

So runs the traditional, limp, liberal defense of all the criticisms of the world organization in its first sixty years. That seems to me too weak a riposte.

If you are going to offer a fair assessment, then you must answer this critical question: What does our world possess today, because of the United Nations organization, that it did not possess in, say, 1942–43, the middle of the Second World War? Any other measure is secondary or evasive, as would be the efforts to avoid some answers to that basic criterion. How about the following:

We have, because of our UN and its infrastructural underpinnings, created a central place where the governments of all nations, large and small, can meet in assembly, raise a common budget, and empower international mechanisms (through the General Assembly and the ECOSOC) to seek to implement our common aims. We have established a town meeting place of the world. Of course, it was imperfect, as doubtless was the town moot portrayed in the Norman Rockwell cartoon. The fact is that the Assembly exists and is observed across the world (and highly respected in many countries), yet it was not there in 1942.

We have a world Secretariat to coordinate the needs and requests of all member states. We all too often criticize it. We always take it for granted. But where was it when the Battles of Midway and Stalingrad were being fought?

We have a central, self-selected world security body that can be summoned day and night in the event of a new emergency and threat to international order. It is as strong or weak as its permanent members wish it to be. At least, the Great Powers remain inside the tent. At best, they can do great things.

We have established international early-warning, assessment, response, and coordination mechanisms for when states fray or collapse; and we are starting to work seriously on the matter of state rebuilding. Whoever thought on those lines in Mussolini's time?

We have powerful international financial instruments in play that, in their negative dimension, can detect, arrest, and turn around an economic crisis in a member state that might have serious spillover effects elsewhere, especially upon vulnerable neighbors. There was nothing like this when the world's banks started to collapse in the great 1931 crisis. Would we really want our present, volatile fiscal and exchange systems without an IMF? I think not.

More positively, we have created myriad international agencies and mechanisms to assist poor- and medium-income economies in their endeavors to escape the poverty trap, transcend their demographic and environmental challenges, and bring them fully into the community of prosperous nations, enjoying but not damaged by the world market.

We have established a stunning array of international bodies to respond to the needs of the world's women and children, especially the poorest and most discriminated against. The early suffragettes and Victorian children's rescue societies would have been amazed. It is not a fair retort to say that much more needs to be done and that so many of the earth's women and children still fall dismally behind. The fact is that a great deal has been done by an impressive mix of UN agencies working alongside NGOs, the churches, and the liberal foundations. Ask any of the latter how the world would look without UNICEF, and you would probably be rolled over.

We have established an international human rights regime that for all its dreadful setbacks may be the single most significant advance in our global mentality—in our way of thinking about the rights of others—since the campaigns against slavery. Whatever beastly threats to freedom may occur in the future, the human rights agenda since the epic statements of 1945 and 1948 can never be eliminated. George Orwell's hero-coward Winston Smith, in the novel *1984*, was wrong.

We are steadily, and with setbacks and grudging opposition, setting up an international monitoring regime to protect our environ-

ments, local, national, and global, and to safeguard future generations from the all too obvious harm that neglect of our ecologies can
bring. Can any intelligent person hold that such cooperative progress—
or, rather, efforts to reverse the damage—can be done without international agencies?

We have, alongside all this institution building, witnessed the
emergence of the idea of an international civil society. It is vague, contested, and always in flux, which is probably a good thing. It has developed thanks to the profound technological, economic, social, and
ideological transformations of the post-1945 era. And it has done so
not apart from international institutions, but in conjunction with
them, as part of a sort of second Enlightenment movement. It criti-
cizes the United Nations system on many grounds and walks hand in
hand with it on others.

And who is the "we"? Certainly it has to be the world citizenry
identified in "We the Peoples," the men, women, and children inhab-
iting this world. But it is not an amorphous, anonymous mass of bodies, even if the majority of humans go through their lives in humble
condition. It is also the many individuals who created and worked
within our global institutions, the idealists like Bunche and Urquhart
and Cassin and Eleanor Roosevelt and Wangari Maathai and Mary
Robinson, who knew that the world simply had to be a better place
than it was before 1945. Of course, they were overly optimistic. All
who roll boulders uphill are. And what they all had in common was
a recognition that without institutions, rules, and operating principles, our crooked humanity would not advance.

This is not a rosy-eyed tale, falling into the trap of believing that
international organization solves (and has solved) all problems. The
United Nations, or at least its major players, have made terrible mistakes, from its paralysis over the Cambodian and Rwandan genocides to the collusion or befuddlement over the food for oil program.
Many actors have a lot to apologize for, though it is hard to see how
the UN itself can apologize, since it is only as strong or as weak as its
major parts. And we all know that certain favorable world developments, like the rise of Asian standards of living, have had little to do
with the deliberate acts of the United Nations, except perhaps to the

degree that it provided frameworks in which commerce and investment could flourish. The ways in which the UN and its many agencies
have interacted with global trends since 1945 give us a mixed record,
but that is the point. If the world body had functioned perfectly, we
would not be having endless debates about reforming it. But those
who ask, "Just what has the United Nations achieved?" might well be
advised to pause and consider the previous list.

We therefore don't need the mantra (which I raised a few pages
earlier) "If a world organization didn't exist, we would have to invent
it." It does exist. It belongs to the governments of the world and,
much more distantly, to its peoples. The human race created it, and
the human race has inherited it. Parts of it have failed miserably, others have performed wonderfully, just like human beings. But to dismiss the UN's record, as do some contemporary critics, is unfair.
Actually, it is absurd.

There is more. The strongest argument for the continued validity
and empowerment of the United Nations lies in the future and in humankind's cry for help early in our present, disturbed new century.
Were all the globe to enjoy a condition like, say, the nations of Scandinavia (peace, prosperity, gender and generational equality, respect
for the environment, the war drums throbbing no longer), we should
probably require only technical support services like the International
Telecommunication Union. But the world is not so happy a place. Billions of people suffer impoverishment, many until the end of their
miserable lives. Population pressures build up; can we really offer justice and freedom from want to a mid-twenty-first-century earth of
perhaps nine billion people, one-third of whom may live in squalor
and desperation? How do we handle our collective human impact on
the environment, with its rising sea levels, collapsing glaciers, and
massive weather turbulences, without multinational work? How do
we manage global fiscal and trading dislocations without strengthening present UN instruments or creating new ones? How do we push
for the advancement of human rights and the displacement of awful
dictatorships except through the summoning of world opinion, pressure, and Security Council sanctions?

So the only answer, as far as I see it, is by trying; by repairing weaknesses, coaxing reluctant governments to accept change, understanding what works best and where international organization has problems—or even should not be involved at all—and not giving up. A hard-nosed realist approach to the world order will not work here. Nor will an overimaginative idealist belief that everything will be okay if we just pull together. The world needs both skeptical intelligence and vision. Mixed properly, as they were between 1942 and 1945, they can work wonders.

Thus, Gladstone was right, both for his time and for ours. The story of the past sixty years has not been one of unremitting setback and failure for the world body that we own. The United Nations organization is not like the great boulder that Sisyphus tried to roll uphill, only to have it repeatedly fall back to the bottom; it has sometimes slipped, but only for a while. When all its aspects are considered, the UN has brought great benefits to our generation and, with civic resolution and generosity by all of us who can contribute further to its work, will bring benefits to our children's and grandchildren's generations as well. But the boulder is only halfway up the mountain, and much effort is needed if it is to be moved further.

Acknowledgments

This book has been a long time in the making, partly because of the extraordinary complexity of the subject, partly because of personal vicissitudes. In August 1993 I was approached by Shepard Forman and Sir Brian Urquhart of the Ford Foundation and asked if my colleagues at Yale and I would assist them in putting together an international commission that would report on the long-term future of the United Nations and produce its recommendations in time for the fiftieth anniversary of the creation of the world body, which had taken place at the signing of the Charter in June 1945. The report thus had to be done within a couple of years.

My knowledge of international organizations at that time was (and probably still is) most shallow, but I was fortunate in having fellow scholars at Yale who could cover for my ignorance. My colleague Professor Bruce Russett, then head of United Nations Studies at Yale, joined me in co-chairing the secretariat to that report. It appeared on time, in 1995, as "The United Nations in Its Second Half-Century: The Report of the Independent Working Group on the Future of the United Nations" (New York: Ford Foundation, 1995). Its distinguished co-chairs, Moeen Qureshi, former prime minister of Pakistan, and Richard von Weizsaecker, former president of the Federal Republic of Germany, gave great leadership, as did the other ten members of that broad international body.

Bruce enlightened me so much on the mechanics of the Security Council and on UN matters in general, not only with his drafts but also his scholarly writings. Our working group had the enormous assistance of several successive chiefs of staff, Isabel Grunberg, Will Hitchcock, and Jean Krasno. All three were wonderful, but I have to note Will Hitchcock's good humor at times when our own project was floundering, as was the UN enterprise itself, in the mid-1990s. Many others at Yale helped us in those days, but my key supports were the then graduate students Robert Chase (later economics Ph.D.) and Emily Hill (later history Ph.D.). They have especial thanks.

Our secretariat enjoyed sage counsel from two voices of much experience. Charles Hill, seasoned U.S. diplomat, political adviser to Secretary-General Boutros Boutros-Ghali, and distinguished fellow and lecturer at Yale, taught us in his pithy manner not to be too ambitious in our framing of a UN reform agenda; his forecasts, as the late 1990s unfolded, turned out to be all too accurate. James Sutterlin, with a similar background in the U.S. foreign service, was later adviser to Secretary-General Javier Pérez de Cuéllar, and then fellow in UN studies and lecturer at Yale. He offered similarly realistic advice, produced crisp new versions of important paragraphs to the report, and kept gently correcting my ignorance. Jim was generous enough to do this again to the present manuscript, which greatly benefited from his criticisms, both factual and substantive. His voice has always been positive, both to my endeavor and, more important in a psychological sense for this author, to encouraging a belief in the future of global cooperation even in the worst of times.

The resources of two great universities, Yale and Cambridge, undergirded this operation with their vast library holdings and with the array of scholars, specialist and nonspecialist alike, who encouraged my work and commented upon my various presentations. In the autumn of 2002 I was honored by being made a visiting fellow of Christ's College, Cambridge, a warm and scholarly setting that permitted me to draft the first three chapters of this book. My debt to the master and fellows of Christ's is huge, and I especially want to thank Professors David Reynolds and Quentin Skinner as well as Mr. Geoffrey Payne. I was greatly helped at that time by Michael Gottesman, a former Yale student then on a graduate scholarship at Cambridge. Three years later this good fortune repeated itself when the master, president, and fellows of St. John's College made me a fellow commoner for the first six months of 2005. Their good fellowship toward me was attended by the provision of a wonderful little residence along the Madingley Road, where I drafted, discarded, and drafted again the remaining chapters of this work. I am especially indebted to the master, Richard Perham, to the president, John Leake, and to fellows Jane Heal, Mary Sarotte, and John Harris for their unwavering support and hospitality. I wish above all to record my massive debt to Adam Heal, my research assistant during those six months—and more than research assistant: It was Adam who sat me down, day after day, and compelled me to rewrite almost all of the manuscript, tightening it up, page after page, in a manner that reminded me of my great editor at Random House, Jason Epstein.

Jason had encouraged me to begin this work, which must surely have seemed to him a curiosity after our collaboration on *The Rise and Fall of the Great Powers* and *Preparing for the Twenty-first Century.* In more recent times his role as editor has been taken over by Will Murphy, who has been patient, supportive, and encouraging when I seemed to fumble through this past year; I am grateful to Will and his whole production team at Random House, and am particularly bound to Sona Vogel for her severe and terrific copyediting. At Penguin Books in London, Stuart Proffitt has been my editor throughout, combining the patience of Job and the willingness to boost an author through choppy waters with a scholarly determination that this manuscript must be right in all its parts. I do not think a single paragraph escaped Stuart's lengthy scrutiny.

I hold a special regard for my friend and literary agent of more than thirty years, Bruce Hunter of David Higham Agency in London. This has been a relationship of which authors can only dream, and my debts to Bruce are, simply, unrepayable.

My chief base at Yale for well over fifteen years has been its International Security Studies program, where I was supported by its first administrator, Ann Bitetti, and then by the wonderful and extraordinary Ann Carter-Drier. Over the past years I have also been privileged to enjoy the support of my secretary Monica Ward, who has assisted and shielded me in every way. Ann and Monica, together with my successive associate directors Will Hitchcock (now a professor at Temple University) and the present associate director Ted Bromund, have provided a remarkable human space in which to research, administer, and teach. We have been aided by many dedicated Yale assistants, but in particular Andrew Levine, Chad Golder, Alastair Gillespie, Jennifer Chang, and Will Chou; I am awfully in their debt.

My chairmen and colleagues at Yale have been wonderfully tolerant, but no one has given me greater encouragement, often through dark patches, than my friend and neighbor John Lewis Gaddis, together with his wife, Toni. Old friends Martin Landy and Ruth Caleb, Joshua Sherman, Eric and Judy Homberger, and Volker and Marion Berghahn never flinched in their encouragement, not to mention provision of food, drink, and a bed at night.

My first wife, Catherine Kennedy, thought it was an odd idea for me to accept the approach from the Ford Foundation in the first place, and perhaps even odder to write a book on the UN; but as she entered her final months she gave me and the enterprise her full moral support. I hope she approves of what I have done.

Unwavering moral backing came, too, from my three sons, Jim, John, and Matthew Kennedy, and John's wife, Cinnamon. My two granddaughters, Catherine and Olivia, didn't have strong opinions on Security Council reform, but they helped me in many other ways. And I truly do not think I would have had the courage to begin this project anew had it not been for my great fortune in marrying again, to my partner, sternest critic, and greatest support, Cynthia Farrar. She, and my wonderful stepdaughter, Sophia Lear, have provided me with all possible encouragement and love.

Paul Kennedy
New Haven and Cambridge
2005–6

Notes

Preface

1. It is therefore consonant with the Yale University–Ford Foundation report entitled "The United Nations in Its Second Half-Century: The Report of the Independent Working Group on the Future of the United Nations" (New York, 1995) that Yale colleagues and Working Group members and I produced a decade or so ago and will be referred to from time to time in the text and endnotes following. But an individual author's "voice" is always different from the agreed-upon texts of a group, and besides, much has happened in the past decade that gives cause for thought.

CHAPTER 1: *The Troubled Advance to a New World Order, 1815–1945*

1. The literature of early ideas about a world federation or a commonwealth of man is massive. The interested reader might begin with W. Warren Wagner's quirky but spirited *The City of Man* (Boston, 1963); and J. P. Baratta, *The Politics of World Federation*, 2 vols. (Westport, Conn., 2004), vol. 1, pp. 27–48.
2. The classic account now of the change in sentiments toward war and peace is P. W. Schroeder, *The Transformation of European Politics, 1763–1848* (Oxford, 1994).
3. For the development of treaties (especially The Hague agreements and ancillary contracts), see G. Best, *Humanity in Warfare: The Modern History of the International Law of Armed Conflict* (London, 1983).
4. The quotation is from J. M. Keynes's brilliant *The Economic Consequences of the Peace* (written and published immediately after the treaty was signed, in 1919; I have used the New Brunswick, N.J., 2003 ed.), pp. 11–12.

5. My translation of German political economist Werner Sombart's classic 1916 text *Haendler und Helden* (Munich, 1915). Sombart's polemic sought to prove that the First World War—the Anglo-German war—was inevitable because Prussian stoic, warrior values stood in direct contrast with British mercantilist, money-grubbing policies.

6. See A. Marwick, *Warfare and Social Change in the Twentieth Century: A Comparative Study of Britain, France, Germany, Russia and the United States* (London, 1974).

7. The Inis Claude quotation comes from pp. 54–55 of his great work, *Swords into Ploughshares: The Problems and Progress of International Organization*. I am using the fourth edition, with a new preface (New York, 1984). This is surely one of the most thoughtful books ever upon the United Nations.

8. The quote comes from p. 359 of Zara Steiner, *The Lights That Failed: European International History 1919–1933* (Oxford, 2005). My summation of the League's achievements and weaknesses relies heavily upon this important new work.

9. Germany, Britain, and Italy repudiated a similar "Eastern Locarno" guarantee that France and Poland desired for the borders to Germany's east and southeast. Gustav Stresemann said he would be assassinated if he signed such a deal. Austen Chamberlain declared the Polish corridor was not worth the bones of a British grenadier, a lousy judgment given September 1939. The British army reminded the cabinet that it didn't possess the regiments to fulfill the Locarno pledges. And the French army started to build the Maginot Line, behind which they would sit when Hitler went east. And Mussolini bided his time.

10. See the fine analysis in D. Reynolds, *The Creation of the Anglo-American Alliance, 1937–1941* (London, 1981), especially the early chapters.

11. Still the best study is Arnold Wolfers's *Britain and France Between the Wars* (New York, 1940).

12. I refer to Ludwig Dehio's marvelous synthesis, *The Precarious Balance: The Politics of Power in Europe, 1494–1945* (London, 1963).

13. Robert Cecil, *A Great Experiment* (London, 1941), passim. And see again Steiner, *The Lights That Failed*, chaps. 12–14; also the standard account by F. P. Walters, *History of the League of Nations*, 2 vols. (London, 1952).

14. Avenol was a Frenchman, interested in social and economic cooperation but distinctly right-wing regarding the Spanish Civil War and the expulsion of the USSR from the League. Lester was competent and judicious, although it is ironic that his previous position had been as high commissioner in Danzig, another Versailles creation made irrelevant by the international events of the 1930s.

15. The first printing was in March 1943; by July 1943 (my paperback edition), it is recorded that more than 1.2 million copies had been printed, making it the fastest-selling book of its generation. Note, on p. 174, Willkie's tart comment that fine and idealistic statements like the "Four Freedoms" speech and the Atlantic Charter will have no lasting meaning unless their purposes are made real. R. C. Hilderbrand, *Dumbarton Oaks: The Origins of the United Nations and the Search for Postwar Security* (Chapel Hill, N.C., and London, 1990), chaps. 1–2, covers these early plans and thoughts.

16. The paragraphs that follow rely heavily upon the confidential 1943–45 correspondence and memoranda of the U.K. Foreign Office that are contained in the Public Record Office (PRO), especially the political files (FO371) and the treaty files (FO475). The British watched the American delegates like hawks, and these records are as interesting for the information on U.S. policy as they are upon British Empire motives. For a sampling, the interested reader might go to the documents in PRO FO371/vols. 35397 and 50723.

17. Vandenberg's role is detailed in various places, but the best source still remains *The Private Papers of Senator Vandenberg*, edited by A. H. Vandenberg, Jr., with J. A. Morris (Boston, 1952). Chapter 11 especially shows Vandenberg's stress upon the United States having the veto, combined with worry that the Soviets would misuse it.

18. For an example of this assumption, see the preface of A.J.P. Taylor's *The Course of German History* (London, 1945), where he makes the remark, "It was no more a mistake for the German people to end up with Hitler than it is an accident when a river flows into the sea," p. vii of the 1961 edition, essentially a restatement of p. 1 of the first edition that German history is "a history of extremes."

19. One should note that Article 2, Part 7, ends with a balancing clause, "But this principle shall not prejudice the application of enforcement measures under Chapter VII"—that is, a Security Council resolution for enforcement. Still, it is the early part of Article 2, Part 7, that is quoted most frequently, especially by regimes most sensitive with regard to their sovereignty and/or wishing to protect their domestic malfeasances.

20. They are defined in Article 18, Part 2, and include electing nonpermanent members to the Security Council, electing the membership of the ECOSOC and Trusteeship Council, and so on.

21. I have relied a great deal upon Claude, op. cit., passim, and upon Hilderbrand's fine *Dumbarton Oaks,* passim. I also benefited from Stephen C. Schlesinger's *Act of Creation: The Founding of the United Nations* (Boulder, Colo., 2003), a good account from the American perspective, though

not using the incredibly interesting unpublished British documents. Another useful, judicious account is Gary B. Ostrower's *The United Nations
and the United States 1945–1995* (New York, 1998).

22. The creation—and later demise—of the Military Staff Committee is best
    discussed in Eric Grove, "UN Armed Forces and the Military Staff Com-
    mittee," *International Security* 17, no. 4 (Spring 1993), passim.

23. For the plans for UN bases, ports, and airfields, see the detailed cor-
    respondence in the Foreign Office's papers (PRO, FO371 series) for
    1944–45.

24. For Bunche's role on Trusteeship Council issues, see Brian Urquhart's
    Ralph Bunche: An American Life (New York, 1993), chaps. 9–10.

25. This may be why some writers see the Charter as being awfully hidebound
    and narrow, whereas others praise its adaptability. Schlesinger, op. cit.,
    pp. 284–85, notes that the radical historian Gabriel Kolko asserts that
    "the new organization failed before it began" because it was a contrivance
    of selfish Great Powers, a belief widespread in the developing world
    today; whereas Sir Brian Urquhart claims that the Charter is "a surpris-
    ingly practical document."

26. A. Deporte, *Europe Between the Superpowers: The Enduring Balance*
    (New Haven, 1986).

27. Truman's address is replicated as an appendix in Schlesinger's *Act of Crea-
    tion;* the exact quote is from p. 294. Hilderbrand, *Dumbarton Oaks,*
    notes Kennan's pessimism on p. 250 and Gladwyn Jebb's on p. 257.

28. For Eisenhower's quote, see Schlesinger, op. cit., p. 287.

CHAPTER 2: *The Conundrum of the Security Council*

1. Vandenberg's account and justification of the Soviet veto is in the *Con-
   gressional Record: Senate,* 79th Cong., 1st sess. (vol. 92, pt. 2), especially
   p. 1694, Vandenberg speech of February 27, 1946. His earlier defense before the Senate of the UN Charter as *not* being a threat to American sovereignty is in ibid., vol. 91, pt. 2, pp. 6981–85, a remarkable address on
   June 29, 1945.

2. The pattern of vetoes in the Security Council in the almost half-century
   after 1945 is traced in Anjali V. Patil, *The UN Veto in World Affairs
   1946–1990: A Complete Record and Case Histories of the Security
   Council's Veto* (Sarasota, Fla., and London, 1992). It is worth noting
   that Patil supports the veto and argues against veto reform or abolition.

3. H. G. Nicholas's phrase about the Military Staff Committee can be found
   on p. 70 of his significant work *The United Nations as a Political Institution* (London, 1959).

4. Brian Urquhart's memoir, *A Life in Peace and War* (New York, 1987), especially chaps. IX–XVI, gives an atmospheric, almost breathless account of the many matters upon which the Security Council was "seized" in these chaotic years.

5. *United Nations, Divided World: The UN's Roles in International Relations,* edited by A. Roberts and B. Kingsbury, 2nd ed. (Oxford, 1993), contains two thoughtful chapters on the secretary-general's roles, by Javier Pérez de Cuéllar (himself secretary-general between 1982 and 1991) and by T. M. Franck and G. Nolte. Nicholas's book has consistent, telling commentary upon both Lie and Hammarskjöld (whose acceptance remark about "filling in the vacuum" is quoted on p. 157). The latter's actions in the Suez, Hungarian, Lebanon, and Congo crises are admiringly captured in Brian Urquhart's *Hammarskjöld* (New York, 1994), chaps. 7, 8, 10, and 15.

6. The UN's role in the Cuban missile crisis is covered in U Thant's personal memoir, *View from New York* (New York, 1978), but it is amply confirmed in the secondary literature, which suggests its limited function. It was useful that it existed; it was probably not vital.

7. The quotation from T. M. Franck and G. Nolte comes from p. 148 of their essay in *United Nations, Divided World.* The rest of that chapter contains an excellent survey of the secretary-general's various "good offices" roles in the 1980s and 1990s.

8. The results of the unfreezing of the Cold War after 1987 are judiciously analyzed in Brian Urquhart's essay "The UN and International Security After the Cold War," in Roberts and Kingsbury (eds.), *United Nations, Divided World.* See also D. Reynolds, *One World Divisible: A Global History Since 1945* (New York, 2000), chaps. 15–16.

9. The struggles and setbacks that faced the United Nations in the middle to late 1990s are personally reflected upon in Boutros Boutros-Ghali's fine (though pompously entitled) memoir, *Unvanquished: A UN-U.S. Saga* (New York, 1999), passim.

10. The chapters in Roberts and Kingsbury (eds.), *United Nations, Divided World,* capture in a highly intelligent way the various ideas current in the early 1990s for improving the world organization. It is not possible here to survey the plethora of writings about UN reform that accompanied the fiftieth anniversary in 1995. The author tried his hand in Paul Kennedy and Bruce Russett, "Reforming the United Nations," *Foreign Affairs* 75, no. 5 (September/October 1995): 56–71, and, as part of a team effort, in "The United Nations in Its Second Half-Century." Another important contemporary analysis was "Our Global Neighborhood: The Report of the Commission on Global Governance" (New York, 1995).

CHAPTER 3: *Peacekeeping and Warmaking*

1. I found the best general introduction on this topic to be P. F. Diehl, *International Peacekeeping* (Baltimore/London, 1993), with an excellent, brief bibliography. His analyses of the Suez and Congo missions are difficult to beat. Also very useful was the UN's own (and therefore anonymous) publication *The Blue Helmets: A Review of United Nations Peace-Keeping* (New York, 1990). Its rather dry text is compensated for by valuable detail and excellent maps. But nothing quite matches Brian Urquhart's memoir, *A Life in Peace and War,* chaps. X–XIV on the Suez and Congo crises.

2. Again, my coverage of the UN peacekeeping operations of the 1960s to 1980s relies a great deal upon operational details in *The Blue Helmets* and shrewd commentary in Diehl, *International Peacekeeping.* Diehl is particularly good in his distinction between "ceasefire effectiveness" and "conflict resolution."

3. Urquhart's coverage of Middle East tensions is in chaps. XVI–XIX, XXII, of *A Life in Peace and War.*

4. Urquhart, op. cit., p. 256.

5. *The Blue Helmets,* appendix III, has two excellent maps of the UN peacekeeping deployments in Cyprus before and after the Turkish invasion and offers a very good account of the whole affair.

6. For this rough-and-ready assessment of peacekeeping missions in the 1980s and 1990s, I relied upon S. Morphet's chapter, "UN Peacekeeping and Election-Monitoring," in Roberts and Kingsbury (eds.), *United Nations, Divided World;* and J. Boulden's splendid work, *Peace Enforcement: The United Nations Experience in Congo, Somalia and Bosnia* (Westport, Conn., 2001). I also found very useful the comments provided in two works of an extremely different political provenance: F. H. Fleitz, *Peacekeeping Fiascoes of the 1990s: Causes, Solutions, and U.S. Interests* (Westport, Conn., 2002); and T. Barry with E. Leaver, *The Next Fifty Years: The United Nations and the United States* (Albuquerque, N.M., 1996). Fleitz carries a huge grievance against virtually anything done by the Clinton administration; Barry is extremely critical of U.S. behavior, especially its unilateralism and disregard of international law. Reading the two side by side is both instructive and a commentary upon our human condition. For a very important and chilling personal memoir, see the Canadian general Roméo Dallaire's *Shake Hands with the Devil: The Failure of Humanity in Rwanda* (Toronto, 2003).

7. As noted in the previous chapter, Boutros-Ghali offers a reasonable defense in his memoir, *Unvanquished,* passim. He had not been dealt a good hand of cards in any case but could do little at all when the Clinton administration turned against him.

8. The report in question, "Human Security Report" (Oxford, 2005), was released in October 2005, general editor Professor Andrew Mack; see www.humansecurityreport.info.

9. The 1995 Yale University–Ford Foundation report, "The United Nations in Its Second Half-Century," pp. 20–21, stressed the real need to get the mandate—and the article in the Charter under which an operation takes place—right at the very beginning of any Security Council resolution. The 1992 document An Agenda for Peace had also asked for greater clarity of mission, as did the Brahimi Report of 2000. It is not an unreasonable suggestion.

CHAPTER 4: *Economic Agendas, North and South*

1. Dadzie's comment about the different language used in the Charter regarding peace, and that regarding development, is made in his essay "The UN and the Problem of Economic Development," in Roberts and Kingsbury (eds.), *United Nations, Divided World*, p. 319.

2. This daunting statement about the UN's complexity comes from the opening substantial paragraph of T. Arnold, *Reforming the UN: Its Economic Role* (Royal Institute of International Affairs, Discussion Paper 57, London, 1955), p. 3.

3. The voting balances in the Bretton Woods institutions—indeed, in all UN bodies—are spelled out in the *United Nations Handbook* (New York, comp. and prod. annually by the New Zealand Ministry of Foreign Affairs and Trade).

4. The comparative World Bank and Marshall Plan aid totals appear on p. 68 of Bruce Rich's important study *Mortgaging the Bank: The World Bank, Environmental Impoverishment, and the Crisis of Development* (Boston, 1993). Pages 70–71 of the same book cover the Bank's decision to be "nonpolitical."

5. Dadzie, op. cit., p. 299.

6. The quote from Lewis is recorded in D. Morawetz, *Twenty-five Years of Economic Development, 1950 to 1975* (Baltimore/London, 1977).

7. The statistics about the rich-poor income ratios are taken from Rich, op. cit., p. 72, footnote.

8. The quotation is again from Dadzie, op. cit., p. 301; he provides a lucid account of the transition to the new (NIEO) way of thinking from the 1960s onward.

9. The quotation about the March 1995 Mid-Term Global Review comes from p. 235 of the *United Nations Handbook*. A mere half hour of reading these lists and details produces severe mental dislocation.

10. Dadzie, op. cit., pp. 302–6, is as usual very good and succinct on the

weakening of the South's position. The IMF's focus on Northern financial problems clearly emerges from Michael D. Bordo, *The Bretton Woods International System: An Historical Overview* (National Bureau of Economic Research, working paper No. 4033, Cambridge, Mass., 1992); from the interminable volumes of the official history of the IMF (almost all authored by Margaret G. de Vries), *The International Monetary Fund, 1945–1965,* 3 vols. (1969), . . . *1966–1971,* 2 vols. (1976), and . . . *1972–1978,* 2 vols. (1985), all published by the IMF itself, Washington, D.C.; and by Harold James's masterful *International Monetary Cooperation Since Bretton Woods* (New York/Oxford, 1996), passim—which itself does not examine the South's problems until chapter 11.

11. Developing countries' debt figures are from R. Fraser and C. Long, *The World Financial System* (2nd ed., London, 1992), p. 151.

12. The Mexican and other debt crises are detailed in James, op. cit., chaps. 11–12,15; and in Margaret G. de Vries, *The IMF in a Changing World 1945–1985* (IMF, Washington, D.C., 1986), pt. 4. The loans to Eastern Europe and Russia are in Fraser and Long, op. cit.

13. For criticism of the IMF and World Bank, see especially Rich, op. cit., throughout; Barry, *The Next Fifty Years,* chap. 6; and John J. Gershman, *Globalization and the Challenge of Governance* (Center for UN Reform Education, monograph no. 16, Wayne, N.J., 2000)—a mere sampling of the massive literature of negative comment. James, op. cit., p. 530ff., has a good analysis of such criticisms. But then compare with the massive right-wing criticisms in, for example, D. Bandow and I. Vasquez (eds.), *Perpetuating Poverty: The World Bank, the IMF, and the Developing World* (Washington, D.C., 1994). One is reminded of the Chinese saying "The man who sits in the middle of road gets hit by traffic from both directions."

14. The Kenya example comes from the June 2001 issue of the UNDP's monthly magazine *Choices,* the Kyrgyzstan case from the September 2001 issue; for more examples, readers can browse the UNDP website at www. undp.org/focusareas.

15. Perhaps the most severe of those critics in the past decade has been the Nobel Prize–winning economist Joseph Stiglitz, especially in his *Globalization and Its Discontents* (New York, 2002). He is particularly vitriolic about IMF policies, more empathetic toward the World Bank, where he was for a while its chief economist. But his language is withering.

16. Gershman, op. cit., pp. 50–59, has a powerful assault upon the WTO.

CHAPTER 5: *The Softer Face of the UN's Mission*

1. This is made clear in Chapters IX and X of the Charter, although, as the next paragraph in the main text explains, there were of course various

specialized agencies like the World Bank group, the World Health Organization, and the International Labour Organization, none of which were created by the General Assembly/ECOSOC or were required to answer to those bodies.

2. *United Nations Handbook,* annual, published by the New Zealand Ministry of Foreign Affairs and Trade, Wellington, New Zealand, remains the best source.

3. I also used the *United Nations Handbook* to date the creation of the various agencies mentioned in the text.

4. Urquhart, *A Life in War and Peace,* p. 96.

5. The quotation comes from p. 3 of R. E. Asher's introductory chapter in *The United Nations and Economic and Social Cooperation,* by Asher et al. (Brookings Institution, Washington, D.C., 1957), an encyclopedic account of the UN's first ten years.

6. The sorry tale of the UNRWA is recounted in ibid., pp. 65–70.

7. The summary quotes from the Brookings report are on p. 532. The remark about the special problems of developing countries is on p. 500.

8. The list of conferences is on p. 5 of M. G. Schechter (ed.), *United Nations–Sponsored World Conferences* (Tokyo/New York, 2001). See also chap. 4, "UN World Conferences and Global Challenges," in L. Emmerij, R. Jolly, and T. J. Weiss, *Ahead of the Curve?: UN Ideas and Global Challenges* (Bloomington, Ind., 2001), an important early work of the UN Intellectual History Project.

9. The scholar in question is Patricia Birnie, "The UN and the Environment," in Roberts and Kingsbury (eds.), *United Nations, Divided World.* The quotation is from p. 327. This is another superb essay showing the shifting patterns of ideas, institutions, and policies in this highly complex and contentious field. I have been using the 1993 second edition of this collection throughout; it is worth noting that the 1988 first edition did not have this chapter on the UN and the environment—a measure, perhaps, of how fast ideas on the significance of this subject have been changing.

10. Birnie, op. cit., pp. 339–50, and Emmerij, Jolly, and Weiss, op. cit., pp. 89–92, both provide fine and succinct accounts of the 1972 Stockholm conference.

11. For the Stockholm conference's resolutions and statements, see Birnie, op. cit., especially p. 349.

12. The quotation is from the UN Department of Public Information's "Revised 23 May 1997" document on the Earth Summit, at www.un.org/geninfo/bp/enviro.html. For somewhat blunter accounts of what happened at Rio, see Birnie, op. cit., pp. 366ff.; and Thomas Yongo's fine essay in Schechter (ed.), *United Nations–Sponsored World Conferences.*

13. The comment upon the UNFCCC text at Rio comes from Jo Elizabeth Butler and Aniket Ghai's article, also in Schechter (ed.), op. cit., p. 157.

14. Fliers on British Airways (for example) will be familiar with the UNICEF bags into which spare foreign currency can be donated. According to UNICEF itself, British Airways' "Change for Good" program has raised £21 million (about $29 million) since 1994; see www.unicef.org.uk/gettinginvolved/corporate/cfg-ba.htm.

15. This paragraph is a summary of the nice description of the Children's Summit in Emmerij, Jolly, and Weiss (eds.), op. cit.

16. This long quotation comes from the UN's own distributed document about the conference, at www.un.org/geninfo/bp/women2.html. The follow-up document, bp/women4.html, cites examples of implementation in various countries.

17. See Amartya Sen's terrifying article "More than 100 Million Women Are Missing," *The New York Review of Books,* December 20, 1990.

18. The Human Rights Watch annual report can be found at www.hrw.org/wr2k1/women/women7.html.

19. There is a good summary of the United States' break with UNESCO in Mark F. Imber, *The USA, ILO, UNESCO and IAEA: Politicization and Withdrawal in the Specialized Agencies* (Basingstoke, 1989), chap. 5, "The UNESCO Case." See also Harold K. Jacobson, "U.S. Withdrawal from UNESCO: Incident, Warning, or Prelude?" *Policy Science* 17, no. 3 (Summer 1984): 581–85.

20. The American return to UNESCO was variously reported in *The Guardian, The Washington Post,* and *The New York Times* (all of September 13, 2002). There was already some mention of assisting in the rebuilding of Afghanistan by Director-General Koichiro Matsuura in 2001. The Blair government brought the United Kingdom back into the organization in 1997.

CHAPTER 6: *Advancing International Human Rights*

1. The idea that human rights were accepted way back into ancient times is demolished in E. Pagels, "Human Rights: Legitimizing a Recent Concept," *Annals of the American Academy of Political and Social Science* 422 (March 1979). It is also dismissed in K. Sellars's fine recent study, *The Rise and Rise of Human Rights* (Stroud, Glos., 2002), which goes on to show how the Marquis de Condorcet, Thomas Paine, and contemporaries at least advanced it as a discussable concept.

2. There is a superb analysis of these early iterations and campaigns in Paul Gordon Lauren, *The Evolution of International Human Rights* (Philadelphia, 1998), a work that this chapter found hard to resist.

3. Its text and those of other crucial documents are assembled in the UN's own official publication *The United Nations and Human Rights, 1945–1995* (New York, 1995), a basic work for this chapter.

4. These paragraphs on the 1948 Universal Declaration are heavily in debt to Lauren, op. cit., chap. 7; but also note Sellars, op. cit., chap. 1; M. Glen Johnson and Janusz Symonides, *The Universal Declaration of Human Rights: A History of Its Creation and Implementation, 1948–1998* (UNESCO, Paris, 1998), pp. 19–75; and Johannes Morsink, *The Universal Declaration of Human Rights: Origins, Drafting and Intent* (Philadelphia, 1999), passim, among the vast literature on this subject. There is some disagreement about the extent of Cassin's role, but none about the intellectual heritage that he brought to the drafting committee.

5. "Cassin's portico," because in one sketch these four parts of the Universal Declaration are represented as four classical pillars, each equal in size (and importance), holding together the entire edifice.

6. The behind-doors maneuverings and the reservations are covered exhaustively in Morsink, op. cit., passim, and Lauren, op. cit., chap. 7.

7. Lauren's judgment about the Universal Declaration's longer-term power is in *Evolution of International Human Rights*, p. 239. The remark by Tom J. Farer and Felice Gaer is in "The UN and Human Rights: At the End of the Beginning," in Roberts and Kingsbury (eds.), *United Nations, Divided World* p. 248.

8. There is a good summary of the decision to create two covenants in *The United Nations and Human Rights 1945–1995*, pp. 42ff. This source is also invaluable in describing the "follow-up" machinery.

9. For the worldwide and heterogeneous nature of the 1960s protests, see once again Suri, *Power and Protest: Global Revolution and the Rise of Détente*, passim.

10. For the tragedies and holocausts of these decades, see Eric Hobsbawm, *Age of Extremes* (London, 1994), pt. 2; and Reynolds, *One World Divisible*, chaps. 7–8,10; as well as the early chapters of Samantha Power's impassioned *"A Problem from Hell": America and the Age of Genocide* (New York, 2002).

11. *The Killing Fields* was, of course, the later movie. The quotation is from Reynolds, op. cit., p. 361, itself quoting Karl D. Jackson (ed.), *Cambodia, 1975–1978: Rendezvous with Death* (Princeton, 1989). For another compelling reconstruction, see Ben Kiernan, *The Pol Pot Regime: Race, Power, and Genocide in Cambodia Under the Khmer Rouge, 1975–79* (New Haven, Conn., 1996).

12. For the Helsinki process and the creation of Human Rights Watch, see again Sellars, *The Rise and Rise of Human Rights*; Lauren, *Evolution of International Human Rights*, chap. 8 (very good on the UN Commission

on Human Rights); Reynolds, *One World Divisible;* and the pertinent sections in W. Keylor, *The Twentieth Century World: An International History,* 3rd ed. (New York, 1996).

13. "The Short Twentieth Century (1914–1991)" is the subtitle of Hobsbawm's book *Age of Extremes.*

14. The description of the Vienna conference comes from Clarence J. Dias, "The United Nations World Conference on Human Rights: Evaluation, Monitoring, and Review," in Schechter (ed.), *United Nations–Sponsored World Conferences,* p. 31.

15. The text itself is on pp. 448–69 of *The United Nations and Human Rights, 1945–1995.*

16. The quotations (and much of my text) assessing the Vienna declaration is taken from Dias, op. cit., especially pp. 31–36, a withering and startling account. See also Farer and Gaer, "The UN and Human Rights," p. 296. Lauren, op. cit., pp. 273–74, has a rather more optimistic assessment of the conference's conclusions.

17. Dias, op. cit., passim, is also very good on the follow-up procedures, as is the 1993 edition of *A Global Agenda: Issues Before the 48th General Assembly of the United Nations* (New York, 1993), pt. V, "Human Rights and Social Issues," written by Charles Norchi, p. 213ff.

18. The statistics on the transitions to democracy in Africa come from Reynolds, op. cit., p. 601. Reynolds also has a fine, brief survey of the Balkan conflicts on pp. 621–24.

19. James Rosenau, "The Relocation of Authority in a Shrinking World," *Comparative Politics* (April 1992), passim, is the key article here.

20. Simply read, for example, Amnesty International Report 2001, which was published in New York in that same year.

21. For the political transformations in Central America and elsewhere in the 1990s, see again Reynolds, op. cit., chap. 16.

22. The quotation is from p. 280 of Lauren's remarkable *Evolution of International Human Rights.*

CHAPTER 7: *"We the Peoples": Democracy, Governments, and Nongovernmental Actors*

1. Discussed, with great subtlety in Inis Claude's *Swords into Ploughshares,* chaps. 18–19.

2. It is interesting to recall that the San Francisco conference took place midway between the Yalta and Potsdam conferences. Of course, the latter two were different in character, subject, and tone from the UN's founding event, but this conjunction of the three sets of negotiations helps to explain better why the Great Powers were content to allow the Charter to

contain so much about the General Assembly. The real decisions, in their view, were being taken elsewhere, by themselves.

3. For example, our Yale University–Ford Foundation report "The United Nations in Its Second Half-Century" had very little to say about the General Assembly. It was a commonplace neglect.

4. President Lula da Silva's address was given to the 58th session of the General Assembly on September 23, 2003.

5. See again the document "Our Global Neighborhood: The Report of the Commission on Global Governance." The stress that they are not arguing for "global government" is made on p. xvi. The two terms are frequently confused. I take *governance* to mean the existence of international rules and organizations that all parties respect; and *government* to mean, literally, some global equivalent to a national government, with corresponding powers.

6. Richard Falk and Andrew Strauss, "Toward Global Parliament," *Foreign Affairs* 80, no. 1 (January–February 2001): 212–20. George Monbiot's unrealistic views are best expressed in his recent book *The Age of Consent: A Manifesto for a New World Order* (London, 2003), chap. 4, and in many of his articles in *The Guardian,* plus his various TV/radio interviews. He certainly is not alone. Anyone using the Google search engine will find 12,400 items under "world parliament," including the website of www.worldparliamentgov.net/constitution.html, encouraging new readers to sign up and become world parliamentarians.

7. For the 1960s agitations and social/intellectual changes, see again Suri, *Power and Protest,* passim.

8. For the "international personality" of NGOs, see Benjamin Cohen's "Of the People, by the People, for the People," pp. 129–37 of *The United Nations: Constitutional Developments, Growth and Possibilities* (Cambridge, Mass., 1961)—an amazingly optimistic and utopian vision of the coming together of all peoples. Clearly, some external observers at the time took the lofty words of the Charter more literally than did the diplomats who had hammered out that very language.

9. I have done a quick scan of the "Index to Country Entries" in the Amnesty International Report 2004 (New York, 2004) for the year 2003, and it appears that only Costa Rica, Denmark, Iceland, Norway, the Netherlands, and New Zealand do not appear. Even Finland gets a mild tap of disapproval.

10. I have taken this information about Médecins sans Frontières from www.doctorswithoutborders.org. Like all of the other NGOs, it has used the communications revolution to produce its own website, which not only spreads the word, but (probably) makes suspicious governments somewhat more cautious about moving against it.

11. Following the attacks in Afghanistan, the MSF was reluctantly scaling down its work in Pakistan because of worries about imitation attacks. And the ICRC has not felt it safe to go into Iraq, though it operated there untouched during the First Gulf War. Thus, three large and very poor peoples, desperately needing this sort of impartial and unselfish work, now suffer from calculated extremism. (See Quentin Peel's fine article "A Humanitarian Crisis of Conscience," *Financial Times,* January 29, 2004, p. 13.)

12. On the MSF's decision to withdraw from Afghanistan, see the important article in *The Guardian* (London, July 28, 2004), by Sarah Left.

13. Details about Greenpeace came from its website, www.greenpeace .org; see in particular "Greenpeace Victories" at www.greenpeace.org/ international/about/history.

14. The two examples of WRI collaboration are taken from their website, www.wri.org, more specifically their two announcements at http:// newsroom.wri.org/newsrelease_text.cfm?NewsReleaseID=292 and ID=293.

15. In all cases, I have taken information from the NGOs' websites (therefore with the usual caveats about objectivity): www.madre.org and, for the specific quote, www.madre.org/mission.html; www.equalitynow.org/ english/campaigns/un/un_en.html for Equality Now's cooperation with UN bodies; and www.globalfundforwomen.org for the Global Fund for Women's activities.

16. On Wangari Maathai and the GMB, see www.greenbeltmovement.org. This is an astonishingly full and sophisticated website and shows how Moi's thugs never had a chance of crushing this movement.

17. As is normal nowadays, these faith-based agencies all have their own extensive websites, as in, for example, www.catholicrelief.org.

18. I relied here upon C. A. McIntosh and J. L. Finkle, "The Cairo Conference on Population and Development: A New Paradigm?," *Population and Development Review* 21, no. 2 (1995): 223–60; also, Yasmin Abdullah, "The Holy See at United Nations Conferences: State or Church?," *Columbia Law Review* 96, no. 7 (November 1996): 1835–75, the latter being an argument to reduce the Vatican's special status. It is not fully clear to me exactly how many UN member states the Holy See has diplomatic relations with, but at one stage during the Cairo conference, the Vatican summoned 120 of the resident foreign ambassadors to convey its opinions.

19. Basic collective data about U.S. foundation giving came from the Foundation Center, both from its recent annual surveys and from its website at www.fdncenter.org. The information about the Ford and Gates foundations came from their respective websites, www.fordfound.org and www.gatesfound.org. Both organizations are extremely prolix and, inevitably, somewhat self-congratulatory about their roles; but the case

studies they report on form the basis for this analysis. There is also an important older article by Peter D. Bell, "The Ford Foundation as a Transnational Actor," in *International Organization* 25, no. 3 (Summer 1971): 465–78.

20. I have relied heavily here on three important revisionist articles: Peter Viggo Jakobsen, "National Interest, Humanitarianism or CNN: What Triggers UN Peace Enforcement After the Cold War?," *Journal of Peace Research* 33, no. 2 (1996): 205–15; Jakobsen, "Focus of the CNN Effect Misses the Point," *Journal of Peace Research* 37, no. 5 (2000): 547–62; and Jonathan Mermin, "Television News and American Intervention in Somalia: The Myth of a Media-Driven Foreign Policy," *Political Science Quarterly* 112, no. 3 (1997): 385–403.

21. Information about the BBC World Service derived from many articles in their 2003–4 annual report, available at www.bbc.co.uk/worldservice/us/annual_review/2003. The Krugman observation is in his column, "The China Syndrome," *The New York Times,* May 13, 2003.

22. I have not been able to find a study that examines the totality of activities by the UN agencies, the churches, the NGOs, the foundations, and others in a single country like, say, Tanzania. But it would be truly interesting to have one. As for convergence, at the 1994 UN Global Conference on Population, staff from the Pew Charitable Trusts not only monitored the proceedings and interacted with those NGOs present who were interested in population/reproductive health issues, but also supplied information and arguments to developing world representatives. On the other side of the fence, as noted in the earlier text, were the Vatican and supporting Catholic governments.

CHAPTER 8: *The Promise and the Peril of the Twenty-first Century*

1. Perhaps best expressed in the Goldman Sachs policy paper "Dreaming with BRICS: The Path to 2050" (London, 2003). (The acronym BRICS refers to Brazil, Russia, India, and China.) It is also captured in a January 2005 report by the U.S. National Intelligence Committee, "Mapping the Global Future," which looks at possible power shifts between now and 2020, though remaining cautiously optimistic about the United States maintaining its edge; and compare with a very optimistic pro-Indian paper by Arvind Virmani, "Economic Performance, Power Potential and Global Governance: Towards a New International Order" (ICRIER Working Paper no. 150, New Delhi, 2004), forecasting the emergence of a tripolar order by 2035—of China, the United States, and India. No doubt the locations from which the respective reports were issued and the differing time horizons chosen (2050, 2020, 2035) explain the varying conclusions.

There is not much discussion of the implications of a solid and more deeply integrated European economic bloc by 2025 or 2050, which would significantly change the rankings. But the basic conclusion remains: Large-scale global power shifts are under way and if anything are accelerating.

2. For the text of some of these reform proposals, see again "The United Nations in Its Second Half-Century"; "Our Global Neighborhood"; and the report issued by the High-level Panel on Threats, Challenges and Change. I shall be referring to these three reports throughout this chapter.

3. The High-level Panel's recommendations on the distribution of Security Council seats can be found on pp. 67–68.

4. To some extent, the idea goes back to the call by the first secretary-general, Trygve Lie, for a "U.N. Legion" in the 1940s and may even be regarded as implicit in Article 43 of the Charter itself.

5. This is a shot in the dark. Much depends on how one puts the numbers together. Someone from the British or French Ministry of Defense could (rightly) point out that they are contributing so many troops to existing peacekeeping and peace enforcement missions that setting up a separate force would be difficult until their units came home; and that the possibilities of double counting are large. The real issue was and is not about numbers, but about whether the Security Council could commit parts of a volunteer UN army into action without reference back to governments and legislatures. A Foreign Legion–type army, with individuals applying to join, would be very different from having, say, battalion-size contributions from the British army who volunteered for UN service anywhere but would still be a British unit loaned to the Security Council.

6. Chapters XI–XIII; and see my observations about it in Chapter One of this book.

7. I have not included abolishing Chapter XI, "Declaration Regarding Non-Self-Governing Territories" (Articles 73–74), since it seemed to me that some of the language might be rescued to assist the world organization's efforts in regard to failed states.

8. Joint cooperation between the Security Council and the General Assembly: see pp. 24–25 of the Ford-Yale report "The United Nations in Its Second Half-Century." The High-level Panel's remarks upon a Peacebuilding Commission are on p. 69.

9. To be sure, there would be IMF advice to the government of Chile, for instance. But that would be minimal compared with the involvement of the Bretton Woods institutions in Africa, Central America/Caribbean, and Eastern Europe.

10. Just to remind: The World Bank's twenty-four-member Executive Board has five members from countries having the largest number of shares; the IMF's Executive Board now includes those eight out of twenty-four coun-

tries (United States, Japan, United Kingdom, Germany, France, Russia, China, Saudi Arabia) that have the largest quotas. The ILO may be smarter here: Ten of the twenty-eight government members of its board are nonelective seats held by "states of chief industrial importance"— Brazil, China, France, Germany, India, Italy, Japan, Russian Federation, the United Kingdom, and the United States; the BRICS have already arrived. All data are from the New Zealand government's *United Nations Handbook.*

11. Regarding ECOSOC commissions and committees mentioned here: See details on pp. 116–21, 130–34, and 150–52 of the *United Nations Handbook.*

12. The High-level Panel's critique of the UN's Commission on Human Rights is on pp. 74–75 of its report.

13. On "the General Assembly's relevance" and possible improvements, see "Our Global Neighborhood," pp. 241–50; The High-level Panel report, p. 65; and the Ford-Yale report, pp. 42–43.

14. I have slightly paraphrased the opening lines of the Charter here.

Afterword

1. "Locksley Hall Sixty Years After" is in Adrian Day (ed.), *Alfred, Lord Tennyson: Selected Poems* (Penguin, 2003 rev. ed.), pp. 96–104. Gladstone's critique is in "Locksley Hall and the Jubilee," *The Nineteenth Century* 119 (January 1887). Queen Victoria's golden jubilee occurred at the same time as Tennyson's lament, just as, logically, her coronation had been in the same year as the original poem. "Locksley Hall Sixty Years After," in effect, was a critique of fifty years of liberal Victorianism. Gladstone's essay was a defense of it. Many years ago, I was introduced to this remarkable intellectual debate (can one imagine an American president writing a long article in, say, *The Atlantic Monthly* with his own hand these days?) by my colleague at the University of East Anglia, Professor R. T. Shannon, in his seminal work, *The Crisis of Imperialism, 1865–1915* (St. Albans, Eng., 1976), pp. 199–202.

   But there has always been a puzzle about the title of the later poem. It was obviously written and published fifty, not sixty, years later. Some literary scholars suggest that Tennyson wished to downplay an exact chronological and ironic relationship to the earlier work and thus employed "Sixty Years Later." Of course, by issuing it just before Queen Victoria's golden jubilee in 1887, he actually drew enormous attention to the notion of a vast gap between early-Victorian aspirations and his own late-Victorian worries.

2. Gladstone's extract can be found in full in Day, op. cit., p. 342.

Appendix: Charter of the United Nations

WE THE PEOPLES OF THE UNITED NATIONS DETERMINED

to save succeeding generations from the scourge of war, which twice in our lifetime has brought untold sorrow to mankind, and to reaffirm faith in fundamental human rights, in the dignity and worth of the human person, in the equal rights of men and women and of nations large and small, and

to establish conditions under which justice and respect for the obligations arising from treaties and other sources of international law can be maintained, and

to promote social progress and better standards of life in larger freedom,

AND FOR THESE ENDS

to practice tolerance and live together in peace with one another as good neighbours, and

to unite our strength to maintain international peace and security, and

to ensure, by the acceptance of principles and the institution of methods, that armed force shall not be used, save in the common interest, and

to employ international machinery for the promotion of the economic and social advancement of all peoples,

HAVE RESOLVED TO COMBINE OUR EFFORTS TO ACCOMPLISH THESE AIMS

Accordingly, our respective Governments, through representatives assembled in the city of San Francisco, who have exhibited their full powers found to be in good and due form, have agreed to the present Charter of the United Nations and do hereby establish an international organization to be known as the United Nations.

CHAPTER I: PURPOSES AND PRINCIPLES

Article 1
The Purposes of the United Nations are:
1. To maintain international peace and security, and to that end: to take effective collective measures for the prevention and removal of threats to the peace, and for the suppression of acts of aggression or other breaches of the peace, and to bring about by peaceful means, and in conformity

with the principles of justice and international law, adjustment or settlement of international disputes or situations which might lead to a breach of the peace;

2. To develop friendly relations among nations based on respect for the principle of equal rights and self-determination of peoples, and to take other appropriate measures to strengthen universal peace;

3. To achieve international co-operation in solving international problems of an economic, social, cultural, or humanitarian character, and in promoting and encouraging respect for human rights and for fundamental freedoms for all without distinction as to race, sex, language, or religion; and

4. To be a centre for harmonizing the actions of nations in the attainment of these common ends.

Article 2

The Organization and its Members, in pursuit of the Purposes stated in Article 1, shall act in accordance with the following Principles.

1. The Organization is based on the principle of the sovereign equality of all its Members.

2. All Members, in order to ensure to all of them the rights and benefits resulting from membership, shall fulfill in good faith the obligations assumed by them in accordance with the present Charter.

3. All Members shall settle their international disputes by peaceful means in such a manner that international peace and security, and justice, are not endangered.

4. All Members shall refrain in their international relations from the threat or use of force against the territorial integrity or political independence of any state, or in any other manner inconsistent with the Purposes of the United Nations.

5. All Members shall give the United Nations every assistance in any action it takes in accordance with the present Charter, and shall refrain from giving assistance to any state against which the United Nations is taking preventive or enforcement action.

6. The Organization shall ensure that states which are not Members of the United Nations act in accordance with these Principles so far as may be necessary for the maintenance of international peace and security.

7. Nothing contained in the present Charter shall authorize the United Nations to intervene in matters which are essentially within the domestic jurisdiction of any state or shall require the Members to submit such matters to settlement under the present Charter; but this principle shall not prejudice the application of enforcement measures under Chapter VII.

CHAPTER II: MEMBERSHIP

Article 3
The original Members of the United Nations shall be the states which, having participated in the United Nations Conference on International Organization at San Francisco, or having previously signed the Declaration by United Nations of 1 January 1942, sign the present Charter and ratify it in accordance with Article 110.

Article 4
1. Membership in the United Nations is open to all other peace-loving states which accept the obligations contained in the present Charter and, in the judgement of the Organization, are able and willing to carry out these obligations.
2. The admission of any such state to membership in the United Nations will be effected by a decision of the General Assembly upon the recommendation of the Security Council.

Article 5
A Member of the United Nations against which preventive or enforcement action has been taken by the Security Council may be suspended from the exercise of the rights and privileges of membership by the General Assembly upon the recommendation of the Security Council. The exercise of these rights and privileges may be restored by the Security Council.

Article 6
A Member of the United Nations which has persistently violated the Principles contained in the present Charter may be expelled from the Organization by the General Assembly upon the recommendation of the Security Council.

CHAPTER III: ORGANS

Article 7
1. There are established as the principal organs of the United Nations: a General Assembly, a Security Council, an Economic and Social Council, a Trusteeship Council, an International Court of Justice, and a Secretariat.
2. Such subsidiary organs as may be found necessary may be established in accordance with the present Charter.

Article 8

The United Nations shall place no restrictions on the eligibility of men and women to participate in any capacity and under conditions of equality in its principal and subsidiary organs.

CHAPTER IV: THE GENERAL ASSEMBLY

Composition

Article 9

1. The General Assembly shall consist of all the Members of the United Nations.
2. Each Member shall have not more than five representatives in the General Assembly.

Functions and Powers

Article 10

The General Assembly may discuss any questions or any matters within the scope of the present Charter or relating to the powers and functions of any organs provided for in the present Charter, and, except as provided in Article 12, may make recommendations to the Members of the United Nations or to the Security Council or to both on any such questions or matters.

Article 11

1. The General Assembly may consider the general principles of co-operation in the maintenance of international peace and security, including the principles governing disarmament and the regulation of armaments, and may make recommendations with regard to such principles to the Members or to the Security Council or to both.
2. The General Assembly may discuss any questions relating to the maintenance of international peace and security brought before it by any Member of the United Nations, or by the Security Council, or by a state which is not a Member of the United Nations in accordance with Article 35, paragraph 2, and, except as provided in Article 12, may make recommendations with regard to any such questions to the state or states concerned or to the Security Council or to both. Any such question on which action is necessary shall be referred to the Security Council by the General Assembly either before or after discussion.

3. The General Assembly may call the attention of the Security Council to situations which are likely to endanger international peace and security.

4. The powers of the General Assembly set forth in this Article shall not limit the general scope of Article 10.

Article 12

1. While the Security Council is exercising in respect of any dispute or situation the functions assigned to it in the present Charter the General Assembly shall not make any recommendation with regard to that dispute or situation unless the Security Council so requests.

2. The Secretary-General, with the consent of the Security Council, shall notify the General Assembly at each session of any matters relative to the maintenance of international peace and security which are being dealt with by the Security Council and shall similarly notify the General Assembly, or the Members of the United Nations if the General Assembly is not in session, immediately the Security Council ceases to deal with such matters.

Article 13

1. The General Assembly shall initiate studies and make recommendations for the purpose of:
   a. promoting international co-operation in the political field and encouraging the progressive development of international law and its codification;
   b. promoting international co-operation in the economic, social, cultural, educational, and health fields, and assisting in the realization of human rights and fundamental freedoms for all without distinction as to race, sex, language, or religion.

2. The further responsibilities, functions and powers of the General Assembly with respect to matters mentioned in paragraph 1 (b) above are set forth in Chapters IX and X.

Article 14

Subject to the provisions of Article 12, the General Assembly may recommend measures for the peaceful adjustment of any situation, regardless of origin, which it deems likely to impair the general welfare or friendly relations among nations, including situations resulting from a violation of the provisions of the present Charter setting forth the Purposes and Principles of the United Nations.

Article 15

1. The General Assembly shall receive and consider annual and special reports from the Security Council; these reports shall include an account of

the measures that the Security Council has decided upon or taken to maintain international peace and security.

2. The General Assembly shall receive and consider reports from the other organs of the United Nations.

Article 16

The General Assembly shall perform such functions with respect to the international trusteeship system as are assigned to it under Chapters XII and XIII, including the approval of the trusteeship agreements for areas not designated as strategic.

Article 17

1. The General Assembly shall consider and approve the budget of the Organization.
2. The expenses of the Organization shall be borne by the Members as apportioned by the General Assembly.
3. The General Assembly shall consider and approve any financial and budgetary arrangements with specialized agencies referred to in Article 57 and shall examine the administrative budgets of such specialized agencies with a view to making recommendations to the agencies concerned.

VOTING

Article 18

1. Each member of the General Assembly shall have one vote.
2. Decisions of the General Assembly on important questions shall be made by a two-thirds majority of the members present and voting. These questions shall include: recommendations with respect to the maintenance of international peace and security, the election of the non-permanent members of the Security Council, the election of the members of the Economic and Social Council, the election of members of the Trusteeship Council in accordance with paragraph 1 (c) of Article 86, the admission of new Members to the United Nations, the suspension of the rights and privileges of membership, the expulsion of Members, questions relating to the operation of the trusteeship system, and budgetary questions.
3. Decisions on other questions, including the determination of additional categories of questions to be decided by a two-thirds majority, shall be made by a majority of the members present and voting.

Article 19

A Member of the United Nations which is in arrears in the payment of its financial contributions to the Organization shall have no vote in the General

Assembly if the amount of its arrears equals or exceeds the amount of the contributions due from it for the preceding two full years. The General Assembly may, nevertheless, permit such a Member to vote if it is satisfied that the failure to pay is due to conditions beyond the control of the Member.

PROCEDURE

Article 20
The General Assembly shall meet in regular annual sessions and in such special sessions as occasion may require. Special sessions shall be convoked by the Secretary-General at the request of the Security Council or of a majority of the Members of the United Nations.

Article 21
The General Assembly shall adopt its own rules of procedure. It shall elect its President for each session.

Article 22
The General Assembly may establish such subsidiary organs as it deems necessary for the performance of its functions.

CHAPTER V: THE SECURITY COUNCIL

COMPOSITION

Article 23
1. The Security Council shall consist of fifteen Members of the United Nations. The Republic of China, France, the Union of Soviet Socialist Republics, the United Kingdom of Great Britain and Northern Ireland, and the United States of America shall be permanent members of the Security Council. The General Assembly shall elect ten other Members of the United Nations to be non-permanent members of the Security Council, due regard being specially paid, in the first instance to the contribution of Members of the United Nations to the maintenance of international peace and security and to the other purposes of the Organization, and also to equitable geographical distribution.
2. The non-permanent members of the Security Council shall be elected for a term of two years. In the first election of the non-permanent members after the increase of the membership of the Security Council from eleven to fifteen, two of the four additional members shall be chosen for a

term of one year. A retiring member shall not be eligible for immediate re-election.

3. Each member of the Security Council shall have one representative.

FUNCTIONS AND POWERS

Article 24

1. In order to ensure prompt and effective action by the United Nations, its Members confer on the Security Council primary responsibility for the maintenance of international peace and security, and agree that in carrying out its duties under this responsibility the Security Council acts on their behalf.
2. In discharging these duties the Security Council shall act in accordance with the Purposes and Principles of the United Nations. The specific powers granted to the Security Council for the discharge of these duties are laid down in Chapters VI, VII, VIII, and XII.
3. The Security Council shall submit annual and, when necessary, special reports to the General Assembly for its consideration.

Article 25

The Members of the United Nations agree to accept and carry out the decisions of the Security Council in accordance with the present Charter.

Article 26

In order to promote the establishment and maintenance of international peace and security with the least diversion for armaments of the world's human and economic resources, the Security Council shall be responsible for formulating, with the assistance of the Military Staff Committee referred to in Article 47, plans to be submitted to the Members of the United Nations for the establishment of a system for the regulation of armaments.

VOTING

Article 27

1. Each member of the Security Council shall have one vote.
2. Decisions of the Security Council on procedural matters shall be made by an affirmative vote of nine members.
3. Decisions of the Security Council on all other matters shall be made by an affirmative vote of nine members including the concurring votes of the permanent members; provided that, in decisions under Chapter VI, and under paragraph 3 of Article 52, a party to a dispute shall abstain from voting.

PROCEDURE

Article 28
1. The Security Council shall be so organized as to be able to function continuously. Each member of the Security Council shall for this purpose be represented at all times at the seat of the Organization.
2. The Security Council shall hold periodic meetings at which each of its members may, if it so desires, be represented by a member of the government or by some other specially designated representative.
3. The Security Council may hold meetings at such places other than the seat of the Organization as in its judgement will best facilitate its work.

Article 29
The Security Council may establish such subsidiary organs as it deems necessary for the performance of its functions.

Article 30
The Security Council shall adopt its own rules of procedure, including the method of selecting its President.

Article 31
Any Member of the United Nations which is not a member of the Security Council may participate, without vote, in the discussion of any question brought before the Security Council whenever the latter considers that the interests of that Member are specially affected.

Article 32
Any Member of the United Nations which is not a member of the Security Council or any state which is not a Member of the United Nations, if it is a party to a dispute under consideration by the Security Council, shall be invited to participate, without vote, in the discussion relating to the dispute. The Security Council shall lay down such conditions as it deems just for the participation of a state which is not a Member of the United Nations.

CHAPTER VI: PACIFIC SETTLEMENT OF DISPUTES

Article 33
1. The parties to any dispute, the continuance of which is likely to endanger the maintenance of international peace and security, shall, first of all, seek a solution by negotiation, enquiry, mediation, conciliation, arbitra-

tion, judicial settlement, resort to regional agencies or arrangements, or other peaceful means of their own choice.

2. The Security Council shall, when it deems necessary, call upon the parties to settle their dispute by such means.

Article 34

The Security Council may investigate any dispute, or any situation which might lead to international friction or give rise to a dispute, in order to determine whether the continuance of the dispute or situation is likely to endanger the maintenance of international peace and security.

Article 35

1. Any Member of the United Nations may bring any dispute, or any situation of the nature referred to in Article 34, to the attention of the Security Council or of the General Assembly.
2. A state which is not a Member of the United Nations may bring to the attention of the Security Council or of the General Assembly any dispute to which it is a party if it accepts in advance, for the purposes of the dispute, the obligations of pacific settlement provided in the present Charter.
3. The proceedings of the General Assembly in respect of matters brought to its attention under this Article will be subject to the provisions of Articles 11 and 12.

Article 36

1. The Security Council may, at any stage of a dispute of the nature referred to in Article 33 or of a situation of like nature, recommend appropriate procedures or methods of adjustment.
2. The Security Council should take into consideration any procedures for the settlement of the dispute which have already been adopted by the parties.
3. In making recommendations under this Article the Security Council should also take into consideration that legal disputes should as a general rule be referred by the parties to the International Court of Justice in accordance with the provisions of the Statute of the Court.

Article 37

1. Should the parties to a dispute of the nature referred to in Article 33 fail to settle it by the means indicated in that Article, they shall refer it to the Security Council.
2. If the Security Council deems that the continuance of the dispute is in fact likely to endanger the maintenance of international peace and secu-

rity, it shall decide whether to take action under Article 36 or to recommend such terms of settlement as it may consider appropriate.

Article 38

Without prejudice to the provisions of Articles 33 to 37, the Security Council may, if all the parties to any dispute so request, make recommendations to the parties with a view to a pacific settlement of the dispute.

CHAPTER VII: ACTION WITH RESPECT TO THREATS TO THE PEACE,
            BREACHES OF THE PEACE, AND ACTS OF AGGRESSION

Article 39

The Security Council shall determine the existence of any threat to the peace, breach of the peace, or act of aggression and shall make recommendations, or decide what measures shall be taken in accordance with Articles 41 and 42, to maintain or restore international peace and security.

Article 40

In order to prevent an aggravation of the situation, the Security Council may, before making the recommendations or deciding upon the measures provided for in Article 39, call upon the parties concerned to comply with such provisional measures as it deems necessary or desirable. Such provisional measures shall be without prejudice to the rights, claims, or position of the parties concerned. The Security Council shall duly take account of failure to comply with such provisional measures.

Article 41

The Security Council may decide what measures not involving the use of armed force are to be employed to give effect to its decisions, and it may call upon the Members of the United Nations to apply such measures. These may include complete or partial interruption of economic relations and of rail, sea, air, postal, telegraphic, radio, and other means of communication, and the severance of diplomatic relations.

Article 42

Should the Security Council consider that measures provided for in Article 41 would be inadequate or have proved to be inadequate, it may take such action by air, sea, or land forces as may be necessary to maintain or restore international peace and security. Such action may include demonstrations, blockade, and other operations by air, sea, or land forces of Members of the United Nations.

Article 43

1. All Members of the United Nations, in order to contribute to the maintenance of international peace and security, undertake to make available to the Security Council, on its call and in accordance with a special agreement or agreements, armed forces, assistance, and facilities, including rights of passage, necessary for the purpose of maintaining international peace and security.

2. Such agreement or agreements shall govern the numbers and types of forces, their degree of readiness and general location, and the nature of the facilities and assistance to be provided.

3. The agreement or agreements shall be negotiated as soon as possible on the initiative of the Security Council. They shall be concluded between the Security Council and Members or between the Security Council and groups of Members and shall be subject to ratification by the signatory states in accordance with their respective constitutional processes.

Article 44

When the Security Council has decided to use force it shall, before calling upon a Member not represented on it to provide armed forces in fulfilment of the obligations assumed under Article 43, invite that Member, if the Member so desires, to participate in the decisions of the Security Council concerning the employment of contingents of that Member's armed forces.

Article 45

In order to enable the United Nations to take urgent military measures, Members shall hold immediately available national air-force contingents for combined international enforcement action. The strength and degree of readiness of these contingents and plans for their combined action shall be determined within the limits laid down in the special agreement or agreements referred to in Article 43, by the Security Council with the assistance of the Military Staff Committee.

Article 46

Plans for the application of armed force shall be made by the Security Council with the assistance of the Military Staff Committee.

Article 47

1. There shall be established a Military Staff Committee to advise and assist the Security Council on all questions relating to the Security Council's military requirements for the maintenance of international peace and security, the employment and command of forces placed at its disposal, the regulation of armaments, and possible disarmament.

2. The Military Staff Committee shall consist of the Chiefs of Staff of the permanent members of the Security Council or their representatives. Any Member of the United Nations not permanently represented on the Committee shall be invited by the Committee to be associated with it when the efficient discharge of the Committee's responsibilities requires the participation of that Member in its work.

3. The Military Staff Committee shall be responsible under the Security Council for the strategic direction of any armed forces placed at the disposal of the Security Council. Questions relating to the command of such forces shall be worked out subsequently.

4. The Military Staff Committee, with the authorization of the Security Council and after consultation with appropriate regional agencies, may establish regional subcommittees.

Article 48

1. The action required to carry out the decisions of the Security Council for the maintenance of international peace and security shall be taken by all the Members of the United Nations or by some of them, as the Security Council may determine.

2. Such decisions shall be carried out by the Members of the United Nations directly and through their action in the appropriate international agencies of which they are members.

Article 49

The Members of the United Nations shall join in affording mutual assistance in carrying out the measures decided upon by the Security Council.

Article 50

If preventive or enforcement measures against any state are taken by the Security Council, any other state, whether a Member of the United Nations or not, which finds itself confronted with special economic problems arising from the carrying out of those measures shall have the right to consult the Security Council with regard to a solution of those problems.

Article 51

Nothing in the present Charter shall impair the inherent right of individual or collective self-defence if an armed attack occurs against a Member of the United Nations, until the Security Council has taken measures necessary to maintain international peace and security. Measures taken by Members in the exercise of this right of self-defence shall be immediately reported to the Security Council and shall not in any way affect the authority and responsibility of the Security Council under the present Charter to take at any time such action as it deems necessary in order to maintain or restore international peace and security.

CHAPTER VIII: REGIONAL ARRANGEMENTS

Article 52

1. Nothing in the present Charter precludes the existence of regional arrangements or agencies for dealing with such matters relating to the maintenance of international peace and security as are appropriate for regional action provided that such arrangements or agencies and their activities are consistent with the Purposes and Principles of the United Nations.
2. The Members of the United Nations entering into such arrangements or constituting such agencies shall make every effort to achieve pacific settlement of local disputes through such regional arrangements or by such regional agencies before referring them to the Security Council.
3. The Security Council shall encourage the development of pacific settlement of local disputes through such regional arrangements or by such regional agencies either on the initiative of the states concerned or by reference from the Security Council.
4. This Article in no way impairs the application of Articles 34 and 35.

Article 53

1. The Security Council shall, where appropriate, utilize such regional arrangements or agencies for enforcement action under its authority. But no enforcement action shall be taken under regional arrangements or by regional agencies without the authorization of the Security Council, with the exception of measures against any enemy state, as defined in paragraph 2 of this Article, provided for pursuant to Article 107 or in regional arrangements directed against renewal of aggressive policy on the part of any such state, until such time as the Organization may, on request of the Governments concerned, be charged with the responsibility for preventing further aggression by such a state.
2. The term enemy state as used in paragraph 1 of this Article applies to any state which during the Second World War has been an enemy of any signatory of the present Charter.

Article 54

The Security Council shall at all times be kept fully informed of activities undertaken or in contemplation under regional arrangements or by regional agencies for the maintenance of international peace and security.

CHAPTER IX: INTERNATIONAL ECONOMIC AND SOCIAL CO-OPERATION

Article 55
With a view to the creation of conditions of stability and well-being which are necessary for peaceful and friendly relations among nations based on respect for the principle of equal rights and self-determination of peoples, the United Nations shall promote:
  a. higher standards of living, full employment, and conditions of economic and social progress and development;
  b. solutions of international economic, social, health, and related problems; and international cultural and educational co-operation; and
  c. universal respect for, and observance of, human rights and fundamental freedoms for all without distinction as to race, sex, language, or religion.

Article 56
All Members pledge themselves to take joint and separate action in co-operation with the Organization for the achievement of the purposes set forth in Article 55.

Article 57
  1. The various specialized agencies, established by intergovernmental agreement and having wide international responsibilities, as defined in their basic instruments, in economic, social, cultural, educational, health, and related fields, shall be brought into relationship with the United Nations in accordance with the provisions of Article 63.
  2. Such agencies thus brought into relationship with the United Nations are hereinafter referred to as specialized agencies.

Article 58
The Organization shall make recommendations for the co-ordination of the policies and activities of the specialized agencies.

Article 59
The Organization shall, where appropriate, initiate negotiations among the states concerned for the creation of any new specialized agencies required for the accomplishment of the purposes set forth in Article 55.

Article 60
Responsibility for the discharge of the functions of the Organization set forth in this Chapter shall be vested in the General Assembly and, under the authority of the General Assembly, in the Economic and Social Council, which shall have for this purpose the powers set forth in Chapter X.

CHAPTER X: THE ECONOMIC AND SOCIAL COUNCIL

COMPOSITION

Article 61
1. The Economic and Social Council shall consist of fifty-four Members of the United Nations elected by the General Assembly.
2. Subject to the provisions of paragraph 3, eighteen members of the Economic and Social Council shall be elected each year for a term of three years. A retiring member shall be eligible for immediate re-election.
3. At the first election after the increase in the membership of the Economic and Social Council from twenty-seven to fifty-four members, in addition to the members elected in place of the nine members whose term of office expires at the end of that year, twenty-seven additional members shall be elected. Of these twenty-seven additional members, the term of office of nine members so elected shall expire at the end of one year, and of nine other members at the end of two years, in accordance with arrangements made by the General Assembly.
4. Each member of the Economic and Social Council shall have one representative.

FUNCTIONS AND POWERS

Article 62
1. The Economic and Social Council may make or initiate studies and reports with respect to international economic, social, cultural, educational, health, and related matters and may make recommendations with respect to any such matters to the General Assembly to the Members of the United Nations, and to the specialized agencies concerned.
2. It may make recommendations for the purpose of promoting respect for, and observance of, human rights and fundamental freedoms for all.
3. It may prepare draft conventions for submission to the General Assembly, with respect to matters falling within its competence.
4. It may call, in accordance with the rules prescribed by the United Nations, international conferences on matters falling within its competence.

Article 63
1. The Economic and Social Council may enter into agreements with any of the agencies referred to in Article 57, defining the terms on which the agency concerned shall be brought into relationship with the United Nations. Such agreements shall be subject to approval by the General Assembly.

2. It may co-ordinate the activities of the specialized agencies through consultation with and recommendations to such agencies and through recommendations to the General Assembly and to the Members of the United Nations.

Article 64

1. The Economic and Social Council may take appropriate steps to obtain regular reports from the specialized agencies. It may make arrangements with the Members of the United Nations and with the specialized agencies to obtain reports on the steps taken to give effect to its own recommendations and to recommendations on matters falling within its competence made by the General Assembly.
2. It may communicate its observations on these reports to the General Assembly.

Article 65

The Economic and Social Council may furnish information to the Security Council and shall assist the Security Council upon its request.

Article 66

1. The Economic and Social Council shall perform such functions as fall within its competence in connexion with the carrying out of the recommendations of the General Assembly.
2. It may, with the approval of the General Assembly, perform services at the request of Members of the United Nations and at the request of specialized agencies.
3. It shall perform such other functions as are specified elsewhere in the present Charter or as may be assigned to it by the General Assembly.

VOTING

Article 67

1. Each member of the Economic and Social Council shall have one vote.
2. Decisions of the Economic and Social Council shall be made by a majority of the members present and voting.

PROCEDURE

Article 68

The Economic and Social Council shall set up commissions in economic and social fields and for the promotion of human rights, and such other commissions as may be required for the performance of its functions.

Article 69

The Economic and Social Council shall invite any Member of the United Nations to participate, without vote, in its deliberations on any matter of particular concern to that Member.

Article 70

The Economic and Social Council may make arrangements for representatives of the specialized agencies to participate, without vote, in its deliberations and in those of the commissions established by it, and for its representatives to participate in the deliberations of the specialized agencies.

Article 71

The Economic and Social Council may make suitable arrangements for consultation with non-governmental organizations which are concerned with matters within its competence. Such arrangements may be made with international organizations and, where appropriate, with national organizations after consultation with the Member of the United Nations concerned.

Article 72

1. The Economic and Social Council shall adopt its own rules of procedure, including the method of selecting its President.
2. The Economic and Social Council shall meet as required in accordance with its rules, which shall include provision for the convening of meetings on the request of a majority of its members.

CHAPTER XI: DECLARATION REGARDING NON-SELF-GOVERNING TERRITORIES

Article 73

Members of the United Nations which have or assume responsibilities for the administration of territories whose peoples have not yet attained a full measure of self-government recognize the principle that the interests of the inhabitants of these territories are paramount, and accept as a sacred trust the obligation to promote to the utmost, within the system of international peace and security established by the present Charter, the well-being of the inhabitants of these territories, and, to this end:

a. to ensure, with due respect for the culture of the peoples concerned, their political, economic, social, and educational advancement, their just treatment, and their protection against abuses;
b. to develop self-government, to take due account of the political aspirations of the peoples, and to assist them in the progressive development of

their free political institutions, according to the particular circumstances of each territory and its peoples and their varying stages of advancement;

c. to further international peace and security;

d. to promote constructive measures of development, to encourage research, and to co-operate with one another and, when and where appropriate, with specialized international bodies with a view to the practical achievement of the social, economic, and scientific purposes set forth in this Article; and

e. to transmit regularly to the Secretary-General for information purposes, subject to such limitation as security and constitutional considerations may require, statistical and other information of a technical nature relating to economic, social, and educational conditions in the territories for which they are respectively responsible other than those territories to which Chapters XII and XIII apply.

Article 74

Members of the United Nations also agree that their policy in respect of the territories to which this Chapter applies, no less than in respect of their metropolitan areas, must be based on the general principle of good-neighbourliness, due account being taken of the interests and well-being of the rest of the world, in social, economic, and commercial matters.

CHAPTER XII: INTERNATIONAL TRUSTEESHIP SYSTEM

Article 75

The United Nations shall establish under its authority an international trusteeship system for the administration and supervision of such territories as may be placed thereunder by subsequent individual agreements. These territories are hereinafter referred to as trust territories.

Article 76

The basic objectives of the trusteeship system, in accordance with the Purposes of the United Nations laid down in Article 1 of the present Charter, shall be:

a. to further international peace and security;

b. to promote the political, economic, social, and educational advancement of the inhabitants of the trust territories, and their progressive development towards self-government or independence as may be appropriate to the particular circumstances of each territory and its peoples and the freely expressed wishes of the peoples concerned, and as may be provided by the terms of each trusteeship agreement;

c. to encourage respect for human rights and for fundamental freedoms for all without distinction as to race, sex, language, or religion, and to encourage recognition of the interdependence of the peoples of the world; and

d. to ensure equal treatment in social, economic, and commercial matters for all Members of the United Nations and their nationals, and also equal treatment for the latter in the administration of justice, without prejudice to the attainment of the foregoing objectives and subject to the provisions of Article 80.

Article 77

1. The trusteeship system shall apply to such territories in the following categories as may be placed thereunder by means of trusteeship agreements:

   a. territories now held under mandate;

   b. territories which may be detached from enemy states as a result of the Second World War; and

   c. territories voluntarily placed under the system by states responsible for their administration.

2. It will be a matter for subsequent agreement as to which territories in the foregoing categories will be brought under the trusteeship system and upon what terms.

Article 78

The trusteeship system shall not apply to territories which have become Members of the United Nations, relationship among which shall be based on respect for the principle of sovereign equality.

Article 79

The terms of trusteeship for each territory to be placed under the trusteeship system, including any alteration or amendment, shall be agreed upon by the states directly concerned, including the mandatory power in the case of territories held under mandate by a Member of the United Nations, and shall be approved as provided for in Articles 83 and 85.

Article 80

1. Except as may be agreed upon in individual trusteeship agreements, made under Articles 77, 79, and 81, placing each territory under the trusteeship system, and until such agreements have been concluded, nothing in this Chapter shall be construed in or of itself to alter in any manner the rights whatsoever of any states or any peoples or the terms of existing international instruments to which Members of the United Nations may respectively be parties.

2. Paragraph 1 of this Article shall not be interpreted as giving grounds for delay or postponement of the negotiation and conclusion of agreements for placing mandated and other territories under the trusteeship system as provided for in Article 77.

Article 81

The trusteeship agreement shall in each case include the terms under which the trust territory will be administered and designate the authority which will exercise the administration of the trust territory. Such authority, hereinafter called the administering authority, may be one or more states or the Organization itself.

Article 82

There may be designated, in any trusteeship agreement, a strategic area or areas which may include part or all of the trust territory to which the agreement applies, without prejudice to any special agreement or agreements made under Article 43.

Article 83

1. All functions of the United Nations relating to strategic areas, including the approval of the terms of the trusteeship agreements and of their alteration or amendment, shall be exercised by the Security Council.
2. The basic objectives set forth in Article 76 shall be applicable to the people of each strategic area.
3. The Security Council shall, subject to the provisions of the trusteeship agreements and without prejudice to security considerations, avail itself of the assistance of the Trusteeship Council to perform those functions of the United Nations under the trusteeship system relating to political, economic, social, and educational matters in the strategic areas.

Article 84

It shall be the duty of the administering authority to ensure that the trust territory shall play its part in the maintenance of international peace and security. To this end the administering authority may make use of volunteer forces, facilities, and assistance from the trust territory in carrying out the obligations towards the Security Council undertaken in this regard by the administering authority, as well as for local defence and the maintenance of law and order within the trust territory.

Article 85

1. The functions of the United Nations with regard to trusteeship agreements for all areas not designated as strategic, including the approval of

the terms of the trusteeship agreements and of their alteration or amendment, shall be exercised by the General Assembly.

2. The Trusteeship Council, operating under the authority of the General Assembly, shall assist the General Assembly in carrying out these functions.

CHAPTER XIII: THE TRUSTEESHIP COUNCIL

COMPOSITION

Article 86

1. The Trusteeship Council shall consist of the following Members of the United Nations:
   a. those Members administering trust territories;
   b. such of those Members mentioned by name in Article 23 as are not administering trust territories; and
   c. as many other Members elected for three-year terms by the General Assembly as may be necessary to ensure that the total number of members of the Trusteeship Council is equally divided between those Members of the United Nations which administer trust territories and those which do not.
2. Each member of the Trusteeship Council shall designate one specially qualified person to represent it therein.

FUNCTIONS AND POWERS

Article 87

The General Assembly and, under its authority, the Trusteeship Council, in carrying out their functions, may:
   a. consider reports submitted by the administering authority;
   b. accept petitions and examine them in consultation with the administering authority;
   c. provide for periodic visits to the respective trust territories at times agreed upon with the administering authority; and
   d. take these and other actions in conformity with the terms of the trusteeship agreements.

Article 88

The Trusteeship Council shall formulate a questionnaire on the political, economic, social, and educational advancement of the inhabitants of each trust territory, and the administering authority for each trust territory within the competence of the General Assembly shall make an annual report to the General Assembly upon the basis of such questionnaire.

VOTING

Article 89
1. Each member of the Trusteeship Council shall have one vote.
2. Decisions of the Trusteeship Council shall be made by a majority of the members present and voting.

PROCEDURE

Article 90
1. The Trusteeship Council shall adopt its own rules of procedure, including the method of selecting its President.
2. The Trusteeship Council shall meet as required in accordance with its rules, which shall include provision for the convening of meetings on the request of a majority of its members.

Article 91
The Trusteeship Council shall, when appropriate, avail itself of the assistance of the Economic and Social Council and of the specialized agencies in regard to matters with which they are respectively concerned.

CHAPTER XIV: THE INTERNATIONAL COURT OF JUSTICE

Article 92
The International Court of Justice shall be the principal judicial organ of the United Nations. It shall function in accordance with the annexed Statute, which is based upon the Statute of the Permanent Court of International Justice and forms an integral part of the present Charter.

Article 93
1. All Members of the United Nations are ipso facto parties to the Statute of the International Court of Justice.
2. A state which is not a Member of the United Nations may become a party to the Statute of the International Court of Justice on conditions to be determined in each case by the General Assembly upon the recommendation of the Security Council.

Article 94

  1. Each Member of the United Nations undertakes to comply with the decision of the International Court of Justice in any case to which it is a party.
  2. If any party to a case fails to perform the obligations incumbent upon it under a judgement rendered by the Court, the other party may have recourse to the Security Council, which may, if it deems necessary, make recommendations or decide upon measures to be taken to give effect to the judgement.

Article 95

Nothing in the present Charter shall prevent Members of the United Nations from entrusting the solution of their differences to other tribunals by virtue of agreements already in existence or which may be concluded in the future.

Article 96

  1. The General Assembly or the Security Council may request the International Court of Justice to give an advisory opinion on any legal question.
  2. Other organs of the United Nations and specialized agencies, which may at any time be so authorized by the General Assembly, may also request advisory opinions of the Court on legal questions arising within the scope of their activities.

CHAPTER XV: THE SECRETARIAT

Article 97

The Secretariat shall comprise a Secretary-General and such staff as the Organization may require. The Secretary-General shall be appointed by the General Assembly upon the recommendation of the Security Council. He shall be the chief administrative officer of the Organization.

Article 98

The Secretary-General shall act in that capacity in all meetings of the General Assembly, of the Security Council, of the Economic and Social Council, and of the Trusteeship Council, and shall perform such other functions as are entrusted to him by these organs. The Secretary-General shall make an annual report to the General Assembly on the work of the Organization.

Article 99

The Secretary-General may bring to the attention of the Security Council any matter which in his opinion may threaten the maintenance of international peace and security.

Article 100

1. In the performance of their duties the Secretary-General and the staff shall not seek or receive instructions from any government or from any other authority external to the Organization. They shall refrain from any action which might reflect on their position as international officials responsible only to the Organization.

2. Each Member of the United Nations undertakes to respect the exclusively international character of the responsibilities of the Secretary-General and the staff and not to seek to influence them in the discharge of their responsibilities.

Article 101

1. The staff shall be appointed by the Secretary-General under regulations established by the General Assembly.

2. Appropriate staffs shall be permanently assigned to the Economic and Social Council, the Trusteeship Council, and, as required, to other organs of the United Nations. These staffs shall form a part of the Secretariat.

3. The paramount consideration in the employment of the staff and in the determination of the conditions of service shall be the necessity of securing the highest standards of efficiency, competence, and integrity. Due regard shall be paid to the importance of recruiting the staff on as wide a geographical basis as possible.

CHAPTER XVI: MISCELLANEOUS PROVISIONS

Article 102

1. Every treaty and every international agreement entered into by any Member of the United Nations after the present Charter comes into force shall as soon as possible be registered with the Secretariat and published by it.

2. No party to any such treaty or international agreement which has not been registered in accordance with the provisions of paragraph 1 of this Article may invoke that treaty or agreement before any organ of the United Nations.

Article 103

In the event of a conflict between the obligations of the Members of the United Nations under the present Charter and their obligations under any other international agreement, their obligations under the present Charter shall prevail.

Article 104

The Organization shall enjoy in the territory of each of its Members such legal capacity as may be necessary for the exercise of its functions and the fulfilment of its purposes.

Article 105

1. The Organization shall enjoy in the territory of each of its Members such privileges and immunities as are necessary for the fulfilment of its purposes.
2. Representatives of the Members of the United Nations and officials of the Organization shall similarly enjoy such privileges and immunities as are necessary for the independent exercise of their functions in connexion with the Organization.
3. The General Assembly may make recommendations with a view to determining the details of the application of paragraphs 1 and 2 of this Article or may propose conventions to the Members of the United Nations for this purpose.

CHAPTER XVII: TRANSITIONAL SECURITY ARRANGEMENTS

Article 106

Pending the coming into force of such special agreements referred to in Article 43 as in the opinion of the Security Council enable it to begin the exercise of its responsibilities under Article 42, the parties to the Four-Nation Declaration, signed at Moscow, 30 October 1943, and France, shall, in accordance with the provisions of paragraph 5 of that Declaration, consult with one another and as occasion requires with other Members of the United Nations with a view to such joint action on behalf of the Organization as may be necessary for the purpose of maintaining international peace and security.

Article 107

Nothing in the present Charter shall invalidate or preclude action, in relation to any state which during the Second World War has been an enemy of any signatory to the present Charter, taken or authorized as a result of that war by the Governments having responsibility for such action.

CHAPTER XVIII: AMENDMENTS

Article 108

Amendments to the present Charter shall come into force for all Members of the United Nations when they have been adopted by a vote of two thirds of the members of the General Assembly and ratified in accordance with their respective constitutional processes by two thirds of the Members of the United Nations, including all the permanent members of the Security Council.

Article 109
1. A General Conference of the Members of the United Nations for the purpose of reviewing the present Charter may be held at a date and place to be fixed by a two-thirds vote of the members of the General Assembly and by a vote of any nine members of the Security Council. Each Member of the United Nations shall have one vote in the conference.
2. Any alteration of the present Charter recommended by a two-thirds vote of the conference shall take effect when ratified in accordance with their respective constitutional processes by two thirds of the Members of the United Nations including all the permanent members of the Security Council.
3. If such a conference has not been held before the tenth annual session of the General Assembly following the coming into force of the present Charter, the proposal to call such a conference shall be placed on the agenda of that session of the General Assembly, and the conference shall be held if so decided by a majority vote of the members of the General Assembly and by a vote of any seven members of the Security Council.

CHAPTER XIX: RATIFICATION AND SIGNATURE

Article 110
1. The present Charter shall be ratified by the signatory states in accordance with their respective constitutional processes.
2. The ratifications shall be deposited with the Government of the United States of America, which shall notify all the signatory states of each deposit as well as the Secretary-General of the Organization when he has been appointed.
3. The present Charter shall come into force upon the deposit of ratifications by the Republic of China, France, the Union of Soviet Socialist Republics, the United Kingdom of Great Britain and Northern Ireland, and the United States of America, and by a majority of the other signatory states. A protocol of the ratifications deposited shall thereupon be drawn up by the Government of the United States of America which shall communicate copies thereof to all the signatory states.
4. The states signatory to the present Charter which ratify it after it has come into force will become original Members of the United Nations on the date of the deposit of their respective ratifications.

Article 111

The present Charter, of which the Chinese, French, Russian, English, and Spanish texts are equally authentic, shall remain deposited in the archives of the Government of the United States of America. Duly certified copies thereof shall be transmitted by that Government to the Governments of the other signatory states.

IN FAITH WHEREOF the representatives of the Governments of the United Nations have signed the present Charter.

DONE at the city of San Francisco the twenty-sixth day of June, one thousand nine hundred and forty-five.

Index

ABOUT THE AUTHOR

PAUL KENNEDY is the author or editor of thirteen books, including *Preparing for the Twenty-first Century* and *The Rise and Fall of the Great Powers,* which has been translated into more than twenty languages. He serves on the editorial board of numerous scholarly journals and has written for *The New York Times,* the *Los Angeles Times, The Atlantic Monthly,* and several other publications. Educated at Newcastle University and Oxford University, he is a former fellow of the Institute for Advanced Studies at Princeton University and of the Alexander von Humboldt-Stiftung in Bonn.

ABOUT THE TYPE

This book was set in Sabon, a typeface designed by the well-known German typographer Jan Tschichold (1902–74). Sabon's design is based upon the original letter forms of Claude Garamond and was created specifically to be used for three sources: foundry type for hand composition, Linotype, and Monotype. Tschichold named his typeface for the famous Frankfurt typefounder Jacques Sabon, who died in 1580.